LIFE AFTER THE
SOVIET UNION

SUNY series in Global Politics
James N. Rosenau, editor

LIFE AFTER THE SOVIET UNION

The Newly Independent
Republics of Transcaucasus
and Central Asia

NOZAR ALAOLMOLKI

State University
of New York
Press

Published by
State University of New York Press, Albany

© 2001 State University of New York

For information, address State University of New York Press,
90 State Street, Suite 700, Albany, NY 12207

Production by Susan Geraghty
Marketing by Patrick Durocher

Library of Congress Cataloging-in-Publication Data

Alaolmolki, Nozar, 1938–
    Life after the Soviet Union : the newly independent republics of Transcaucasus and
Central Asia / Nozar Alaolmolki.
        p. cm. — (SUNY series in global politics)
    Includes bibliographical references and index.
    ISBN 0-7914-5137-2 (alk. paper)—ISBN 0-7914-5138-0 (pb : alk. paper)
        1. Asia, Central—Politics and government—1991– 2. Transcaucasia—Politics and
government—1991– 3. Middle East—Politics and government—1979– 4. World
politics—1989– I. Title. II. Series.

DK859.56 .A4 2001
958'.04—dc21
                                                                                    00-068764

10 9 8 7 6 5 4 3 2 1

CONTENTS

FOREWORD

Before the dissolution of the Soviet Union, scholarship on the region somewhat imprecisely termed "Central Asia" was universally informed by the perspective of Russian and Soviet studies. This viewpoint was certainly conditioned by the Russian conquest of those lands in the nineteenth-century and their forcible incorporation into the Soviet Union after 1917 and subsequent reconfiguration and redefinition. Thus, prior to 1991, it can be said that modern Central Asia, with its politics, history, and culture, was seen through the comprehension, interpretation, policies, and ideology of the power that had colonized it, whether such studies were published in the USSR or abroad.

In this book, Nozar Alaolmolki refers to these newly independent nations of Central Asia as "the Newly Independent Republics," by which he means the states of Kazakhistan, Uzbekistan, Kyrgyzstan, Tajikistan, and Turkmenistan lying to the east of the Caspian Sea along with the Transcaucasian republic of Azerbaijan on its southwestern shore. This designation points not only to the fact that these nations share a common religion with their neighbors to the south but also implies a common history and a common culture. We need only glance at a historical atlas to realize that *Azerbaijan* once referred to a much larger geographical entity that is now bisected by the Iranian frontier or that in the past Turkmenistan, Uzbekistan, and Tajikistan were frequently linked with polities based in eastern Iran or northern Afghanistan. Likewise, we should note that the peoples of Central Asia are bound linguistically to the larger communities of Iranian and Turkic speakers of western and southern Asia.

In addition to political and economic uncertainties, the republics are also beset internally by a number of problems of ideology and self-definition. On the one hand, in at least two of the republics, there is continuity with the Soviet period in that the presidents of Uzbekistan and Kazakhstan were both leaders of the Supreme Soviets of their respective polities before 1991. On the other hand, all republics are grappling with the issues of remembering, recovering, and inventing their histories and identities. One of the best-known examples of this process is the emergence of the cult of Tamerlane in Uzbekistan.

Since 1991, a number of studies on contemporary Central Asia have been published that purport to move our understanding of this important region beyond the colonized-colonizer paradigm of Sovietology by considering these factors. Unfortunately, too often the authors of these works do not possess the requisite training in the languages of Central Asian history and culture or a firm grasp of the premodern history of the region itself to enable them to open these new vistas. One recent book on the Central Asian states, for example, confuses the Sasanian imperial dynasty that ruled Iran from 224 to 651 with the.Central Asian state of the Samanids that controlled Samarqand and Bukhara from the ninth to the eleventh century.

Nozar Alaolmolki provides us a clear and comprehensive view of this dynamic region, balancing sound empirical research with clear analytical interpretation. After providing an overall geographical, cultural, and historical context for Central Asia as a whole, he examines in detail each of the constituent republics, focusing on contemporary politics, economy, society, and international relations. It is in this last category that I believe he makes one of his most significant contributions to this emerging field by showing us how the region and the several republics function and relate interregionally. This is particularly relevant today as old notions of area studies undergo revision and rethinking in the United States. Finally, he also demonstrates how Central Asia figures in the conflicting ambitions and aspirations of Iran, Saudi Arabia, and Turkey.

With this book, Nozar Alaolmolki has contributed substantially to the body of our knowledge on contemporary Central Asia and has established a benchmark for future research.

John E. Woods

ACKNOWLEDGMENTS

This volume is the result of a conference convened at the University of Edinburgh, Scotland, in Summer of 1991. I presented more papers about the regions at the annual International Studies Association and numerous other professional conferences. Then I received a Fulbright Teaching Scholars grant that took me to Kyrgyzstan and Kazakistan in 1995.

I would like to express my appreciation and thanks to my Vancl-Carr Student scholars, Tricia Hill, Heidi Froelich, and Sarah Chase. And special thanks to Hiram College for its generous assistance and support to conduct and complete the project. A special thanks to John Stack (Falsgraf Teaching Fellow) who graciously offered to read the first draft of this book. Special thanks to my wife, Kathleen, for her continuous encouragement and support while working on this project. The last but not least of many thanks to all those colleagues in Kyrgyzstan and Kazakistan who offered unique insight to the culture and social and political aspects of those regions.

INTRODUCTION

The demise of the Soviet Union ended the cold war, established several different independent states, and brought forth the emergence of a multipolar international system. Events in the Soviet Successor States (SSS, or the former Soviet republics), a legal term used generally to describe legal consequences resulting from a change in sovereignty over territory,[1] specifically in the former Soviet republics, will have significant implications for them as well as their immediate neighbor, Russia, and the international community.

This study examines the former Soviet republics: their dilemmas, the regional and international implications of their location and rich resources, and their potential for economic and political development. It also describes their political, social, and economic conditions, as well as their relations with Russia and other countries in their immediate region and in the overall international system in order to provide a framework from which to understand what is happening in this region. Highlighted, particularly, are the relations of these republics with American and other global oil and construction corporations that have acquired oil and natural gas concessions from Azerbaijan, Kazakistan, and Turkmenistan. It demonstrates the attempt by the West, particularly the United States, to diminish Russia's dominant rule. This study will be examined within the context of national identity and nation-state building, which are important factors because most of these republics have never had any experience at being nation-states, even prior to the Russian and the Soviet (Communist) domination.

LOCATION

The location of the two regions of the Caucasus and Central Asia signifies the importance of this study. It is an area rich in natural resources but filled with conflict as the newly formed countries come to grips with their new identities, battle with tensions in their surrounding neighboring states, and face growing attention from the international community.

1

THE CAUCASUS REGION

The Caucasus region is faced with numerous conflicts: Azerbaijan with Armenia over Nagorno Karabagh, as well as Chechnia's (Chechnistan, meaning "land of Chechens," or "Icheria" as the Chechens call it) and Daghistan's (Daghistan, meaning "land of mountains") struggle for independence from Russia. The Transcaucasus is a volatile region that will have a direct impact on the pipeline routes from this area to the international market. The northern Caucasus is an intricate web of shifting loyalties and borders, as well as ethnic and religious animosities reaching back for centuries. The 1990s has seen the poor, mountainous region of Russia's southern border ravaged by wars, ethnic rivalries, and growing lawlessness.

STRUGGLES IN CHECHNIA OR THE CHECHNIA CONFLICT

Chechnia, a rugged, mountainous autonomous area made up of ethnically different people, has been struggling on and off for one hundred and fifty years to break away from Russia. The attempt for independence reached a head shortly after the collapse of the Soviet Union and turned into a war, which ended in August 1996 when battered Russian troops withdrew, leaving sixty thousand dead and Chechnia devastated. The war resumed, however, when the Russians invaded Chechnia in 1999 after the military incursion in Daghistan by the Chechen fighters and numerous apartment bombings in Russia. Russia and Chechnia have failed to come to any resolution. Chechens continue to demand independence. Yet, all the while, Russia insists that Chechnia remain a part of the Russian Federation as a semiautonomous republic.

Chechnia is in ruins following its twenty-one-month war with Russia. Poverty is creating lawlessness, which in turn fuels banditry, kidnapping, and drug and gun smuggling. Russia has failed to compensate Chechnia as promised to rebuild the country.

One consequence of the war in Chechnia has been a strain on already tense relations between Russia and Georgia. The tensions grew after the outbreak of war in Chechnia in 1999, when the Russians proposed stationing troops on the Georgian side of the border with Chechnia. Russia's objective was to seal the southern route to the Chechen highlands—where Chechen fighters can easily hide—but the Georgians refused, balking at being drawn into the Chechen conflict. The labyrinth of complications in north Caucasus is exacerbated, especially for Georgia, by South Ossetia, located in the northern part of Georgia, which has been struggling to secede from Georgia and merge with North Ossetia, a Russian autonomous republic.

DAGHISTAN'S PREDICAMENT

Daghistan, another problem area in the region with an important pipeline, is falling into violence and lawlessness. This land of 2 million people has about 70 percent of Russia's Caspian Sea shore and its major port. Daghistan controls the main pipeline taking Caspian oil west through Russia. It also shares a long mountain border with its rebellious neighbor, Chechnia. In addition, it shares long borders with its southern neighbor, Azerbaijan.

Violence and lawlessness in Chechnia have directly impacted this area. Militant Daghistanis have begun calling for independence from Russia. The bombing of a marketplace in the troubled Caucasus on 19 March 1999, another Russian military campaign started in September 1999 when the Chechen forces attacked Daghistan, and a string of apartment bombings in Russia were the latest incidents in a series of escalating turbulent conflicts in the northern Caucasus that Russian leaders fear may one day unleash their worst nightmare—the unraveling of Russia.

POLITICAL AND ECONOMIC RAMIFICATIONS

A powerful bomb went off in Vladikavkaz, capital of North Ossetia, killing fifty-one and seriously wounding more than one hundred people. Russian Interior Minister Sergei Stepashin characterized the bombing as an "act of sabotage aimed at destabilizing the situation in the North Caucasus and throughout Russia," he added, "at instigating a clash between the peoples. A possible fueling of ethnic strife must be prevented." According to the Russian Federal Security Services, the bombing, because of its location and timing, was meant to be "intimidating and was aimed at destabilization."[2]

The bombing was the worst violence in northern Ossetia since its 1992 war with ethnic Ingush in which hundreds were killed. This conflict has yet to be resolved. Occasionally, clashes still flare up between the Ossetians and the ethnic Ingush living in the republic.

It would not be unreasonable to speculate the possible hand of Chechens in this recent bombing. This bombing, along with recent kidnappings in Chechnia and other violence in the region, serves as a reminder of how little control Moscow has over its southern autonomous republics. Nevertheless, the recent violence has generated international concern, particularly after kidnappers cut off the heads of four employees of a British telecommunications company who had been among the handful of foreign hostages held by Chechen kidnappers in early 1999.

In another incident, a gunman kidnapped the representative of the Russian Interior Ministry in Chechnia, Major General Gennady Sigun, in early March 1999, and at the time of this writing, he has not been released. The kidnappers have demanded a large sum of money for his release.

The Russian weakness, which has permeated every aspect of life since the collapse of the Soviet Union, is encouraging the ethnic rivalry and separatism fueled by existing widespread anti-Russian sentiments among the approximately 4 million Muslims in the Northern Caucasus. Moscow claims the unrest is imported, which is a "very narrow view," as Alexander Iskandarian, deputy director of the Center for Caucasian Studies in Moscow, points out. "Of course, all different groups involved in challenging Moscow do support and assist each other in the regional revolts in addition to those outside agitators from the Muslim world and other places. But most of the rebels are from the region, as are the causes of their uprising." Iskandarian points out that "revolts are due in part to mass poverty that is widespread since the collapse of the Soviet-era subsidies and development. Unemployment is estimated to be as high as 80 percent. This is not unique to the Caucasus region. All over the underdeveloped world, young men become radicalized when there is no land, no money, no jobs, and no prospects." Therefore, Islam, as a worldview, can easily become a temptation for those anti-Russian groups, as an easy, identifiable core to rally around. This worldview, throughout the region's history, has been perceived as a threat to the Russian way of life.

The economic situation has been cited as a major cause of the unrest in this region. "The combination of committed, radical intellectuals and a mass of poor, angry young men is social dynamite," says Iskandarian. That combination is prevalent in Daghistan, Chechnia, and throughout the North Caucasus today, particularly in the rural areas of the region.

According to official figures, between 50 and 80 percent of the population is living under the poverty line. Farm production in 1990s was just 80 percent of what it was in the early 1990s, and industrial production is six times worse than in 1990, before the collapse of the Soviet Union. "Comparing with the rest of Russia, we are lagging behind. Indicators for the standard of living and development are three or four times worse than the Russian average," points out Daghistan's economic minister. Almost 80 percent of the youths in Daghistan and the Caucasus region are unemployed and could be lured into the ranks of the fighters seeking to bring a major change to the whole region. "It's unemployment which pushes the young people toward the independent seeking Muslim movements," claimed Russia's former prime minister Sergei Stepashin in late June 1999.

The conflict in the Caucasus is not an isolated case, says Sergei Kazyennov, an analyst with the Institute of National Security and Strategic Research. "The people are not Russian, and the government in Moscow has not pursued policies that incline to make them feel Russian. Moscow makes them identify more with outside forces, with the ideology of Islam and the countries of the Muslim world. To change the view of these people would take massive economic investment and a whole set of new policy ideas for the region." He points out that neither of these resources seems to be available today.

Since the collapse of the Soviet Union, not only are the rich getting richer, but, in fact, the poor are getting poorer. "The top 10 percent is reckoned to possess 50 percent of the state's wealth; the bottom 40 percent, less than 20. Somewhere between 30 and 40 million people live below the poverty line—defined as around $36 a month. The GDP has shrunk every year of Russia's freedom, except perhaps one—1997— when it grew, at best by less than 1 percent. Unemployment, officially nonexistent in Soviet time, is now officially 12 percent and may really be 25 percent. Men die, on average, in their late 50s; diseases like tuberculosis and diphtheria have reappeared; servicemen suffer malnutrition; the population shrinks rapidly," observed John Lloyd in "The Russian Devolution."

The aftermath of the August 1998 financial crash—when the Yeltsin government announced it would no longer try to prop up the Russian currency causing the ruble to slide from its exchange rate of six rubles to a dollar to a rate of twenty to a dollar and even more—has been replete with bad news, according to the Russian Federal Agency for Statistics. For example:

1. the Russian *ruble* lost 70% of its value;
2. the banking sector remains in a state of virtual collapse;
3. unemployment is up 30% over June 1998. Russians who are employed earn, on average, only 77% as much as they did in June 1998. For pensioners, buying power has fallen to one-third of its 1998 level;
4. Inflation reached 118% from August 1998 through July 1999. Foreign investments fell to $2.2 billion in 1999, down from $3.5 billion in 1998 and
5. ongoing political instability.[3]

CENTRAL ASIA

In Central Asia, problems such as Kazakistan's efforts to assimilate its large Russian ethnic population and the Kyrgyzstan's Uzbek ethnic minority in the regions of Osh and Jalalabad remain a concern for both republics. And the problem of the Tajik minority in Uzbekistan and minority problems in Kyrgyzstan have presented an arena for the overall existing problem of the armed Islamists movement in the Ferghana Valley.

The hostage taking in Kyrgyzstan in August 1999 is one of the latest activities in this region. This was the work of hundreds of guerillas, identified as followers of the notorious Uzbek Islamic leader Juma Namangani, who stormed into Kyrgyzstan and took thirteen hostages, including four Japanese geologists. The underground Islamic opposition to President Islam Karimov aims to establish an Islamic state in the Ferghana Valley. Early in August 1999, more than three dozen armed Islamists entered into southern Kyrgyzstan from their bases in Tajikistan. Demanding safe passage to enter Uzbekistan, the majority of these Islamist militants were from Uzbekistan. When the Kyrgyz authorities refused their demand, they took hostage four Kyrgyz officials and extracted a ransom before releasing them. The Uzbek air force bombed the group and their bases in Tajikistan but had little, if any, effect on them. The Kyrgyz army tried to force them back into Tajikistan but failed. By then, the insurgents had grown to more than seven hundred and took over several Kyrgyz villages in Osh Oblast. Kyrgyz authorities expressed their desire to ask for Russian military assistance to drive them out. The prolonged Tajik civil war destroyed the country's economy, social fabric, and political process. Although it has ended, peace and stability are the major concerns for all states involved. The civil war in Tajikistan has subsided somewhat, but the Islamist groups in Tajikistan are moving into Kyrgyzstan and Uzbekistan in order to spread the Islamic worldviews. Uzbekistan has been the main target of these groups.

The possible spread of the autonomy movement in the Xinjiang[4] province of China, coupled with the developments in Afghanistan and Tajikistan, have also added significance to the region. Afghanistan has been wracked by an ongoing civil war among rival religious and ethnic groups for more than twenty years. On 27 September 1996, an orthodox Islamist group calling itself "Taliban" ("Religious Students"), with the direct support from Pakistan, Saudi Arabia, and the United States, took over Kabul. Talibans continued their war with the former Afghan government forces under the command of Ahmad Shah Masood and the warlord General Abdul Rashid Dostum, who is not involved there any longer. After taking over the government, the Taliban movement imposed harsh restrictions on women and girls, especially from going to school or working outside the home. Forced prayer is also a significant part of this movement. The Taliban's late 1998 decree involves the banning of the use of televisions and other electronic entertainment instruments from home and public. Such developments have alarmed the Central Asian republics, which are considering whether there is a need to have a unified policy toward the group in Kabul. General Abdul Rashid Dostum, a former Communist who controls the northern part of the country, came out in support of President Burhanuddin Rabbani's government. The recent development in Afghanistan has alarmed the Kremlin so much that officials are seriously discussing options regarding the protection of Russia's "Near Abroad" and coordination of its strategy with the front line countries. However, Russia lacks the capability to mount a military response if the Afghani skirmishes were to penetrate into Tajikistan and Uzbekistan.

CHINA: ANOTHER PLAYER

Chinese interests in the area include concerns about cooperation and improvement of stability along the border. China has also been keen to boost trade ties with the former Soviet republics. For instance, in November 1997, Yeltsin and Jiang Zemin signed an economic accord in Beijing to boost economic development in the border areas, primarily in Russia's Far East. In July 1998, Jiang Zemin traveled to Almaty, where he and Nazarbaev discussed the construction of a Chinese auto plant in Kazakistan and various other construction projects in the new Kazak capital of Astana.[5]

China is the world's second largest energy consumer. The U.S. Department of Energy estimates that Chinese consumption will rise from 3.3 million barrels a day in 1996 to 4.6 million by the year 2000. By 2005, it projects Chinese consumption to be at 10.5 million barrels a day. If these estimates are accurate, China will soon have the highest energy consumption in the world. Therefore, it is not difficult to see why China is becoming a key strategic player in global oil economics. Because of its proximity to Central Asia and the Caspian Sea region, it will become a major competitor for profit and influence in the region.

China's economy has grown rapidly in the last twenty years, and this growth is expected to continue for some time in the future. China needs energy to sustain its development. Since 1978, China's overall annual economic growth rate has been somewhere in the area of 8 to 9 percent. At a more sustainable rate of growth of 6 percent per person,

China would reach an average of ten thousand dollars per capita income by the year 2030, and its economy would then total an estimated $16 billion, or twice the size of the 1998 American economy.[6] China has committed billions of dollars to underwrite production-sharing agreements overseas. It plans to spend $100 billion annually with foreign aid capital over the next twenty years to expand domestic energy production. More than $20 billion will be spent on the world's largest hydropower dam, the Three Gorges on the Yangtze. Massive government spending has paid off, boosting China's economic growth to 7.6 percent in the third quarter, according to the State Statistical Bureau. But what China needs most is a guaranteed supply of oil.[7] The deal the Chinese struck with Kazakistan should signal to Washington that the U.S. and international oil corporations are not the only players in this region.

Along with Iran, Turkey, and Saudi Arabia, China's expansion of economic and trade activities with the Central Asian republics was accentuated by the twelve-day trip of Chinese Prime Minister Li Peng to these republics during 1994. This visit brought to light the major influences of China in this region.

Premier Li Peng, during his one-day visit on 24 September 1997 to Almaty, Kazakistan, signed an estimated $9.6 billion deal on oil shipments and the construction of two pipelines. According to the agreement, the China National Oil Corporation (CNOC) will build a 3,000-kilometer pipeline from Kazakistan to China's western border and a 250-kilometer pipeline to the Turkmenistan border. The CNOC will also continue development of the Uzen and Aktyubinsk oil fields in western Kazakistan on the east Caspian Sea. Combined, there are an estimated 1.5 billion barrels in oil reserves. The $9.6 billion deal mandates that the pipelines will begin operating within five years.

During his visit to Kazakistan on 3 July 1998, President Jiang Zemin of China signed a border agreement with Kazakistan, Kyrgyzstan, and Tajikistan regarding the implementation of a previous border agreement signed in Shanghai in 1996. This was coupled with the military reduction accord signed in Moscow in 1997. The four leaders agreed that the accords have laid the foundation for boosting bilateral and multilateral trade. Jiang Zemin noted that his country is prepared to act as a "bridge" for railroad traffic and pipelines to the Pacific Ocean. A separate agreement was signed between China and Kazakistan on 4 July 1998, which finally resolved the outstanding disputes over the two countries' 1,700-kilometer border by dividing the area evenly. Nazarbaev announced at the end of the summit that his country had become the first of the four countries that border northern China to have settled once and for all the territorial disputes dating from the

Soviet era. Jiang Zemin reaffirmed his country's commitment to the agreement signed with Kazakistan in the summer of 1997 on the issue of connecting an oil pipeline from Kazakistan to China. Nazarbaev noted that the feasibility studies on that project are already under way. He added that a gas pipeline would be built to run parallel to the oil pipeline.

On 25 August 1999, the heads of state of Russia, China, Kazakistan, Kyrgyzstan, and Tajikistan—known as the Shanghai Five—signed an eleven-point declaration in Bishkek, capital of Kyrgyzstan. The leaders pledged cooperation in fighting terrorism, drug trafficking, arms smuggling, illegal migration, national separatism, and religious extremism. They also agreed to "prevent the use of their territories for activities detrimental to the sovereignty, security, and public order" in the member states. At the request of China and Kazakistan, the draft declaration was amended to state that the signatories undertake not to intervene in the internal affairs of other states under the pretext of protecting human rights. Overall, the discussion focused on regional security problems, expanding trade, and reviewing the implementation of an earlier agreement. This Shanghai Five summit was the fourth such meeting since April 1996, when the leaders first met in Shanghai, China, and agreed on a series of confidence-building measures along the border. The five leaders agreed that their next summit will be held in May 2000 in Dushanbeh.

On the sidelines of the Bishkek summit, Jiang Zemin, Nazarbaev, and Askar Akaev signed what Akaev termed "a final agreement" on demarcating the frontiers between the three countries where they converge at the Khan-tengri peak. China signed a similar agreement in May 1999 with Russia and Kazakistan. Boris Yeltsin and Jiang Zemin met privately at this time. Their meeting was characterized as a "very warm and friendly atmosphere," as noted by Russian foreign minister Igor Ivanov, "Our relations are now at a peak, and that meets the interests of both nations as well as the interests of regional and international stability."

OTHER ASIAN INTERESTS

Asian interests in Central Asia are not limited to China or for that matter, to oil and natural gas. Korean conglomerate Samsung has bought up copper mines and smelter plants, which have been recently privatized by Kazakistan. A Japanese company, Chori Limited, plans to double the capacity of a railway linking Kazakistan to China. Kazakistan's government has a plan to generate a revenue of about $400 million by privatizing more industrial facilities,[8] such as Aktobemunaigaz and Mangys-tau Munai Gas oil companies, Kazakhmys (country's largest copper producer), Kazakistan Chromium, Kazakistan Zin, and some other mining plants. It should be noted that numerous grandiose plans for economic development in the Caspian and Central Asian republics have made it past the drawing board. Therefore, the region continues to depend on the goodwill of, and the competition between, foreign governments to ensure that its resources find a market.

Azerbaijan, Turkmenistan and Kazakistan are able to play investors against one another. If the former republics are to free themselves from Russian dominance, they must avoid the traps of the new contending countries and corporations, by taking advantage of any opportunity to export their own natural resources, that is, oil and gas.

It should be noted that despite current export problems, the potential rewards to be gained from the former republics are so enormous that no international oil company, or China, can afford to walk away. According to reports, two major U.S. oil companies, Unocal and Amoco, wanted the same two large oilfields as their CNOC rivals. Despite lobbying from Washington, they could not match the noncommercial terms guaranteed by the Chinese, who agreed to fund the pipeline.

THE AMERICAN FACTOR

It is also exceedingly useful to present the U.S. foreign policy objective toward this region. The United States remains the main regional and international actor. Without such a presentation, this study would have serious shortcomings and thus make it difficult, if not impossible, for the reader to evaluate the direct connection in this study. The readers' attention will be drawn to the regional policies of the United States whenever applicable.

On 17 March 1999, Ambassador Stephen Sestanovich, a special advisor to the U.S. secretary of state on the former Soviet republics, told members of Congress that "the cornerstone of American policy in Central Asia is securing the sovereignty, independence and territorial integrity of the states." To advance these objectives American diplomacy focuses on four key issues:

1. the formation of democratic political institutions, as they are the long-term guarantors of stability and prosperity.

2. promotion of market economic reform.

3. cooperation and greater integration of these countries into the Euro-Atlantic and international communities.

4. advancement of responsible security policies, including weapons nonproliferation, antiterrorism, and drug trafficking.

Ambassador Sestanovich continued by pointing out that perhaps the toughest challenges are developing democracy in the region. Other difficulties include the economic performance of these republics in connection with Russia's economic performance and development. In relation to the development of democracy, he criticizes the January 1999 presidential election in Kazakistan as falling short of international standards. He said: "We've been specific with the government on the need to repair the damage to our relations and Kazakistan's reputation through a program of reforms that improve the climate for elections and advance democracy generally." In connection with the second challenge, Sestanovich said: "The global and Russian financial crises, coupled with sharply declining commodity prices, have undermined reforms and set back economic revival." Sestanovich pointed out, "Throughout Central Asia, leaders are on edge about instability in Afghanistan and Tajikistan. They fear an expansion of Iranian influence and the rise of violent extremism in their countries. They are wary of reliance on Russia." He said, "much work remains before we can safely leave the legacy of the Soviet Union behind us in Central Asia."[8]

HOW THIS BOOK IS ORGANIZED

This book is organized into four parts. Part 1 looks at the background of these newly independent states from its roots as part of the Soviet Union to their current economic conditions and activities. Part 2 focuses on each republic independently, covering historical, political, social, and economic development implications. Part 3 goes on to analyze the neighboring influences on this region. Part 4 offers insight into the future of this region.

Therefore, we begin with an overview of the former sovereign republics. Russian policy statements and behavior in relation to the former Soviet republics will be incorporated along the way.

PART I

The Background

CHAPTER 1

Caspian and Central Asian Nations: The Battleground

Situated along the borders of the former Soviet Union with Iran, Afghanistan and the People's Republic of China, the newly independent republics are attempting to reassert their independence and identity. Tsarist Russia began its dominance of these republics back in the 1850s, and the domination continued for seventy years under the Soviet system, which came to power in Russia in 1917.[1] In the 1920s, the Soviet Union created the Central Asian Soviets and drew the boundaries between these republics. With the collapse of the Soviet Union, a complicated new geopolitical situation has arisen. A historical overview of Russian expansion and the involvement of other regional and international players in this area contribute to our understanding of the area's present day significance and configuration. The Caucasus remains a battleground. The Caspian and Central Asian regions have a long history of geopolitical struggles, which continues today.

PRE-RUSSIA

Numerous people, who have left as their heritage a complex mixture of races, languages, and culture, have invaded Central Asia. Throughout the centuries, the original, predominantly Iranian, people in the region either have been displaced or have merged with various invading peoples. Greeks (under Alexander), Persians, Arab Muslims, various Turkic tribes, and the Moghuls (Mongols) have, like the rivers of Central Asia, "flowed into the region, found no outlet, and remained."[2]

The periodic incursions of the Turk or Moghul nomads into the agricultural cities and towns in the Farghana valley were almost a law of nature. Sometimes these nomads were able to defeat the rulers of the region and take their places, after having them executed. The nomad leader would then adopt the title of khan of China, shah of Persia or sultan of Rum. In China, he would become half-Chinese, in Ispahan or Rai, half Persian. The descendants of Chenghiz (Chengiz) Khan were either entirely Sinocized in the Far East or Islmo-Persianized in present day Uzbekistan or Iran. In Russia, the nomad leaders were to be the representatives on earth of *Tangri* ("Khaghan"or "Eternal Heaven").

In protohistoric time, the movements of people were most often in the direction of east and southeast. It is believed that nomads of Iranian stock, or Indo-European stock, called the "Sycthians" and "Sarmatians," who were identified by Iranian inscription as Saka, must have traveled a long way northeast, perhaps even as far as the regions of Pazyrk and Minusinsk. Other Indo-Europeans populated the Tarim oases, from Kashgar to Kucha, Kara Shahr, and Turfan, perhaps even all the way to Kansu. It is certain, however, that from the beginning of the Christian era, people traversed from east to west. The Huns came to establish a proto-Turkic empire in southern Russia and in Hungary. They were followed by the Avars, a Moghul (or Mongol) horde who had fled from Central Asia under pressures from the Chinese in the sixth century. The Avars would later come to dominate the same regions, first Russia and later Hungary. In the seventh century came the Khazar (Qazar) Turks, in the eleventh the Petcheneg Turks, and in the twelfth the Cuman Turks, all following the same route. Last, the Mongol Chengiz Khan, a ruthless marauder who ruled over land spanning from Peking to Kiev in the thirteenth century, was followed by Timurlane (Timurlame). The latter established the Timurid Empire in the fourteenth century.[3]

The conquests of the Iranians, Greeks, Romans, Mongols (Chenghiz Khan), Timurlame, and even the Byzantine Empire to the eighteenth-century expansionist drive of the Russian Empire demonstrate just what a battleground this area had become. In the Caucasus, Russian expansion led to a clash with Iranians and, to a lesser extent, with Ottoman Turks. In fact, in the early twentieth century, offensive Ottoman, German, and British troops intervened in the region in an attempt to undermine the Bolshevik revolution and to bring the region back under the sphere of influence of the intervening countries.

RUSSIAN EXPANSION

Russian history is replete with attempts to expand its control over Caspian and Central Asian regions with aims to enlarge the empire and to secure access to Iran, India, and China and to directly challenge the Ottoman Empire. Between 1710 and 1721, Peter I dispatched several expeditions into Asia (east and south) in search of mineral resources and an easy route to China and India. In order to establish bases, he ordered the building of such towns as Omsk (1713) and Smipaliatinsk (1718). He extended Russian expansion into the Caspian Sea area and in the direction of the Caucasus. This expansion led to a successful war against Persia (1722–1723). As a result of this war, Baku, Ashabad, and Darband ("lock gates" in Persian) were brought under Russian control. These acquisitions had enormous economic and strategic value, as they provided Russia a base from which to launch attacks against the Ottoman Empire. However, fourteen years later, under the 1735 Treaty of Rasht, the Russians withdrew from Baku and Darband and abandoned claims on Astrabad and Gilan, which they had never managed to control effectively.

In the late eighteenth century, Catherine II approved of the Oriental Project, which called for the Russian occupation of the Caucasus. This would adequately position Russia to attack Persia in the south and east, thereby allowing Russia to establish a direct link with India. The project also included attacking the Ottoman Empire to the west, which would enable the Russians to reach Constantinople. Consequently, the Russians were able once again to occupy Baku and Darband; however, the Oriental Project was abandoned by Catherine II's successor, Paul.

Tsar Alexander made territorial gains in the Caucasus through a campaign he started in 1801. Fearing a Persian invasion, the Kingdom of Georgia voluntarily accepted Russian protection. Russian annexation of the khanates and principalities in the region included the following principalities: Mingrelia in 1803; Imertia, the principality of Guria and the Khanate of Ganjah in 1804; the khanates of Karabagh, Shirvan, and Shaki in 1805; the Ossetian region and the khanates of Kuba, Baku, and Darband in 1806; and the principality of Abkhaz (Abkhazia) in 1810. Persia viewed these successes as threatening, and from 1804 to 1813, the two empires went to war. With the Treaty of Gulistan (12 October 1813), Persia, having lost the war, was obliged to acknowledge all of Russia's annexations. This treaty ended up dividing the Azerbaijani population between Russia and Persia. The Persians, who had hoped to recover the lost territories, promptly started another war, which they quickly lost. They were compelled to sign the Treaty of Turkmanchai on 22 February 1828, which set the Russo-Persian frontier along the Aras River. The Aras River marks the present day border between Iran and Azerbaijan. With this treaty, the Russians also secured full navigational rights to the Caspian Sea. In fact, by 1828, Russia had annexed or had been awarded by treaty all of present day Azerbaijan, Georgia, and most of present day Armenia. However, a majority of the Armenian population at that time resided across the border in the Ottoman Empire.

THE GREAT GAME

During the nineteenth century, Central Asia became the battleground for the "Great Game," primarily between the Russians and the British rulers in India. Russia's southern expansion threatened the British position in India. Consequently, Britain consistently opposed this Russian expansion. The Russo-British rivalry is described as an "almost chronic disease; it had an occasional crisis now and then but it was essentially a disease to which the British government and public opinion were accustomed." The reckless British colonial expansion in India and its rivalry with the Russian imperial expansion are evident in its military campaign in the nineteenth century.

In the summer of 1839, a British army of 15,500 (most of them native recruits), along with about 38,000 helpers and camp followers, as well as a large number of camels, mules, and donkeys, marched toward the Khaibar pass from India into Afghanistan. Beyond the Khaibar pass were situated the rugged hills of Afghanistan and further north, the vast steppe of Central Asia, which extended from the borders of Russia to China, through whose deserts, mountain ranges, and the cities of Mary, Bukhara, Samarkant, and Tashkent the old silk road had run. The military campaign was encouraged and supported by those in London who believed changing the frontiers of British India would send a signal to the Russian Tsar and would bring the local Khans and rulers under the British rule.

This invasion turned out to be one of the greatest debacles in British history. First of all, almost none of the British troops returned alive. Second, it set the stage for a power struggle for domination between the Russians and the British that lasted over a century. The power struggle—the Great Game—took place over two thousand miles of unknown territory that was hostile terrain—mountainous, frozen—which divided British India from the Russian expansion. However, at the end of the eighteenth century, when the British colonial empire was consolidating its control over India, Chinese closed Tibet to the outside world.[4] Nonetheless, the sudden appearance of Napoleon in France and the pressure of Imperial Germany in Middle Eastern affairs would throw the rivalry into deep confusion. This confusion was so great that the British would even compromise with the Russians in order to deal with France and Germany.

During the reign of Nicholas, Russia had pushed its Siberian frontier farther south by conquering the nomadic Kazak tribes, which had roamed the steppe between the northern end of the Caspian Sea and Lake Balkhash. Russian conquest set off a chain reaction in Central Asia, which continued through and beyond the reign of Alexander II.

The Russian expansion extended the country's boundary against the Muslim Khanates of Khiva, Bukhara, and Kokand, where the ethnic people began to attack Russian military barracks as well as the Kazak tribes who had recently accepted Russian rule. The city of Orenburg remained a Russian frontier for more than one hundred years. It marked the furthest point of Russia's advance against the Kyrgyz people, Turkmans and the Khanates of Bukhara, Khiva, and Kokand. The Russian Empire contended, in its response to the European powers, that Russian security would be attained in Central Asia when Russia established common boundaries with countries such as Persia, Afghanistan, and China.

With security as an alleged justification for its expansion, the Russian government ordered General Michael Cherniaev to lead an attack on the Central Asian khanates. In 1865, Tashkent, one of the largest cities of the region, succumbed to a Russian assault. During 1868, the ancient city of Samarkant (ancient Afrasiab) was taken over, and the conquest of the Kokand Khanate was complete. The Khanate of Bukhara, named after the city of Bukhara, was attacked during the same year. Khiva was conquered in 1873. Later revolts against Russian occupiers were ruthlessly suppressed, and the khanates were either incorporated into the Russian Empire or became protectorates controlled from St. Petersburg. Situated on the eastern shores of the Caspian Sea, Russian forces overwhelmed the Turkman tribes of the area and then pushed on southeastward to overrun the district of Marv (Mary) in 1884. The Russian boundaries on the eastern shores of the Caspian now reached Persia and Afghanistan. The Trans-Caspian Railway, begun in 1879, soon stretched to the very borders of Persia and Afghanistan. The United Kingdom nervously observed the Russian expansion as a possible base toward the Russian possession of India. In fact, in 1891, a Russian military contingency moved into the Pamir mountain ranges, in present eastern Tajikistan, almost within sight of India.

THE BATTLEGROUND

The Central Asian region known before 1917 as Russian "Turkistan" (land of Turks) is a large territory (1.5 million square miles) stretching eastward from the Caspian Sea and the lower Volga, along the northern frontiers of Persia, Afghanistan, and India. Finally, this region meets with the western borders of Xinjiang (also called "Eastern Turkistan"). Today, the region is made up of Kazakistan, Kyrgyzstan, Tajikistan, Turkmenistan, and Uzbekistan. Except for the high mountain ranges of the Tien Shian in Kyrgyzstan and the Pamir-Alai in southeast Tajikistan, the region is mostly desert and prairie with no high altitudes in the north. Most of the rivers of the region are fed by melting snow from the mountains in the southeast, such as the Pamir-Alai. Several smaller rivers combine to make up the larger Amu Darya (Oxus Rover) and the Syr Darya (Jaxartes River), which emerge, as it were, from the mountains and make their way across the desert plains, draining into the Aral Sea. The Ili and several smaller streams flow into Lake Balkhash. Other streams such as the Chui, Talass, Zarafshan, Murghab, and Tezhen are sucked dry by the hot weather or drained by irrigation and eventually disappear into the deserts. Since the republics in the Central Asian region are geographically landlocked, the access of the people to other lands is hindered.

RESISTANCE AGAINST RUSSIA AND SOVIET RULE

Russian expansion encountered fierce and prolonged armed opposition in the Caucasus and later in the Central Asian region. Moscow had for many years been well aware of the difficulty of bringing the Caucasus under its control. The people of the region, as the Russians soon learned, were the hardest of all peoples to Russify and absorb. There was only one effective way of Russifying the Caucasus: to colonize the region. Several failed attempts were made in the midnineteenth century (1844–1854) to settle Russians in the Caucasus. Afterward, Moscow decided to help an estimated one hundred thousand Armenians, who had emigrated from Persia and Turkey, to settle in the Caucasus region. However, Moscow also began to make definite plans to try once again to settle Russians in the area. The third time proved to be a success. During the first decade of the twentieth century, several thousand Russians were living in different parts of the Caucasus region.

The treaties and the termination of the war with Persia in the nineteenth century did not bring peace, only a prolonged guerrilla war against the Russian presence. Various indigenous ethnic populations of the Caucasus supported the Persians' armed struggle. In 1830, the Circassians began a conflict in the western Caucasus, and in the eastern part in Daghistan, opposition was led by Muslims known as *Muridun* (Devotees). The *Muridun* embodied a combination of religious fanaticism, social discontent, and an intense hatred of the Russians for their confiscation of land. The Chechens, Avars, Abkhazians, Ossetians, and other ethnic populations of the mountainous region were attracted to this opposition movement.[5]

The Soviet revolutionaries encountered opposition that was known as the Basmachi rebellion (a generic Turkish name that derives from *baskini*, meaning "attacker," which was first used for bands of outlaws). The Basmachi rebellion appealed to a pan-Turanism and to the Islamic sentiment of the population, which was fueled by an intense hatred of the Russian colonialists. Taking to the mountains, they caused problems for the Soviet regime until 1922.[6] In the chaotic period after World War I and the Bolshevik revolution, the Caucasus nations of Armenia, Georgia, and Azerbaijan rejected the Bolsheviks as illegitimate and set out on their own. The result was the formation of the Republic of the Trans-Caucasia. The union lasted only five weeks during the spring of 1918, at which time the individual nations began to pursue independence. Following brief periods of Turkish, German, and British occupations during and after World War I, the Caucasus was finally taken over by the Bolshevik army in 1921.

The Caucasus republics' national languages of Armenian, Georgian, and Azerbaijanis were given special status by the Soviet Union. In the early 1920s, the populations of these nations were among the most highly educated in the Soviet Union. Despite the educational, scientific, and technological benefits these republics would receive from the former Soviet system, other aspects of their national identities and community lives would be devastated. Sadly, this happened throughout the Soviet Union, which has made it difficult for the newly independent republics to rebuild their nations.

Immediately after the Turkistan ASSR (Autonomous Soviet Socialist Republic) was proclaimed in April 1918, a fierce struggle ensued throughout the ASSR. This struggle pitted the Bolshevik revolutionary forces against the anti-Bolsheviks and indigenous Basmachi forces. In central and southern Tajikistan, Enver Pasha led the Basmachi forces, which remained active, despite some setbacks, until 1926. Sporadic Basmachi activities in Tajikistan continued through 1931, mainly consisting of isolated incursions from their bases in Afghanistan. In Turkmenistan, the Basmachis came to power in 1918 but were driven out soon thereafter by the Bolsheviks. Basmachi in Turkmenistan continued to resist the Soviet system until 1936.

Soviets ruled Armenia, Georgia, and Azerbaijan as a federation until 1936, when they were made republics. However, the process of setting inter-Soviet Socialist Republican boundaries was controversial. For example, Nakhjivan (Nakhichevan) and the enclave of Nagorno Karabagh were incorporated into Azerbaijan, but the enclave was surrounded completely by Armenia and was largely populated by Armenians.

Central Asia and Azerbaijan remained relatively out of the reach of Russian influence until late in the nineteenth century with the introduction of the cotton crop. The proliferation of cotton planting in Farghana, which was imposed by the Tsarist government at the expense of cereal cultivation,[7] resulted in a deterioration of economic conditions. Cotton farming was imposed to compensate for the loss of the U.S. cotton supply in the 1860s. Russia's growing textile industry was in need of an alternative source of cotton. It should be noted that during the Soviet regime, Central Asia's environmental concerns were sacrificed for cotton production, due to pesticide poisoning and an irrigation system, which resulted in the near loss of the Aral Sea. This increased anti-Russian sentiment in the region and the activities of the Basmachi group.

The discovery of oil[8] in Azerbaijan attracted the Russians to the area, particularly to the city of Baku (Budkoobeh, meaning the "Windblown").

CONSEQUENCES OF RUSSIAN AND SOVIET RULE

The former Soviet republics suffered extraordinarily under Russian and Soviet rule. Forced Russification in the late nineteenth century and the exploitation of the former Soviet republics' natural resources by Tsarist Russia for its own use only harmed the people living in the former Soviet republics. Tsarist rule did little to improve the material standard of living or the general educational level of these people.

The forced and brutal Soviet collectivization imposed by Stalin wrought disaster for the former Soviet republics. People living in the former Soviet republics at the time were forced to quit using their native language in public in favor of the Russian language, as the use of their native languages was only permitted inside their households. The Russian language became the language of administration, industry, the workplace, and science, as well as the medium of instruction for the educational systems of these republics. Prior to Gorbachev's rule, and in the two decades following the Khrushchev era, the main emphasis was to ensure a predominant role for the Russian language and to develop a high level of bilingualism. However, since 1985, in the former Soviet republics, the language question has become even more controversial. In recent years, there has been a growing movement toward requiring Russian-speaking people living in these republics to learn the native languages.

A major part of the former Soviet republics' cultural heritage, *miras* (an Arabic word for heritage from *irs*, meaning "inheritance"), customs, and habits, *"adat and odat,"* and historical identities were linked directly with Islam. By 1928, the Soviet Union's fierce antireligious campaign was underway. Islamic *madressahs* (seminaries or schools) and courts were phased out; and the mosques were closed down, only to be transformed into clubs or recreation centers. Islamic literature,

Adabiyat, was confiscated and destroyed, and functionaries of the mosques were persecuted. The Soviet system deliberately tried to sever all Islamic linkages through the banning of religious activities and practices throughout the Soviet Union and its republics. Thus, all visible signs of religion, Islam in particular, were wiped out. It even became dangerous to admit publicly to being a Muslim.[9]

Although most of the Muslims live in the republics, many of the urban-educated professionals are not practicing Muslims. Religion generally has a very low profile in the republics. However, the people still consider their cultural tradition to be Islamic. The revival of Islamic movements in these republics can be attributed to an anti-Russian sentiment and a sense of national identity, which is expressed as a demand for the use of native languages in literature, adabiyat, or in cultural and traditional, *sunna* or *sunnat*, activities. In contrast, the young intellectuals and professionals draw a clear distinction between themselves and the older generation and tend strongly to support a secular system.[10]

ARDUOUS TASK OF BUILDING NATIONS ANEW

Due to its long history of foreign domination, the former republics face problems with forging a national identity. Central Asian scholars and intellectuals insist that the people of this region have suffered from being the subjects of a "colonial regime." Mamas Kozibayev, the director of the Institute of History and Ethnology at the Turkmenistan Academy of Science, during a conference sponsored by UNECO in November 1992, made the following remarks, "Our memory has been emptied and our history was taught in an imperial way, leaving a blank spot on Iranian and Turanian influences. The origins of our people were not studied, and nomads were considered second-class citizens." He adds that his people need assistance in writing new history books, which will give "a proper place to pages written with the blood of the people."[11]

"We were a colony and we remain a colony," explains Rostam Azimov, the chairman of Uzbekistan's National Bank for Foreign Economic Activity. Russia, still the most powerful foreign presence in the former Soviet landscape,[12] continues to encourage the leaders of the former Soviet republics to maintain the status quo and limit political democracy. However, the result has been widespread discontent. There are rising frustrations among the numerous ethnic minorities, the native populations, and the newly emerging business groups in these countries. Neo-Communist bureaucrats and high-ranking officials erect obstacles in the paths of the up and coming merchants and business groups, thereby temporarily thwarting their attempts to create a market economy. Moreover, power remains highly centralized, which in this case, has stymied political development and the move toward a market economy. It has also kept a large number of people outside of the political process. This exclusion and centralization has contributed to ever-increasing internal political problems.

Former diplomat Bahadir Abdurazakhov maintains that the difficulties faced by Uzbekistan are different than those experienced by countries that grappled with European colonialism. Russian colonialism was different in essence from that of other European nations. It was much more brutal and repressive, even before the 1917 revolution. Russian colonialism would never permit the type of open political opposition, which in 1947 resulted in the granting, by Britain, of independence to India and Pakistan. "Our lack of political freedom in the past means we have political leaders who have no direct experience of democratic processes and procedures. The Communist Party had a monopoly of power, never sharing power with other groups, and this authoritarian tendency is still strong. . . . In reality, we still have only a nominal independence. It has to be made real." He then went on to highlight the consequences of Russian dominance that were followed by Soviet control over the region.[13]

Some believe that "traditional patterns of belief, life-styles, behavior, and attitudes toward work successfully resisted Soviet-style modernization."[14] However, this view is contrary to the considered judgment of most Central Asian scholars and intellectuals. "Across Central Asia, the Uzbeks and Tajiks, the Kazaks and Kyrgyz, the heirs of the 'Mongols,' Turks and Persians who conquered the world many times over, are rediscovering a heroic past that Communism had tried but clearly failed to destroy."[15]

The revival of ancient histories and literatures is part of a broad change being implemented in these countries. "With Communist ideology abandoned but with Communist elite still in power across the entire region, a new political battle is being fought between Islamic fundamentalists [sic] on the one hand and secular nationalists on the other. Liberal democrats occupy a weak position in the middle." Government officials, most of whom are former Communists, generally try to cater to both the nationalists and the fundamentalists by working to strike a balance between the two that will provide some stability for their non-democratic governments. For the people of these countries, the revival of old glory is "more than just a flashback, it is a way to create a better understanding of how to build a still uncertain future."[16]

The debate over language in Kazakistan illustrates the attempt to forge a national identity. In an effort to weld together a new nation consisting of more than one hundred ethnic groups (Kazaks comprise 52 percent of the population, Russians 35 percent, Ukrainians 5 percent, and Germans 3 percent, while other ethnic groups round out the remaining 5 percent of the population), Kazakistan is attempting to impose a common language on the country. A new law after heated debate passed in the Parliament (Majlis) in November 1996 requiring all 16.6 million citizens of the country be able to speak, read, and write in Kazak. Similar debate continued in the upper chamber (Oli Majlis or Upper Parliament), the senate, in January 1997, and large parts of the draft law were rejected. Consequently, the bill was sent back to the Majlis. The part of the bill that generated the most displeasure was Article 23, which gives ethnic Kazaks working in the government until 2001 to master the language. Yet the deadline for ethnic Russians is 2006.[17] Many officials and experts doubt that the deadlines could be met without greater efforts to promote the use of Kazak. In a country where 52 percent of the population is Kazak and only about half of the Kazaks claim to be fluent in the language, this issue will probably remain bothersome for some years to come. Most of the population in Kazakistan as well as in other republics converse in Russian.

The adoption of the language law by itself and the deadlines it imposes will not ensure that Kazak will be accepted as the common language. The governments of Kazakistan and the other republics do not have the financial capabilities and the other resources necessary to promote native languages. However, it is not likely they will be able to acquire the resources for this demand in the near future.

Some ethnic Kazak people contend that language may be the wrong tool for nation building, at least in this particular case. Nurbulat Masano, a political scientist, wants no part of the drive to promote Kazak, which he views as a language of nomads unsuitable for modern times. "There are dozens of words to describe a camel," he points out, but "no words for modern technology or science."[18]

In the republics, literature and histories were written in an Arabic script for centuries. The Soviet authorities introduced the Latin alphabet in 1928, only to replace it in 1940 with a Cyrillic alphabet. The Soviet Union, especially during the Stalin era, worked hard at molding the native populations of these republics. With the aim of transforming these people into new "Soviet citizens," Moscow created national administrative units established along the ethnolinguistic divisions of these republics.

Former Soviet ambassador Bahadir Abdurazakove points out that Kazakistan more than the other four Central Asian republics (Uzbekistan, Turkmenistan, Tajikistan, and Kyrgyzstan) has common borders with Russia. Kazakistan is attempting to become a dominant regional country with a comparatively large economic potential. This is due to the possession of large natural resources, especially oil. The former Soviet republics have emerged from backgrounds of ideological, cultural, and economic confrontations. Currently, they are attempting to find their national identities and to develop prudent foreign policies in light of their relationships with the rest of the world, either separately or in a regionally collective form. Internal conflicts and external uncertainties shape the character of the new republics.

CHAPTER 2

Economic Conditions and Activities

In comparison to the developing countries, these republics have been characterized as the Soviet Union's "third world." They are backward and exploited, lagging behind the former Soviet industrial center's economic and social development (see table 2.1). From the 1970s until the collapse of the Soviet Union, the Muslims of the former Soviet Union have had the highest birth rate in the USSR. They have also been the poorest and the most rural. Outside the capitals of these republics, prosperity is a distant dream. Industry and agriculture have been only slightly restructured after decades of Soviet central planning. Banks are starting from scratch in learning about letters of credit, trade, and checking accounts.

The former Soviet republics have taken steps to establish their sovereignties. These republics, with the exception of Tajikistan, replaced the old Soviet ruble in 1993.[1] However, Tajikistan adopted what became known as the Tajik ruble in 1995. Their currencies have been on a free fall ever since, with no agreements with Russia or any other countries to allow their new currencies to be transferred or converted. Inflation has skyrocketed since the region's new currencies have been introduced. Despite an official exchange rate of one to one, the Russian ruble is worth more than these new currencies. On 30 October 2000 the new currency Samani was introduced.

The Caspian and Central Asian republics' economy and life conditions have declined drastically since the collapse of the Soviet Union. There are widespread shortages in these countries, and there are especially great needs for basic medical supplies, including disposable needles, anesthetics, antibiotics, and numerous other pharmaceutical products. Consequently, health conditions have declined drastically. A visit to a hospital or a clinic in any of the major cities of these republics graphically reveals the problems confronted by the officials and ultimately the people. At the same time, widespread corruption at every level, along with a significant increase in crimes, organized as well as petty, make it very difficult, if not impossible, to conduct any business in the countries.

Whatever changes have been introduced since independence are mere reflections of the whims and contrasting priorities of each autocratic ruler. Consider, for example, the oil-rich republics of Azerbaijan and

TABLE 2.1
Economic Indicators for the Former Soviet Republics

Countries	Azerbaijan	Kazakistan	Kyrgystan	Tajikistan	Turkmanistan	Uzbekistan
Total Pop. (1000)	7655	16832	4480	6045	4235	23656
Major Languages	Azeri & Russian	Kazak & Russian	Kyrgyz, Russian, & Uzbek	Tajik, Uzbek, & Russian	Turkman, Russian, & Uzbek	Uzbek & Russian
GDP (Mil. US$ 1995)	2417	16730	1475	713	1308	9908
Life Expectancy (males) 1995	66.5	65	65	67.3	61.5	66
Life Expectancy (females) 1995	74.5	73.9	72.8	73	68.5	72.2
GDP Per Capita (US$ 1994)	176	120	222	131	2023	187
Growth Rate of Population (1990–95)	1.2	.52	1.68	2.86	2.28	2.24
Urban Population (% 1995)	55.78	59.71	38.94	32.2	44.88	41.28
Workforce (males)	73.79	76.06	73.34	73.22	77.36	73.97
Workforce (females)	53.26	60.55	59.73	55.09	60.94	60.84

Sources: Compiled from the United Nations Statistics Division, 1997, and the French Institute for Central Asian Studies (FICAS), March 1998.

Kazakistan, both of which have signed production-sharing contracts worth billions of dollars with international oil companies. Even they have done little to improve their crumbling Soviet-era infrastructure. Such dilapidated infrastructures exist in other republics in Central Asia as well. Independence has not been financially beneficial to the ordinary people of these republics. It is possible for a few people to get rich quickly in the former Soviet landscape. However, as is so often the case, the elite of these societies are the major beneficiaries of independence.

THEIR SAVING GRACE?

Most of the former Soviet republics are rich in natural resources. Mineral wealth, including that of gold, silver, oil, gas, coal, copper, and uranium is extensive there.[2] Therefore, oil, natural gas, and coal are seen as the keys to prosperity in these resource-rich countries. However, underdeveloped economies will continue to be major inhibiting factors to growth and prosperity. Under Soviet rule and since declaring independence in 1991, these republics have hardly benefited from their natural wealth. It is still the case that the new republics, except for Kazakistan and Uzbekistan, are poorly developed in the production of iron, steel, coal, and oil.[3] Neither heavy industry nor mining is well developed, again except in Kazakistan and Uzbekistan. The great bulk of manufactured goods and oil products in the former Soviet republics still comes from Russia.

Agriculture remains by far the most important source of wealth and employment throughout Central Asia. The cotton crop is crucial, particularly in Uzbekistan. Much of the region's manufacturing industry is limited to cotton processing and cotton products.

OIL AND GAS

The exploitation of natural gas and oil plays a significant role in the economies of Azerbaijan, Kazakistan, and Turkmenistan. These countries have been able to attract large volumes of direct foreign investment despite their slow pace of economic reforms.[4] The Caspian Sea is of unsurpassed significance to the littoral states. Excluding Russia's natural gas reserves, the Caspian Sea's gas deposits are estimated at 57.1 trillion cubic meters, ranking third in the world. The oil reserves are estimated at 59.2 billion barrels.

Unfortunately, among all of the former Soviet republics, only Kazakistan, by producing 19.9 million tons of oil (5 percent of the total 1992 CIS (Commonwealth of Independent States) oil production of 396 million tons, has maintained efficient exploration and production facilities. Kazakistan even managed to slightly increase its oil production from 1991 through 1992. Moreover, its combined production of oil and liquid gas for 1999 was reported at 30,043,323 tons, 15.8 percent more than 1998 production.

On 18 May 1992, an agreement was signed between the Kazakistani government and the Chevron Corporation. This agreement created a fifty-fifty partnership in developing the Tengiz oil field, one of the largest in the world. The Tengiz field, approximately as rich as Prudhoe

Bay in Alaska, is to become the property of the joint-venture Tengizchevroil company, which was formed in January 1993. The terms of this venture might serve as precedents for the giant oil deals that are sought by oil companies such as Exxon, B.P. (British Petroleum), Texaco, and Marathon. No other area in the world has so much untapped oil as Russia and Kazakistan. Yet, until the Chevron agreement, only small foreign ventures had been undertaken, involving less than $30 million each. Chevron was the first large Western oil company to undertake a project in Central Asia.

In the 1990s, Kazakistan pumped oil to a refinery in Russia through a pipeline that can handle fewer than 200,000 barrels daily. The Tengiz field, however, is expected to produce up to 700,000 barrels a day. This figure is much closer to Chevron's 1992 worldwide output of 1 million barrels. Chevron agreed to invest $750 million into Kazakistan throughout the first three years and $10 billion over the twenty-five-year life of the agreement, and Kazakistan agreed to invest an identical amount. A total investment of $20 billion over twenty-five years will be needed for the project.

Tengiz, which is estimated to yield between 6 and 9 billion barrels, is actually small in comparison to what might lie offshore under the Caspian Sea bed. However, oil production at the Tengiz field climbed to the average of 215,000 barrels per day in late 1999, and is scheduled to reach 260,000 in the summer of 2000, when additional production capacity is completed.[5]

Ironically, with its massive oil and gas deposits, Kazakistan is a major energy exporter in the region, yet it is not an energy-independent country. Kazakistan's energy resources are located in the western part of the country, near and offshore the Caspian Sea. The only existing pipelines lead north to refineries in Russia. However, the urban and industrial centers of Kazakistan are concentrated in the east. These are connected to the oil production facilities, which must import oil via pipelines from Siberia since its own refineries are mainly thousands of miles away.

Kazakistan has three oil refineries that supply the northern (at Pavlodar), western (at Atyrau), and southern (at Shymkent) regions of the country. Kazakistan has two separate pipeline systems. These systems are fragmented and consist of two export pipelines in the west, an import pipeline in the east, and a smaller internal line in the south. The Pavlodar and Shymkent refineries are kept supplied by a crude oil pipeline from Western Siberia. The Pavlodar refinery was idle for much of 1999 due to shortages of crude oil. The Atyrau refinery, the only one in the west, runs solely on domestic crude from northwest Kazakistan. This refinery is a World War II vintage plan and is in dire need of new equipment. All three refineries have reduced production due to the decline in the oil production and all three refineries are badly in need of upgrading, requiring large amounts of international funding.

Clearly, Russia controls Kazakistan's outgoing and incoming oil. Moreover, Kazakistan needs to limit its oil exports in order to have enough supply for its domestic needs. In 1999, the country's oil exports caused a steep decline in oil supply to the refineries for the domestic consumption. This action was taken due to the increase in the international oil prices. In the first ten months of 1999, the country exported 19.2 million tons of oil.[6] During 1999, Kazakistan's refineries processed just 5.35 million tons of oil, 32.1 percent less than that of 1998.

CHALLENGES

Chevron has found that getting to the resources is only half the battle. Exporting the oil to the consumer is the real challenge. In this region, Russia still dominates the playing field of the twenty-first-century game. This is partly due to the White House's policy of limiting the pipeline route options that are available to the regional countries, particularly in the case of Chevron and the oil from Kazakistan. The interplay between U.S. foreign policy and corporate interests has become a serious obstacle to the transportation of the regional resources.

The Caspian Sea region of Kazakistan was under Russian control as early as the seventeenth century. Since the disintegration of the Soviet Union, Russia has not been shy about using its leverage to negotiate a higher number of contracts ensuring Russian participation in oil projects involving international oil corporations. Russia has traditionally controlled Central Asia by controlling access routes for the region's resources. Virtually all of the pipelines and railways, which transport oil, gas, metals, and cotton from the region, pass through Russia. According to Azerbaijan's foreign minister Hasan Hasanov, the Russians want all oil to flow north, through Russia.[7]

The existence of natural resources such as oil and natural gas and the manner in which the oil is transported to the consumers has generated many struggles between those hoping to gain a foothold in the industry. Russia feels strongly about its claim to oil in Central Asia, and, in particular, about its claim to oil in Kazakistan. After all, not many years ago, Azerbaijan, Kazakistan, and Turkmenistan were all part of the Soviet Union.[8] However, these republics, especially Azerbaijan, are attempting to minimize the role of Russia and Iran in the transshipment of their oil to distant markets. These republics decided that revenues earned from their minerals would remain in the republic rather than go to Moscow. Azerbaijan's strategy has received financial support from America to help the former Soviet republics carry out this attempt.

Moscow has responded by demanding an agreement that would place the entire Caspian Sea, except for a narrow strip along the coastline, under the joint control of its five littoral countries. To support its strategy in this regard, Russia is flaunting the treaties signed between Iran and the Soviet Union in 1921 and 1940 that gave each country a ten-mile coastal fishing zone with shared jurisdiction over the rest of the Caspian Sea. The current government in Moscow claims to be the inheritor of the Soviet Union's rights under those treaties. Moscow rejects the 1982 Law of the Sea, which states that the landlocked Caspian Sea can be carved up among the littoral states. Moreover, Moscow realizes that the aging Haidar Aliev, president of Azerbaijan, will not maintain his dictatorial grip over the country and its foreign policy much longer. After his departure, Azerbaijan is likely to be a volatile country.[9] Thus, Russia's foreign ministry has the opportunity and time to play its own game, even though, sometimes, it is perceived by the international oil investors as overly receptive to the wishes of Baku.

On 27 April 1996, Boris Yeltsin and the president of Kazakistan, Nursultan Nazarbaev, presided over the signing of a new agreement for a Caspian Pipeline Consortium. The plan is to build a $1.5 billion pipeline to export oil and gas from Kazakistan through Russia to the Black Sea and then to the rest of the world. Moreover, in May 1997, Russia finally agreed to permit a new pipeline from the Tengiz, which would snake around the northern tip of the Caspian Sea through Russian territories and wind up in the Black Sea. It will be completed by the year 2001, and the first tanker is scheduled to load Tengiz crude oil for the international market by September 1999. However, if the past few years are any indication of what lies ahead, regional instability and ethnic bloodshed will continue to divert the oil flow to other routes and perhaps even block the flow of oil and gas from the former Soviet republics. Azerbaijan, Kazakistan, and Turkmenistan especially would be affected. Currently, however, limited oil is being pumped through pipeline and then transported by barges and railroad.

A diplomatic row was triggered by the agreement signed on 4 July 1997 between Russian oil companies Rosneft and LUKoil and Azerbaijan's state oil company, SOCAR, on jointly exploring and developing a Caspian Sea offshore oil field, Kyapaz/Sardar (in Turkmenistan). The argument over the accord involved Russia, Azerbaijan, and Turkmenistan. The quarrel highlights the ongoing dispute over the legal status of the Caspian Sea and the ownership rights to the oil reserves beneath the sea. The five littoral states have been disputing, for the past few years, over whether the body of water should be legally defined as a sea or a lake.

Turkmenistan had initially sided with Kazakistan and Azerbaijan against Iran and Russia, but as of late fall 1996, it switched. However, in November 1996, Russia modified its position by proposing that the sea be divided into zones. Each littoral state would have the exclusive use of resources within its territorial waters. These waters would be extended from ten to forty-five miles. All five countries would jointly use resources beyond that point. Iran and Turkmenistan agreed with the Russian proposal. In early 1997, however, Turkmenistan switched back to its original position, claiming that the Azeri and Chiraq fields lie in the Turkmen sector of the sea. Interestingly, Iran and Russia seem to either coordinate their approaches to the regional issues, conflicts, and other developments or see resolution of the conflicts in a compatible manner. For example, while the West criticizes Russia's military incursion in the Caucasus, specifically the Chechen, Russia has hardly been criticized by the Muslim countries. In fact, it has received the strongest support from the Islamic Republic of Iran. Moscow sees Iran as an important strategic partner and counterweight to the Western and Turkish influence in the Caspian. Kamal Kharazi, Iran's foreign minister, has vowed "effective collaboration" with the Kremlin against what Iran described as "terrorists bent on destabilizing Russia." Russia went further and thanked Iran for using its chairmanship of the Organization of the Islamic Conference in 1999 to present Russia's view regarding Caucasus.

Issuing a statement on 5 July 1997, the day after the agreement was signed, Turkmenistan immediately protested the signing of the Russian-Azerbaijani agreement in Kyapaz/Sardar. Turkmenistan contested Azerbaijan's ownership of the field, located 180 kilometers east of Baku and only 100 kilometers from the coast of Turkmenistan, and demanded the annulment of the agreement. In late July, Russian officials informed the Turkmen leadership that the Kyapaz contract would be annulled, and the Russian Foreign Ministry issued a statement confirming the annulment on 5 August 1997. Two days later, Russian president Boris Yeltsin told Turkman president Saparmurat Niyazov, during the latter's visit to Moscow, that the signing of the agreement between the Russian companies and the Azerbaijani State Oil Company had been a mistake on the part of the Russian oil companies involved. Russia's actions succeeded in placating President Niyazov, a potential ally, while simultaneously embarrassing President Aliev of Azerbaijan, who was on an official visit to the United States at the time.[10]

During an official visit to Russia in April of 1997, the speaker of Iran's Parliament (Majlis), Ali Akbar Nateq-Nuri, accused Washington of encouraging Baku to disagree with other littoral states on the status of the Caspian Sea. He was quoted as saying, "The United States has an historical dream of establishing itself in the Caspian Sea after it did it in the Persian Gulf. The superpowers always use local factors to penetrate one region or another." He warned that President Aliev of Azerbaijan "is making an historic mistake by laying ground for U.S. interference." He added that Iran, Russia, and Turkmenistan shared similar views on the Caspian Sea and that the three countries had tried hard but failed to reach a compromise with Azerbaijan and Kazakistan.[11]

As of mid-1998, the only pipeline to the Western market runs through Russia. This severely limits Kazakistan and Turkmenistan's access to the market. Recently, numerous pipeline routes have been suggested by Western oil companies and their governments in order to loosen Russia's hegemony by providing transport routes through Georgia and Turkey. These lines will traverse east to China and south through Afghanistan. However, these alternative routes remain to be realized because of numerous violent local oppositions in the countries where the alternative pipeline will be constructed.

The oil agreements signed with China on 24 September 1997, worth an estimated $9.5 billion, will offer other pipeline option routes to Kazakistan, thereby diminishing Russian pressure on Almaty—now Astana. At the heart of these agreements is the building of a 3,000–kilometer (1,860–mile) pipeline from the southwestern oil fields of Kazakistan to the Chinese province of Xinjiang. In return, China is awarded the right to develop some of the largest oil fields of Kazakistan. Western oil experts estimate that the eastern shores of the Caspian Sea, southwest of Kazakistan, may contain up to 200 billion barrels of oil, a quantity large enough to fuel the U.S. economy for thirty years. These shores also contain an enormous amount of natural gas. Kuwait, by comparison, has proven reserves of 97 billion barrels. It is conceivable that Kazakistan may become the fourth or fifth largest oil-producing country in the twenty-first century.[12]

As the Caspian supply of energy lies outside OPEC (the Organization of Petroleum Exporting Countries), the organization is unlikely to have any significant direct impact on the price of that energy. If it has any appreciable impact, the diversity of sources may keep pump prices down and help prevent the "kind of economic stranglehold" that OAPEC (the Organization of Arab Petroleum Exporting Countries) inflicted in the 1970s.[13] However, major consumers are well aware of the problem of the transshipment of oil from the Caspian Sea area and the Central Asian countries. This remains a serious obstacle to maintaining lower oil prices. The oil exported from Kazakistan still travels either via small tankers across the Caspian Sea to railroad tankers in Baku, capital of Azerbaijan, or via the Russian pipeline.

Working the shores of the Caspian Sea involves more than oil exploration and production. It is a geopolitical chess game that involves a
number of players with different objectives.

PIPELINE ROUTES

New transportation routes will be very important to carry oil and natural gas from the Caspian and Central Asian regions to the world market.
The existing routes were built and designed to run throughout Russia
and to supply the Soviet Union with oil. The existing Russian pipelines
do not have the capacity to absorb all of the oil and natural gas the
Caspian Sea and Central Asian regions can produce. Most existing oil
pipelines terminate at the Russian Black Sea port of Novorosiisk, requiring tankers to transit via Bsporus (Bosphorus) to the Mediterranean and
world markets. Questions remain as to whether or not the Mediterranean is the right place to send all of the forthcoming Caspian Sea and
Central Asian oil and natural gas. The energy demand for the next ten
to fifteen years will be different in the European and Asian markets.
Energy experts expect the oil demand in Europe in the next ten to fifteen
years to increase by more than 1 million bpd, while the Asian markets
are expected to increase by 10 million bpd over the same time period.
Therefore, the number, capacity, and direction of these pipeline routes
are of very important business and economic concerns.

The nations of the Caspian/Central Asian regions, Azerbaijan, Iran,
Kazakistan, Turkmenistan, and Uzbekistan, are already major energy
producers. The discoveries of energy reserves in the regions have
attracted the global energy competitors to the area. Most of Azerbaijan's
oil resources, proven as well as possible reserves, are located offshore.
Thirty to 40 percent of the total oil resources of Kazakistan and Turkmenistan are offshore as well. Oil production in these countries will
increase with additional investment in technology and export facilities,
assuming the return on the investment will be attractive for the investors
even in light of the current oil glut and low world prices. Proven oil
reserves for the entire Caspian Sea region are estimated at 16 to 32 billion barrels, which is more than the U.S. and the North Sea reserves.
Kazakistan, Turkmenistan, and Uzbekistan have very large proven natural gas reserves. However, the gas fields of Kazakistan, Turkmenistan,
and Uzbekistan are located far from potential markets. There is also the
lack of a sufficient infrastructure to export the gas. This further prevents
these countries from utilizing their natural resources for possible economic development. The alternative pipeline routes for these countries
are through the existing or expanded Russian system, Caspian Sea

marine pipeline to Baku and from there to follow either existing pipelines or new ones, through Iran (which is target of U.S. sanctions and investment limitations), war-torn Afghanistan and the "East route" through China.

Among the competitors is the United States, which is in the strongest position. As noted before, getting the energy to the world market is the foremost concern of the investors and the United States. Russia, Iran, Turkey, and China are the other major competitors in the region. These rivalries have turned the region into the newest stage of power politics. The official position of the United States is to support cooperation in the region, but the United States does not want Iran to benefit from the development.

At the same time, countries are also seeking to limit Russia's role in the region. This reminds us of the modern version of nineteenth-century Great Game, in which the United Kingdom and Russia competed for dominance in the region. An American diplomat in the region is quoted as saying, "This is where we prove we're—Americans—still the big boy on the block. China, Europe, Iran, Russia, and all the others want to see if they can take us down. All of our so-called friends and all of our so-called enemies want control of this region." Today's game is over oil, natural gas, and the pipeline routes.[14]

The White House's vigorous lobbying for a pipeline route that would run from Baku via Georgia to the Turkish port of Ceyhan and on to the Mediterranean finally succeeded. On the sidelines of the OSCE summit in Istanbul, the presidents of Azerbaijan, Georgia, and Turkey on 18 November 1999 signed agreements that constitute the legal framework for the construction and operation of the Baku-Ceyhan pipeline. Construction of the 1,730 kilometers (1,080-mile) pipeline will begin after a feasibility study is completed (probably in 2001) and must be completed in three years. However, the energy companies point out that the U.S.-backed route is too expensive to build without a government subsidy exceeding $1 billion. Oil company calculations clearly favor the route across Georgia to the Black Sea, which would cost more than half. Since these companies will pay for whatever pipeline is built, it places the companies in a stronger position. The industries have the potential to drive the geopolitics rather than the governments. A number of American oil, gas, and pipeline company executives believe the best export route for the regional energy is through Iran. However, they cannot choose that route at present because of sanctions imposed by the U.S. Congress, which forbid large investments in Iran. These executives are reluctant to write off the Iranian option, preferring to stall, while the oil prices are low in the hope that the sanctions will be lifted.

Lobbyists for American energy companies are pressing for an end to the sanctions, and some prominent individuals support them. In a speech during January 1999, former secretary of state, Cyrus Vance urged for new overtures to Iran.[15]

The regional nations do not share the United States' policy to isolate Iran. These countries must live with Iran as neighbors. Logically, these countries would rather cooperate than feud. Moreover, energy executives are well aware that their pipeline route options are limited for bringing out to the world market oil and natural gas from the land-locked Caspian Sea and the Central Asian regions.

The landlocked regions of the Caspian Sea and Central Asia have several pipeline options available to them. The current pipelines, as noted before, have capacity limitation. Thus, when the oil companies begin to expand production, the new pipelines must have the capacity to absorb the future production levels. This assumes that the market, in the near future, will have a sufficient demand for larger production.[16]

Varying opinions have been presented, as in this writing, that the Caspian region is blessed with a fabulous reservoir of oil. Tapping this would bring vast wealth to the impoverished and unstable region where the United States, Russia, and Iran, not to mention Turkey, China, and others, compete for influence. Optimistic studies and forecasts regarding the Caspian Sea basin still remain mere speculations. Despite the speculations, on 2 December 1999, then Prime Minister Putin met with the leading members of the Caspian Pipeline Consortium, including LUKoil president Vagit Alekperov and Chevron Overseas President Richard Matzke. Alekperov told the meeting that construction of the 1,580-kilometer pipeline from Tengiz to Novorossiisk will be completed on schedule in June 2001. The pipeline, he added, will be able to handle all Kazakistan's current export requirements.

The low oil prices during the first eight years of the 1990s began to increase by 1999 and continue to increase. During the month of January 2000, the oil prices reached the highest level ($26.30) since the Persian Gulf War. The price increase is attributed to the production cuts of 4.3 million bpd by OPEC and the decline in the U.S. oil inventories by more than 136 million bpd in 1999, a 12.7 percent plunge from 1998 and the highest since 1950, according to the American Petroleum Institute (API). The API suggested that this price level might decline by spring and added that such price increases will hurt numerous countries in Asia, Africa, and Latin America, which will force them to curb their demand for oil. Moreover, there are strong indications that there might be an oil glut, and the oil companies must seriously rethink their plans for investments in the region. In fact, some oil companies are pulling out or paring down operations, citing high transport costs and questionable deposits. Others are delaying projects. Stephen O'Sullivan, a Moscow-based oil analyst with the United Financial Group, has this to say on the current situation, "With the price fall, people are more cautious about spending money and are walking away from exploration projects. Maybe expectations of a pot of gold in the Caspian were a little ahead of reality. Now realism is creeping in. It's clear it's not the bonanza it was thought to be." Pessimism deepened in Baku in February 1999 when a consortium, International Petroleum Company, led by the American oil company Penzoil pulled out after drilling three exploration wells. The reserves of oil and gas were not sufficient to justify the $3 billion project.[17]

These conditions and developments would make it unattractive for international oil companies to opt for pipeline routes that would require large investments. Consequently, the Iran pipeline route—190 miles to Tabriz in northwest Iran—becomes the most desirable one even though the White House is adamant in its insistence of the Baku-Ceyhan, a 1,080–mile pipeline route. In fact, Washington's favorite route could cost less if it were to go via Iran to the port of Ceyhan in Turkey. The Clinton administration argues that this route would limit dependence on Russia and undermine Iranian competition for an alternative route. The White House's special envoy to the Caspian region, Ambassador Richard Morningstar, during his visit to Moscow on 25 February 1999, in support of Baku-Ceyhan said, "We believe that the East-West transit corridor is the way to go. We think that it is good for the region and . . . it is good for all countries in the world." In connection with Morningstar's view, Carl Burnett, president of Mobil Oil Kazakistan Incorporated is quoted as saying, "He has a tough case to argue, with estimates that the pipeline will cost up to $4 billion to build. So far, international consortia working in Azerbaijan have not found test-drilling results that would justify such spending. We think the potential is there. But we don't know if there is need for another route."

In December of 1988, the involved American oil companies, Chevron, Mobil, and Royal Dutch Shell agreed to carry out a study about the feasibility of using Baku-Ceyhan. This study was highly encouraged by Washington, D.C. However, oil industry sources repeatedly point out that the oil companies favor the shorter cheaper route to Georgia's Black Sea port of Supsa, or one via Iran. The White House maintains that the pipeline will cost no more than $2.4 billion to build, but AIOC members, who have to bear most of the cost, contend the route could cost up to $3.4 billion. "The pipeline scenario depends on the volumes of additional oil discovered," says Phil Meek, president of Chevron Munaigas Incorporated, based in Almaty, Kazakhstan. However, financing the pipeline remains to be a major hurdle. The director of International Affairs of BP/Amoco, the main oil company involved, has set a deadline of October 2000 for raising financing and commitments to use the pipeline by the producers. But if financing is not in place in time, he noted, BP/Amoco can try to get the oil shipped by a different route, by expanding the Baku-Supsa pipeline. It is also possible that BP/Amoco "might just delay the next phase of oil production in the Caspian Sea if the structure of the pipeline was still not settled."[18] The Baku-Supsa pipeline carries an annual capacity of approximately more than five tons and will bring modest annual revenues of $7 million and $10 million to Georgia and Azerbaijan, respectively. Pumping oil through this pipeline resumed on 4 December 1999. During November 1999, pumping was suspended after torrential rains in western Georgia washed away the ground from under a fifty-meter section of the pipeline. Any break in the pipeline could cause an ecological disaster for the area. Both Azerbaijan and Georgia are counting on a far greater income from the possible construction of a so-called main export pipeline through their territories and down to the Turkish port of Ceyhan on the Mediterranean. However, security is of a major concern for the oil companies. Georgia's security is threatened from within by an ongoing conflict with the separatist region of Abkhazia, as well as the Turkish territory, where the Kurdish ethnic nationality are concentrated in the eastern part of the country where the pipeline will enter the Turkish territory. The latter situation should be viewed within the context of the Kurdish Workers Party (Party Kargaran Kurdistan; PKK) and Ankara's persistent policy of ignoring Kurdish demands for autonomy.

The recent revelations and developments in the Caspian basin, as noted, in addition to the slumped oil prices and possible oil glut, may in fact encourage the oil companies involved in the Caspian and the Central Asian regions to renegotiate their agreement with the regional countries.

CONSEQUENCES OF OIL EXPLORATION IN THE CASPIAN SEA

The Caspian Sea, an inland body of salt water, is home to 90 percent of the world's sturgeon. Most of the known sturgeon species are in the northern part of the sea, which lies on the Russian side. The sea has been overfished, fouled by pollution, and threatened by constant oil exploration. Experts say Russia's caviar industry, the largest in the world, may collapse within a few years. The fishing stock is shrinking at an alarming rate. Dwindling stocks of sturgeon in 1996 and 1997 have increased caviar prices in the West by 35 percent in three years. Experts worry that the recent rush for massive oil exploration and drilling in the Caspian Sea by Azerbaijan and Kazakistan will severely damage the environment of the Caspian Sea and lead to the extinction of sturgeon. "If they fully develop the oil industry in the Caspian, one can safely say there won't be any more sturgeon," says Lidia Vasiliyeva, the director of a sturgeon hatchery south of Astarkhan.[19]

During the Soviet era, the production of caviar, like everything else, was a state monopoly, and the data on the output was tightly controlled. Poaching was rare and quality control strict. However, pollution was a major problem during the Soviet era, and dams hindered sturgeon from reaching spawning grounds they had used for thousands of years. Iran and the Soviet Union signed the only fishing agreement that existed in this area.

With the dissolution of the Soviet Union in 1991 and the increasing levels of poverty and industrial stagnation in the former Soviet republics, which spread through the Caspian region, many people saw sturgeon as a source of instant currency. Consequently, widespread poaching has cut the official sturgeon catch in the Caspian Sea from twenty-five thousand tons a year in the mid-1980s to only thirty-four hundred tons in 1996. This has also reduced caviar production by more than 80 percent in the same period.

The lawlessness in Russia has also contributed to an increase in poaching. Poorly paid police officers can easily double or even triple their monthly salaries by selling a few kilograms of caviar. In fact, corrupt police officers often work with the smugglers and poachers. Illegal and unlawful activities are widespread throughout the former Soviet republics. In the autonomous republic of Daghistan, situated north of Azerbaijan, an all-out caviar war between Russian border guards and local smugglers was underway during the fall of 1996. This dispute was eclipsed when a bomb targeting a barracks killed sixty-seven border guards and their family members, including twenty-one children. "The local Mafia, perhaps backed by the police, is the prime suspect." A year and a half later, during May 1997, "the police officer in charge of caviar interdiction in Dagistan (Daghistan) was murdered."[20]

RUSSIAN IMPACT

A significant number of people living in these republics are from other parts of the former Soviet Union. For example, over 40 percent of the Kazakistan population are Slavs. Thus, these republics have a significant number of non-Muslim, nonindigenous populations. Approximately 10 million Russians live in the newly independent states of Central Asia.

The Russian elite in these republics has found itself to be an unwelcome minority in the middle of a nation-building process that is based on the ethnic majority. Economic chaos in the republics and the fear of a return to an Islamic political system have made many Russians skeptical about their future in Central Asia. Since 1985, it is estimated that more than 500,000 Russians have emigrated from Uzbekistan, while upward of 90,000 people have left Tajikistan. Tajikistan is the Central Asian republic where the Islamists have had the greatest influence on the government. Between 1989 and after mid-1992, an estimated 185,000 Russians have departed from Kyrgyzstan.[21] However, departure of the Russians from these republics has declined since 1995. Of some 900,000 Russians living in Kyrgyzstan in the early 1990s, some 650,000 remain in the country. These departures have had an enormous negative impact on the affected republic's economic activities. Many Russians were attracted to Central Asia or were sent by Moscow there during the 1950s and up through the 1970s. They tended to hold down skilled and relatively high-paying jobs. In fact, Russians accounted for up to 90 percent of the work force of many industries.

On 9 February 1995, Russian Foreign Minister Andrei Kozyrev met with Kazak President Nursultan Nazarbaev and Foreign Minister Tuleutai Suleimanov. They agreed to set up working groups addressing the questions of dual citizenship, military cooperation, and the future of the Baiknur space complex. Nazarbaev later articulated his opposition to dual citizenship, maintaining that non-Kazak Russians living in Kazakistan should hold Kazakistani citizenship. On 3 October 1995, he issued a decree harmonizing the country's citizenship law with the new constitution, which does not provide for dual citizenship. On a more positive note, he agreed to lease the Baiknur cosmodrome to the Russians for twenty-five years at $150 million annually, which will go toward payment of Kazakistan's debt to Russia. Under the agreement, Russian soldiers stationed at the cosmodrome will no longer be subject to Kazak law.[22]

IMPACT OF HOSTILITIES

The new power holders in Kabul have become a major concern for Russia, Iran, and Central Asian countries. The civil war in Tajikistan arose out of the chaos created from the coalition of democrats and members of the Islamic Resurgence Party (IRP) ("Hezib-e Nehzat-e Islami"), which aimed at overthrowing the pro-Communist regime of former President Rahman Nabiev in September 1992. Akbarshah Iskandarov became interim president but later made way for the return of Nabiev in an attempt to reconcile pro-Communists with the IRP-democrat alliance. Shortly after Nabiev was chosen as president, the pro-Communist warlords from Kulyab began a drive to capture Dushanbeh from the former Iskanderov government. Then, the Tajik military and Islam Karimov, president of Uzbekistan, aided Nabiev's government. Pro-Communist forces captured Dushanbeh in early December 1992 and began eliminating the members of the IRP and democratic groups. In a terrible civil war, Tajikistan was almost pulled apart by nine months of bitter fighting between the coalition of Islamists and democrats versus pro-Communist forces. Tragically, this civil war was further compounded by ethnic hostilities and clan rivalries. The war uprooted hundreds of thousands of people, and the government changed hands three times during the conflict. In late December 1992, Tajik officials announced that there were 537,000 registered refugees in the country, almost 10 percent of the total population of 5.5 million.[23]

The coalition government was ousted by the intervention of Uzbekistan and the CIS military forces, along with additional support from Kyrgyzstan, and pro-Communist power was restored to Dushanbeh. Consequently, the military coalition was forced to retreat into the mountains, and a large number of coalition leaders and their supporters fled into Afghanistan.[24]

The outcome of the civil war in Tajikistan and the recent developments in Afghanistan, especially the takeover of two-thirds of the country, including Kabul by Taliban forces in 1996, further exacerbated the existing uneasiness in the area. The United States, Pakistan, and some of the Persian Gulf states, especially Saudi Arabia, were involved with the change in Afghanistan. Developments in the region and reports from foreign diplomats during 1998 indicate that Moscow has returned to Afghanistan and is secretly engaged in the Afghan war. The Russians, according to these reports, ironically, are supporting the Afghan Mujahideen, the Islamic guerrillas who are under the leadership of Ahmad Shah Massood. Massood fought the Soviet military in the 1980s with the backing of the CIA, Pakistan, and Saudi Arabia. In this campaign, the Russians find themselves cooperating with Tehran in their opposition against the Taliban ruling theologians. The latter development is partly because Moscow and Tehran have an overlapping interesting in Central Asia. The anti-Taliban Northern Alliance is viewed as a buffer between the Taliban and the Afghan border with the Central Asian republics. Moreover, the continuation of a civil war prevents international oil corporations from building pipelines through Afghanistan.[25] It could be argued that the continuation of conflicts in the Transcaucasus region, Central Asia, and Afghanistan increases the probability of having Iran and Russia as the only "safe" and available pipeline routes. However, the continuation and in some cases the escalation of violence in the region of the Transcaucasus—for example,

Chechnia and Daghistan—will diminish Russia as a safe pipeline route.

In early January 1993, leaders of the five Central Asian republics met in Tashkent, Uzbekistan, and agreed to enhance cooperation on regional security and to provide humanitarian aid to weary Tajikistan. The one-day Tashkent summit was the second regional summit of the five presidents held since the disintegration of the Soviet Union. The first summit, which discussed Tajikistan and other regional issues, was held in early 1992 in the Kazak capital of Almaty—the capital later was moved to Astana. Since then, several regional meetings have been held regarding Tajikistan, the spread of Islamic "fundamentalism," and the narcotic trafficking coming into these republics from Afghanistan.

REGIONAL COOPERATION

The heads of these republics have discussed ways to coordinate economic activities so as to minimize inflation and curb the alarming fall in industrial production. They also discussed regional security issues and agreed to hold meetings on a regular basis, scheduling the next meetings to take place in Ashqabad, Turkmenistan, and other capitals. Among the leaders of the republics, Nazarbaev is the strongest advocate of close integration within the CIS. At the summit, he suggested that the presidents should either turn the CIS into a fully fledged confederation or admit that it is a failure and go their separate ways. It was suggested at the Tashkent summit that the Central Asian countries might turn their backs on the CIS and create their own regional confederation, in the hopes of bringing about stricter regional security measures and closer economic integration.

In early January 1994, inspired by the newly created regional economic organization, Nursultan Nazarbaev of Kazakistan and Islam Karimov of Uzbekistan agreed to create their own system of economic cooperation. This agreement, if implemented, would allow for the free flow of goods, services, and capital between the two countries and establish "coordinated policies" for credit, finance, budget, tax, customs, and duties (including currency) from 1994 until 2000. This agreement, if it were to be carried out, would serve as the first firm economic agreement within the CIS. However, addressing a news conference in London on 22 March 1994, Nazarbaev contended that increased Western investment toward helping to stabilize Kazak's currency would constitute the most effective safeguard for his country's sovereignty.

During 1996, Azerbaijan, Georgia, and the Ukraine motivated by their pro-Western orientation and mistrust of Russia decided to form a regional alliance. Azerbaijan and Georgia's dissatisfaction with

Russia's record of mediation and involvement in the Nagarno Karabagh and Abkhaz conflicts added to their desire to cooperate. They also wanted to benefit from the export of Azerbaijan's oil through Georgia and Ukraine. Later, Moldova also joined the group, which loosely formed the Azerbaijan and Moldova (GUAM) group. The formation of the group was first announced in mid-October 1997 by the presidents of Georgia, Ukraine, Azerbaijan, and Moldova in Strassbourg, France. This all took place on the sidelines of the Council of Europe summit.

GUAM leaders declared their intention to deepen political and economic ties and cooperation, both on a bilateral basis and within regional organizations. They also affirmed their mutual interest in possible regional security issues—which could not be addressed by the CIS. They rejected Russia's suspicions about the purpose of the union, stating that the group is not an anti-Russian alliance. The statement underscored the economic potential of GUAM, specifically Ukraine and Moldova's interest in the TRASECA project intended to create a coordinated transport corridor from Central Asia via Transcaucasus to Europe and in the possibility of exporting Azerbaijan's Caspian oil through Ukraine or Romania.

However, in a later meeting in Baku, it was announced that the primary topic of discussion was regional security. Azerbaijan advocated coordinating a security policy within the parameters of NATO's Partnership for Peace program.

On 24 April 1999, at a ceremony in Uzbekistan's embassy in Washington, D.C., on the outskirts of the NATO summit, Uzbekistan formally became the fifth member of the Georgia, Ukraine, Azerbaijan, and Moldova alignment. The grouping would, henceforth, be known as GUUAM. The presidents of the member states issued a joint statement affirming their support for one another's territorial integrity. They also announced their support for both regional transport corridors and cooperation within the framework of international organizations such as the Euro-Atlantic Partnership Council. The statement stressed that their cooperation is not aimed against third countries or groups of countries. It is not farfetched to speculate that this may be the primary step toward leaving the CIS.

In an interview with the *Washington Post* during early May 1999, Eduard Shevardnaze, president of Georgia, in connection to the group said, "All these countries—Azerbaijan, Uzbekistan, Ukraine—the main problem they have is retaining their independence. It's quite clear that [Moscow] will try to make them walk the path that Belarus has walked [toward reintegration with Russia]." Then he went on to say that is why leaders, on the fringes of NATO's fiftieth anniversary celebration, were promoting GUUAM. These countries have in common their Soviet past and their desire not to be dominated again by Moscow. Shevardnaze passionately urged the West to support the members of GUUAM, even if many of its leaders fall short of democratic ideals. "Without the help of the West, we will not survive."

PART II

The Republics

CHAPTER 3

Azerbaijan

Azerbaijan consists of 33,400 square miles, with a population of 7.4 million and a relatively high population density. The country is divided into two parts. There is a small portion, Nakhjavan, situated in the southwest and separated by Armenia. Azeri people trace their roots to the Medes who ruled Persia and later moved north and settled in an area to the southwest and another area directly west of the Caspian Sea.

The name *Azerbaijan* is rooted in the word *azarabadegan* or *azarbayegan*, which means "the land of eternal flames." Legend has it that Zoroaster (the prophet of Zoroastrianism) was born in present day Azerbaijan. This country was the site of a major Zoroastrian fire temple in the ancient city of Tabriz, as Zoroastrianism was the dominant religion of the region prior to the Islamic invasion.

THE BID FOR INDEPENDENCE

In the nineteenth century, Azerbaijan, which was part of Persia, was divided between the Russian and Persian Empires. Currently, the part formerly belonging to Russia is independent.

In June 1992, the Azerbaijani Khalq Jebhasi or Azerbaijani Popular Front (APF), then the largest political organization in the state, was the first group to declare independence for the republic from the former Soviet Union. This move by a group of Azerbaijani people ought to be evaluated within the context of the bloody events of 19 January 1990.

When Azerbaijan first declared independence in 1990, families poured across the newly opened border with Iran to meet long-lost relations, but within days, the Soviet tanks crushed the independence movement. The Soviet army rolled through the city of Baku, killing more than one hundred people, mostly civilians, and injuring more than seven hundred. A declaration of emergency and an imposition of curfew were then imposed on the Azeris. The next day, the people reacted to the Soviet army's atrocities by burning their Red Communist Party membership cards, the keys to prominent careers and status in the community. This response was a radical turning point in the life of the Azerbaijani people as it marked the rejection of the Soviet system.

The use of brute force by the Kremlin fueled anti-Russian feelings and further fueled the Azeris' desire for independence. In light of the increasing nationalist sentiment, it is likely that the 20 million Iranian Azerbaijanis will demand some form of autonomy. This option may become particularly attractive for Iranian Azeris in the face of deteriorating social, economic, and political conditions in Iran. The contempt for the Iranian regime was apparent when the Islamic Republic of Iran's former president Hashemi Rafsanjani visited Baku's main mosque in early July 1989. About three thousand people greeted him, which was disappointing because a much larger turnout was anticipated. The less than enthusiastic response to Rafsanjani's visit manifests the Azeris' contempt for the regime, although they are historically adherents of Shi'ite Islam, which is similar to Shi'ism in Iran. The AFP, a secular movement, has enunciated reservations about the nature of the Islamic Republic and its leadership in Tehran. The chairman of the Azerbaijan Parliament said in regards to the reunification issue: "I'd like the same relations between Azerbaijan and Iran as there are in the European Community. Then there would be no necessity to talk of reunification."[1]

The Soviet army invaded Baku in 1990 to prevent further deterioration of the system and to smash any movement toward independence. Nevertheless, APF leader Abulfazl Elchibey (died in Turkey on August 22, 2000) was voted in as president of the republic with more than 59 percent of the votes. The APF opposed the CIS and refused to sign any military pact with it. The APF government contended that the failure of CIS to resolve the Nagorno Karabagh conflict, involving some of the bloodiest battles in the former Soviet Union, was the major reason for its opposition.

During 1991–92, Turkey and Iran were involved in a quiet struggle for influence in the Turkish-speaking area of the former Soviet Union. Iran succeeded in enacting a short-lived truce in Nagorno Karabagh. However, the election of nationalists in Azerbaijan made Baku friendlier toward Turkey. Elchibey denounced Iran's peacemaking efforts as an attempt to help Armenia at the expense of Azerbaijan. During a visit to Turkey in 1992, Elchibey presented himself as a soldier and follower of Ataturk, and he called for the overthrow of the Islamic Republic of Iran. On 7 November 1992, his remarks provoked a scathing threat of retaliation from Fatemeh Homayon Moqadam, a member of Iran's Parliament (Majlis).[2]

In April 1993, the military defeat of Azerbaijani forces, at the hands of Armenians, undermined the government of Elchibey, which had already begun to encounter internal divisions after its inception in June1992. Elchibey had promised during his election campaign to prevent Armenia from advancing in the battlefield, and failing to deliver on that promise, he dismissed Rahim Qaziev, the defense minister. The internal political struggles of Azerbaijan were complicated by the involvement of some thirty political parties. In fact, several of these parties went so far as to refuse to recognize the country's fifty-member Parliament, which was established during Elchibey's rule and consisted of former Communists and their opponents. The government in Baku rejected repeated demands for new elections on the ground that the country was at war. Such demands came from Elchibey's former supporter Etibar Mamadov of the National Independent Party, who broke with the Front the year before, accusing Elchibey's government of abusing its power.[3]

During June and July of 1993, Armenian forces attacked and captured the town of Agdam in Azerbaijan. The inability of the Azeris to stop the Armenian forces caused their anger to be projected toward the government of Abolfazl Elchibey. Rebel soldiers under the leadership of Surat Husseinov marched on Baku and forced then President-elect Elchibey to flee to his home village in the autonomous province of Nakhjavan. Parliamentary speaker Haidar Aliev, a former Communist Party member and KGB boss, took over the presidency, and Suret Husseinov was named prime minister and the minister of the interior and security. President Aliev had spent much of his career in the KGB, rising to the rank of general and running its apparatus in Azerbaijan.[4] This change in leadership was not enough to stop the Armenian advancement, which by 19 August 1993 was only ten kilometers from the Iranian border. Azerbaijan's military, allegedly backed by the Afghan Mujahideen, was unable to put an end to the Armenian assault.

By 13 November 1993, Armenia controlled one-fifth of Azerbaijan's territory, including Nagorno Karabagh. Nearly 1 million lives were lost in the war. When Nagorno Karabagh's Armenian leaders offered to grant freedom for displaced Azeris in exchange for land, Azerbaijan refused. Lacking the military capability to retake the land, Azerbaijan turned to Russia for help.[5] On 12 May 1994, thanks in part to Russian mediation, a cease-fire was signed by Armenia, Azerbaijan, and self-proclaimed Nagorno Karabagh. The cease-fire has now lasted for four years.

ALIEV'S GOVERNMENT

The government of Haidar Aliev is similar to those of other former Soviet republics insofar as it does not tolerate any opposing views from contending political opponents. In fact, opposition leaders are forced to go underground because they are either hunted down and arrested or forced to flee the country. They are usually members of the Musavat Party. Most are former Communists who strongly disagree with the ruling government's policies. They are often accused of "insulting [the] honor and dignity" of the president, which violates the country's criminal code. Show trials are used to intimidate journalists and the opposition. "[Aliev] is a classic Soviet leader," said Laila Yunusova, a human rights activist. "He perfectly understands our people and the slave mentality we have fallen into over the last seventy years. His tools are control over people's livelihood, blackmail, corruption, and propaganda and, if nothing else works, police repression."[6]

Another clear indication of Aliev's abuse of power to muzzle the opposition was the Milli Majlis national parliamentary election in November of 1995, which barred a number of candidates from the election. The central election commission endorsed seventy-two of the one hundred deputies to the new parliament, elected in single-candidate constituencies. The approved candidates included Aliev's son, his son-in-law, and his brother, Jalal Aliev. Forty of them were members of the president's "*yeni*" (new or modern) ruling party. According to reports claiming the names were approved of in advance, the list of candidates was virtually identical to one circulated before the elections by the former presidential advisor Nemat Panahov.[7] Aliev and his yeni party won the election despite, or perhaps because of, use of violence and intimidation against the opposition. During Aliev's visit to the White House in the summer of 1997, President Clinton encouraged him to hold elections free of governmental bias. While in the United States, Aliev committed himself to advocating political pluralism by holding free elections.

It should be noted that uncertainty over Aliev's eventual succession is among the more significant issues concerning the country and the region. The government in Baku has made no visible provisions for succession. President Aliev is close to eighty years of age and oversees every aspect of the government. The opposition groups contended that the government would manipulate the election if Aliev ran for the presidency again. He did and, as expected, was reelected in October of 1998. President Aliev was reelected for another five-year term amidst the accusation of fraud and ballot rigging. He received 76.11 percent of the votes. His closest challenger, Etibar Mamedov, received 11.6 percent, and Independent Azerbaijan Party chairman Nizami Suleymanov, 8.6 percent. Aliev said the election showed the world that Azerbaijan was "on the road of democratic development." Five opposition candidates boycotted the elections, predicting the election would be rigged. Mamedov was reported as saying the results were falsified.

Aliev, undoubtedly, has such tremendous power in his hands that if he were to die suddenly, the country might fall into chaos. Azerbaijan is also vulnerable because of its large oil resources, which are located in a region where every warlord and regional actor longs to participate in the oil business. "When he is out of the country everything stops," observed a foreign ambassador posted in Baku. "People hardly even dare to fix a leaking toilet without his approval."[8]

Reports indicate that President Aliev's son Ilham Aliev (aged thirty-seven) is in line to replace his father and, therefore, maintain Aliev's rule over Azerbaijan. It has been suggested that Ilham has the innate ability if not innate right to take over when the time arrives.[9] Papers describe President Aliev as one who bears the hallmark of a "national patriarch" who currently enjoys all powers of a latter-day "Qajar" shah. This implies that the top job in Azerbaijan should stay in the family. However, officials at the president's office deny this as a sheer fabrication. It should be noted that there are two possible contenders to Aliev's dynasty. One is Rasul Guliev, a former speaker of Parliament who is reluctant—as of this writing—to return from the United States because he is under investigation for alleged embezzlement. The other presidential contender is Etibar Mamedov, who came second in October 1998's presidential race and is one of a number of powerful Azeris with roots in Armenia.[10]

RUSSIAN PRESSURE

Azerbaijan, like Georgia, is under pressure to sign an agreement with Moscow allowing the reestablishment of Russia's military bases. Pro-Turkish nationalists of the Popular Front, who held power in Baku until May 1993, succeeded in forcing the last Russian soldiers to withdraw from Azerbaijan. President Aliev is still reluctant to allow the full-scale return of the Russian military. However, he has agreed to allow Russia to deploy inspection forces in the country after the Armenians withdraw, even though the Armenians are refusing to budge without substantial guarantees on Nagorno Karabagh. Before committing troops to Azerbaijan, Moscow wants to recover its old bases in the republic and resume surveillance of its borders with Iran and Turkey.[11]

In early February 1996, President Aliev issued a presidential decree mandating that the Gabala radar station is the "property of Azerbaijan." The country's defense minister, Safar Aliev, interpreted the decree to mean that the Gabala station will "never be a Russian military base."[12] Both the Soviet Union and the Russian Federation have used Gabala as an early warning station against missile attacks and to intercept communications to and from the Caucasus and beyond. One thousand Russian military personnel, at one time or another, have been posted at the station. If the station were once again to serve as a Russian military base, a few thousand Russian military personnel and their families would be there.

OVERTURES TO TURKEY

President Aliev went to Turkey on 8 February 1994 for an official visit, after allowing some time to pass following the collapse of the Popular Front government of Abolfazl Elchibey. A ten-year treaty of friendship and cooperation with Turkey was signed, in which Azerbaijan and Turkey pledged mutual assistance in consultation with the United Nations and other international organizations. This treaty obligates Ankara to assist Azerbaijan in case of aggression initiated by a third party. Fifteen other documents were also signed, which promote trade and investment and further cooperation and development in science and culture.

ECONOMIC CONDITIONS

Azerbaijan is not as industrialized as its Caucasus neighbors, Armenia and Georgia. It resembles the Central Asian republics insofar as a majority of its population is nominally Muslim, with a high level of structural unemployment and a low standard of living. Most of its economy is dominated by the oil industry and the production of natural gas and cotton.

Azerbaijan, and more specifically the city of Baku (Badkoobeh), is the most important place in the Caucasus region, because of its offshore oil fields. Oil has been bubbling out of the ground since the beginning of recorded history. When the Arab Muslims conquered the place in the seventh century, they used the oil as a skin ointment. Baku can be characterized as the first oil town. Prior to the Bolshevik takeover, most Azeris were peasants, but a very small group of nobility and merchant class dominated Baku.

The oil fields were discovered and exploited by the Russian tsars[13] and later by the Soviet Union. By the end of the nineteenth century, the Russians had helped to make Baku the leading oil producer in the world. The Rockefellers and the Swedish Nobel family made fortunes in this city. The increase in the exploration and production of oil through the centuries has made Baku a cosmopolitan city with all the trappings of cultural diversity.

However, Azerbaijan's oil production has declined since the collapse of the Soviet Union, but its 1994 ratification of a $7.5 billion oil agreement with a consortium of oil companies, a majority of which are Western, has generated the funds needed for future industrial developments. As is the case with other former Soviet republics, Azerbaijan is struggling to make the transition from a centrally planned economic system to a market economy. The country may use its energy resources to fuel its long-term economic development, despite the probability that the current global oil glut will make the region less attractive to oil companies.

The Azerbaijan republic produces about 450,000 tons of raw cotton and 200,000 tons of fiber-cotton annually. Due to insufficient cotton-processing industries in Azerbaijan, it possesses only 18 percent of the cotton crop market. Experts believe that it would require $400 million to create the infrastructure and machinery necessary to process a complete annual harvest.[14]

As of this writing, international investors are committed to spending over $30 billion toward Azerbaijan's long-term economic development, especially in the oil industries. The money has yet to make the country rich, let alone the Azeri people. Oil is not expected to flow in large amounts from the oil wells until the year 2003. According to some reports, it could be another ten years before the oil begins to flow at full speed. If everything goes smoothly, the oil will bring in substantial revenue. Azerbaijan's oil exports could exceed 1 million bpd by 2010 and 2 million bpd within twenty years. From 1994 through June 1998, the Azerbaijan oil sector attracted only $1.8 billion in direct foreign investment, which is equivalent to about 40 percent of the country's GDP.

The country's oil revenues are projected to be roughly $80 billion over the thirty-year life of the Azerbaijan International Operating Company (AIOC), and Azerbaijan will realize 80 percent of these revenues. AIOC as of this writing remains the country's only working consortium. It intends to develop three offshore fields with estimated reserves of about 630 million tons and projected investment of more than $10 billion.

The oil sector represents more than 65 percent of the country's exports and more than 80 percent of Azerbaijan's direct foreign investment. Azeri government officials say they hope to earn about $100 million from sales of oil in 2000, which would allow Baku in part to cover the country's growing deficit. Azerbaijan, similar to other republics, lacks the institutional capacity to manage the money responsibly.

A governmental decree on 1 January 1994 introduced the national currency, the manat, at the exchange rate of one manat to ten rubles. At that time, the U.S. dollar was exchanged for two hundred-ninety manats, but within two weeks, the U.S. dollar sold for three hundred and twenty-seven manats. In 1999 the exchange rate reached five thousand manats to a U.S. dollar. The Azeri currency declined due to political and economic problems brought about chiefly by Azerbaijan's war with Armenia.

Unfortunately, oil production data showed a declining trend at least through the end of 1997. Despite the direct foreign investment, Azerbaijan produced 9 million tons of crude oil in 1997, down from 12.5 million in 1990. It is doubtful that this country will become a major oil producer on the world market in the near future. The country's real (adjusted for inflation) GDP declined by 55 percent from 1991 to 1997, a downward trend that finally halted between 1996 and 1997.[15] Foreign investment in Azerbaijan has remained low outside of the oil industry, and it is expected this trend will continue in 2000.

In his New Year's Day address of 1997, President Aliev described 1996 as a year of peace and stability. Ironically, in that very year, some opposition leaders were accused of attempting a military coup that was backed by the KGB. Aliev said that although the country survived "attempts mounted by internal and foreign forces" to destabilize it, much has been accomplished in building a democratic, secular, and law-abiding country. As for the country's economic condition, he pointed out that the economy grew for the first time since independence, albeit by only 1.2 percent. He also claimed that the overall rate of decline in production slowed somewhat, while agricultural output increased by 3 percent.[16]

The government in Baku is doing little to improve the country's economy. As estimated, half of Azerbaijan's population of 7 million lives below the poverty line. More than eight hundred thousand Azeris are refugees, mostly as a result of the war over Nagorno Karabagh. Government salaries and pensions are so low that in many cases pensioners cannot cope with daily needs. The poor economic condition means that there have been little funds to spend on health care. Hospitals are in poor conditions. The hospitals have no money for medicine. After admission to the hospital, a patient's family must provide food, nursing care, and usually the drugs and disposables. The hospitals fall far short of international standards.

The roads and railways are in terrible, and, in many cases dangerous conditions. Throughout the country, there is a constant shortage of electricity. In most places outside Baku, blackouts are daily affairs. In 1997, people living in Ganjah, Azerbaijan's second largest city, had to carry on with only two hours of electricity a day. In fact, on 25 January 2000, Azenerg, Azerbaijan's state power generating company, announced that electricity supplies would be cut daily between the hours of 7 to 9 A.M. and 7 P.M. to midnight, effective immediately.[17] The rationing was imposed because of the failure or refusal of 70 percent of all customers to pay their electric bills. The country continues to suffer from badly needed repairs to transmission lines and transformer stations throughout the country. A large number of factories across the country have been shut down. As noted before, the majority of the rural areas of Azerbaijan have received sporadic power supplies for several years, which lead to numerous widespread protests.

CHAPTER 4

Kazakistan

Kazakistan is geographically the largest of the newly independent Central Asian republics. Kazakistan shares borders with the Russian Federation, the Caspian Sea, Turkmenistan, Ubzbekistan, Kyrgyzstan, and China. Despite its considerable size, Kazakistan is completely landlocked.

Kazakistan has a heterogeneous population of 16.8 million, the vast majority of whom support President Nazarbaev. The population of Kazakistan consists of 52 percent Kazak, 35 percent Russian, 5 percent Ukrainian, and 3 percent German, with the remaining ethnic groups making up 12 percent of the population.

BACKGROUND

This country came into existence when various nomadic tribes immigrated to the area during the sixteenth century. These tribes called themselves "qazaq" (renegades), which is the root of the Russified name *Kazak*. Russian Tsars began encroaching on the Kazak khanate in the early eighteenth century. By the midnineteenth century, they dominated the area. The Kazak people are a Turkic people—from Golden Horde—with a mixture of Mongul (Moghul) blood. In the midnineteenth century, they were the most numerous (estimated at over 2 million) of the nomadic peoples of the region. The Kazak people were nomads in a patriarchal society, and they once occupied the steppe region from Siberia as far south as Syr Darya. Their ancestors were among the numerous regional Turkish tribes who were conquered by, and who later came to make up, a predominant part of Jenghiz (Chengiz) Khan's army.

The breakup of the Mongol Empire in the fifteenth century resulted in the formation of a new group from the steppe stragglers who became known as the Kazaks or Qazaqs, which derives from a Turkic term meaning "wanderers" or "fugitives." Although the literal translation of Qazaq is "White Goose," no one has any definite knowledge as to the source of such a name.

The Kazak people, like most of the natives of Central Asia, are

Sunni Muslim. However, because of their nomadic lifestyle and their long-held negative attitude toward the sedentary urban lifestyle, they were lax in many religious observances. They had no mosques, and historically their spiritual worldview included earlier Shamanist and animist belief systems, which had been incorporated into their acceptance of Islam. Present day Kazaks have a similarly lax attitude toward Islam and religious observance. Their tribal and nomadic customary law, Odat, remained the principal rule that governed the behavior of the members of the tribe. As a result, the Islamic Sharia' (or Sharia't) remained on the periphery.

The Kazak people divide themselves by tribes or hordes, however the term they use is *zhooz*, which literally means "hundred," while the word in Kyrgyz is *Juz*, which also signifies hundred. The Kazaks and their Kyrgyz cousins are more closely related than are any of the other Central Asian nationalities. Legend has it that there was a family with three sons who later created three tribes, each consisting of a hundred people. The three tribes became known as three *Zhooz*. The eldest son became the chief or khan of the Oly Zhooz or Great Horde, which ruled the southeastern part of the land. The middle son became the khan of the Orta Zhooz or Middle Horde, which governed the central and the northern lands. The youngest son became the khan of the Kishi Zhooz or Small Horde, which oversaw the western part of the country. It should be noted that each of these tribes or "Hordes" divides into different clans.

The study of this region is complicated by the fact that, historically, the Russians referred to the Kazak people as "Kyrgyz," which is actually the name of another nomadic tribe. The Kyrgyz who occupied the mountainous region of Ala-Tu, in the vicinity of Lake Issy-Kul ("Warm Water") are closely related to Kazaks in language, ethnic composition, and socioeconomic organizations. The Russians wanted to avoid confusion with the "Cossack" people, who were Orthodox people of predominately Slavic stock. The Cossacks were originally vagabonds, freebooters, and runaways who had fled the onerous conditions of life in old Muscovy to form bands of irregular cavalry. Cossacks later become pioneers who colonized farms, villages, and towns throughout the upper region. Ironically, both *Cossack* and *Kazak* (Qazaq) derive from the same Turkish word, and the terms even had identical spellings before the emergence of the Soviet Union. In the 1920s, the term *Kazak*, with a slight change in spelling and pronunciation, became *Kazakh*. *Kazak* is used in this study. The land and people gradually became part of the Russian Empire as the Moghul (Mongol) Empire disintegrated. In 1936, Moscow declared Kazakistan a Soviet Socialist Republic, and it remained as such until it achieved its independence in 1991 upon the collapse of the Soviet Union.

POLITICAL DEVELOPMENTS

Kazakistan held its first election in 1990, while still a Soviet republic. In March of 1994, the second election was held for a new, full-time parliament of 177 deputies to replace the mostly useless old Supreme Soviet's 360 part-timers. Relations between the Russians and the Kazaks, generally good in the past, seem to have worsened during the Kazak government's carefully controlled election campaign. The Russians complained about the top jobs in the country increasingly being filled by Kazaks. Kostantin Zatulin, the head of a group of Russian legislators who monitored the election, described the process as unfair. He criticized the "ethnocratization" of power in Kazakistan, pointing out that the Kazaks received 60 percent of the seats in the new parliament, though they made up only 43.2 percent of the population. In contrast, Russian candidates won only 28 percent of the seats, despite constituting 36.4 percent of the population.[1]

The official results released on March 10 showed that the Union of People's Unity of Kazakistan (Kazak acronym SNEK) won thirty seats in the new 177–seat Parliament. Independent candidates, most of whom support Nursultan Nazarbaev's policies, secured sixty-six seats, while opposition candidates acquired only twenty-three. Forty-two seats were distributed by direct presidential appointment. The official Federal Trade Unions took only eleven seats, and the remaining eleven seats went to others.[2]

Kazakistan's president and ruling party would do almost anything to prolong their rule and enhance their power. A clear indication of this was the constitutional referendum and the country's parliamentary elections. The constitutional referendum of 30 August 1995, according to the official reports, overwhelmingly approved the new Constitution, which enhanced the power of the presidency. Officials maintained that 89 percent of the people who voted favored the new Constitution. This was out of the 90 percent of the eligible voters who, reportedly, turned out. However, a coalition of opposition groups, the Salvation Front, alleged that there were widespread voting irregularities and that only 30 percent of the registered voters actually turned out.[3]

Later in 1995, parliamentary elections were held for the Senate Oli Majlis (upper chamber) and the Majlis (Parliament). Reports indicate that a majority of the elected deputies were friendly to the president and that there was an absence of opposition to him in both chambers. In response to the reports, Nazarbaev stressed the need for cooperation between the government and Parliament in times of crises. He noted that his office had passed about seventy decrees, including laws on taxation and land ownership, which "for years were being held up by the deputies."[4]

In early January 1996, shortly after the parliamentary elections, Nazarbaev signed a decree that substantially enhanced his power. It makes the president the only authority that can initiate constitutional amendments. It also allows him to "appoint and dismiss ministers without the consent of parliament; to dismiss the government in its entirety and suspend or invalidate governmental decisions; to dissolve parliament and call regular or anticipated parliamentary elections; and to call referenda at his discretion."[5] His power also extends over the appointment and dismissal of justices of the constitutional courts, the chairman of the national bank, and regional and city administrators.

His solid political power was clearly indicated in the January 1999 presidential election. President Nursultan Nazarbaev's reelection in January 1999 was certain. No rival was in position to change the election outcome.

The most prominent challenger was Akezhan Kazhegeldin, a former prime minister (1994–1997), who also once worked for the KGB and became a businessman after independence and amassed millions of dollars. During his tenure as prime minister, Kazhegeldin was responsible for privatization and the sale of state enterprises to foreigners. Numerous questions have been raised regarding the origin of his wealth, which he contends were made before joining the government. Kazhegeldin was ruled ineligible by a lower court to run because he had participated in an illegal political meeting. On 24 November 1998, the Supreme Court of Kazakistan upheld the decision of the lower court.

In theory, Nazarbaev could have faced several possible contenders who have passed the mandatory Kazak language test and have been approved by the Central Election Commission. However, these candidates—Gany Kasymov, chairman of the Customs Committee; Engels Gabbasov, parliamentary deputy; and Serikbolsyn Abdildin, chairman of the Communist Party—were also required to secure 170,000 signatures and to come up with the registration fee of $30,000, in a country where the minimum average wage is about thirty U.S. dollars. Nazarbayev, in connection to the presidential election, told a small group of journalists while on a tour of the northern industrial heartland, "Fifteen hundred companies are working here and no one wants a different president. Do you understand this? Write about it." He was reelected president of Kazakistan in the 10 January 1999 elections. According to results, he gained 79.78 percent[6] of the vote. Judging by the number of television ads, posters, and flyers, this president had the most money at his disposal in addition to the government apparatus. None of the other candidates had been able to afford a single poster.

"The US has a lot of diplomatic means to influence Kazakhstan [sic.]. But [Washington] was more interested in the economic sphere than human rights and democracy. They decided to overlook small violations of human rights and this gave President Nazarbaev the impression he could do what he wanted,"[7] says Yevgeny Zhovtis, director of the Kazakistan International Bureau for Human Rights and Rule of Law, in connection to the 10 January 1999 presidential election. Concern by the Western countries came to a head when Nazarbaev brought elections forward by two years, giving the opposition scant time to campaign. In a sign of protest, the Organization for Security and Cooperation in Europe (OSCE) decided not to send official international observers to the election and refused to recognize the results. Judy Thompson, coordinator of the OSCE's local assessment mission, was quoted as saying that authorities had used the country's lack of freedom of assembly to intimidate opposition groups and had in many cases openly backed Nazarbaev's campaign.

Why did Nazarbaev move forward the election? If he had waited until 2000/2001, presumably he knew he would have had a harder time of winning. During his campaign, Nazarbaev issued repeated warnings that the country faced huge economic difficulties in the next two years. Low prices for oil, metals, and wheat—the country's main exports— would be reflected in the economy. Another difficulty, he said, was the financial plight of Russia, which he barely mentioned.

Leaders in the former Soviet republics regularly use elections, fear of domestic as well as external "Islamic" threats, and the poor economic condition of the country to legitimize and even enhance powers rather than promote democracy that would enable them to further the nation-state building and expansion of public participation in the political process. The October 1999 election for the lower house of parliament was marked with serious violations of civil liberties and freedom of assembly. The authorities prevented opposition from having election rallies, ballot boxes stuffed, and opposition observers excluded—to ensure a favorable majority in the lower house of Parliament.

However, consternation boiled into outrage when a Kazak employee of the U.S. embassy, who served as a liaison with human rights groups, was badly beaten on 22 December 1998, by what is widely assumed to have been progovernment attackers. In order to cover up the abuses in Kazakistan, Nazarbaev took a full-page advertisement in the *New York Times* and enlisted the help of a consulting firm, Western Strategy Group, to help press his case. Similar complaints were filed by the opposition leaders and outside observers in connection with the October 1999 election for the lower house of Parliament.[8]

Over the years, Nazarbaev has consolidated his ruling power, and, similar to other Central Asian head of states, he frequently reshuffles the government positions to thwart any possible rival. Theoretically, freedom of press is officially guaranteed, but many Kazak journalists, writers, and commentators apply self-censorship.

In response to criticism by American and West European officials, he tried to justify the expansion of his power based on democratic, pragmatic, and cultural considerations. He pointed to the 1995 referenda, which extended the power of his office and approved the new constitution, giving him a popular mandate to establish presidential rule. He then contended that strong presidential rule is the most effective way to promote reform unencumbered by resistance from "backward looking" forces or special interest groups. Finally, he argued that the Central Asian countries lack the tradition and political culture of parliamentarianism. Although he made these points chiefly to justify his actions, the general evidence supports his view that these republics lack the background and experience for nation building.[9] Thus, the lack of actual experience of national identity may present an obstacle to nation building.

NEW CAPITAL

In 1995, President Nazarbaev selected the city of Akmola in northern Kazakistan to be the country's new capital. This took effect in October of 1997. Although some of the government offices had already moved to Akmola by this time, as planned, it is not clear when the transfer will be complete. Moving the capital involves a large amount of funds, about $500 million to $1 billion. The transfer costs estimated will undoubtedly be higher. Akmola, with a current population of three hundred thousand people, is located on an endless flat land, which is prone to strong winds and harsh winters. Temperatures have been known to drop as low as forty degrees below zero. Almaty, the former capital, is nestled in the foothills of the beautiful snow-laden mountains. Almaty is situated near China and the Kyrgyz capital, Bishkek.

The president decided to switch the capital to Akmola for two reasons. First, the new capital's location is more central than Almaty's, and it is also closer to the industrial and resource-rich regions of the country. Second, and perhaps the main reason for transferring the capital, is the burgeoning and potentially secessionist Russian population in the northern part of the country. Since the economy of northern Kazakistan had been under the control of the Soviet Union's Department of Industry and Metallurgy, the subsequent control of more of the northern area by the Kazak government is likely to stimulate an already growing Russian secession movement in northern Kazakistan. In an attempt to counter this movement, President Nazarbaev is trying to win the loyalty of ethnic Russians by creating privatization laws that favor them. He is also turning over the property of the former Communist Party to the Socialist Party, which is led by Russians. The Russians are increasingly coming to dominate the population of Akmola, making up more than 70 percent of its citizenry. Other non-Kazak ethnic nationalities residing there include Ukrainians and Germans. There is reason to believe that the transfer of the capital is intended to guard against Russia's attempt to annex the northern region.

Most Russians living in Kazakistan tend to support Nazarbaev. Although a Kazak, he is still trying to regulate the "Kazakization" of the country in such a manner as to ensure that ethnic differences do not tear the country apart. Most of the Russians who lived in Kazakistan are remaining there despite the fact that they are losing their governmental positions. The Russians still strongly influence the economy. "They dominate the vast oil and gas industry, which will be the key to the country's future economic progress."[10]

Interestingly enough, on 7 May 1998, President Nazarbaev issued a decree changing the name of the new capital city from Akmola to Astana. Government officials complained about the media's mistranslation of the name *Akmola* as "white tomb" despite its literary meaning of "white plenty." The word *Astana* in Kazak means "capital."

ETHNIC CONSIDERATIONS

Language variations are the cause of many problems for Kazakistan. More than 60 percent of those living in Kazakistan speak Russian as their first language. At present, the Kazak language is the "state" language, whereas Russian is the language of "interethnic communication," a concept Russians find objectionable. President Nursultan Nazarbaev, whose main focus is to hold the country together, has proposed that Russian be made an "official" language, though still inferior to Kazak.

The president realizes that problems in the country could lead to divisions along ethnic lines. To balance these developments, Nazarbaev sponsored the formation of a party for the popular consolidation of Kazakistan, headed by prominent Supreme Soviet Deputies Olzhas Suleimanov and Mukhtar Shakhanov. It appears that Nazarbaev hopes that a Kazak national consolidation party dominated by established intellectuals will help diffuse the growing appeal of the legally recognized non-Communist Kazak nationalist Azat (Azad) "Free" Party. "He would also like to undermine support for the unregistered Islamic Hezibsi Alash party (the term derives from *Alash Urda* "Alash Army"), whose goal is the creation of the Islamic State of Turkistan. However, the ethnic Kazak people view the conditions of the country differently than do those holding down jobs with the government. In a survey conducted between 26 August and 26 September 1994, 46 percent of those surveyed described the economic situation as bad and 38 percent as very bad.[11]

On 3 October 1995, Nazarbaev issued a decree amending the country's citizenship law in order to make it comply with the new constitution, which does not provide for dual citizenship. The amended law stipulates that "Kazakistan does not recognize the citizenship granted by another state to a Kazakistani citizen residing on Kazakistan's territory. A Kazakistani may be deprived of citizenship if he serves in the armed forces or security service of another country."[12]

FOREIGN POLICY

Kazakistan is now trying to develop bilateral and multilateral ties with neighboring states and other countries. It has worked to cultivate an especially strong relationship with Uzbekistan. The former Kazakistani foreign minister Tuleutai Suleimonov carried out this policy.[13] He said that while good relations with China are a primary task, Uzbekistan is "an equally important priority of our foreign policy in the Asian sector." Suleimonov maintained that a Kazak-Uzbek alliance would benefit not only the two countries but also all of Central Asia and perhaps even beyond. He also indicated that cooperation with Turkey, Iran, Pakistan, and India would be a key step in developing a strong regional base. Each of these countries has also shown interest in Kazakistan and has apparently assigned it an accordingly high status in their own foreign policy agendas.

Kazakistan has signed agreements with these four countries in order to increase the likelihood that it will become a more prosperous nation. Anticipating the influence of a Kazak-Uzbek power base, backed by nations such as Turkey, Suleimenov intimated that other neighboring countries would play a greater role in the future of Central Asia. "More extensive friendly relations with Kyrgyzstan, Turkmenistan and Tajikistan will be important in this respect," he claimed. Kazakistan also recognizes the value of open relations with China, Germany, France and the United States. Suleimenov believes that Asian countries, particularly China, will "play a leading role in the evolution of the world in the next century."[14] In Europe, strong ties with Germany and France will have to be balanced by relations with Britain, Italy, Spain, the Netherlands, and the Scandinavian countries. Kazakistan hopes to engage in growing bilateral relations with organizations such as the EU, the WEU, and

NATO. In dealings with the United States, Kazakistan's concerns of international security are at the forefront. Former U.S. Secretary of State Warren Christopher voiced support for a meeting among the foreign ministers of Asian countries in order to establish confidence between the countries and to shore up support for foreign policy decisions emanating from the region. Kazakistan's foreign policy may be overly ambitious at this point, but Nazarbaev and Suleimonov are not far from realizing their dream of a new, strengthened, and independent Central Asia. The country would like to be recognized as a viable regional power and maintain close and friendly relations with nearly all states.[15]

On 31 October 1992, President Nazarbaev went to Iran directly from an Ankara summit where he had met with leaders from the five former Soviet republics. Each of these republics has a large Muslim population and close ethnic and linguistic links with Turkey. His visit to Tehran, immediately after the Ankara meeting, was regarded as an indication that he did not want to be seen as favoring either Turkey or Iran as they struggle for influence in the region. The Turkish media claimed the draft communiqué that included extensive agreements on customs harmonization, a regional development bank, and a pact on the transport of oil and gas across Turkey to Europe were rejected because the five Turkic leaders, especially Nazarbaev, did not want to offend Moscow. In addition, they were offended by Ankara, which sought to impose on them a communiqué that they had no role in drafting. Apparently, the communiqué was drafted by government leaders in Ankara before the summit and simply handed to the visiting presidents for their approval.

Sulayman Demirel, who was then the prime minister of Turkey, suggested that the Turkic-speaking countries should seek to standardize their spoken languages to a mutually comprehensible form of Turkish. In response to this suggestion, President Nazarbaev told a concluding news conference that "the creation of a separate community based on ethnic or linguistic lines does not bring people closer; it merely disunites them." It was Demirel who, shortly after the collapse of the Soviet Union, declared that Turkey should be at the helm of "a Turkic-speaking world stretching from the Great Wall of China to the Adriatic." Turkey has not gained as much influence in these nations as the leaders of Turkey hoped. However, with the help of the United States, and Azerbaijan's leader, Aliev, Turkey has made some headway.[16]

Tehran rolled out the red carpet for Nazarbaev, who met former President Hashemi Rafsanjani and signed several bilateral agreements on 2 November 1992. The president of Kazakistan also met with Khameneh'i, the country's "supreme religious leader," and with Ahmad Khomaini, the son of the late Ayatollah Khomaini. The agreements

signed in Tehran called for the creation of a joint commission for cooperation in the areas of economy, transport, and culture. In addition, letters of understanding were signed for collaboration with regards to oil,
energy, and banking.

Nazarbaev, as president of the largest of the former Soviet republics
and head of one of the four new nuclear powers arising out of the USSR's
collapse, made a state visit to France in 1993. He confirmed that there
were differences of opinion among the members of the CIS on the future
of nuclear weapons, which the West would like to see under exclusive
Russian control. Noting that Kazakistan's position on nuclear weapons
had not changed, he stated: "We have formed unified armed forces and
Kazakistan's strategic weapons are under unified CIS command." He
defended his country's policy by saying that Kazaks were not the ones
who brought in nuclear weapons in the first place, but it was now their
goal to become a nuclear free state. On 24 October 1993, Nazarbaev told
former U.S. Secretary of State Warren Christopher that he would dismantle the nuclear weapons for $140 million of aid and a full signing cere-
mony with President Clinton. This proposal raised quite a few objections
among the Kazak nationalists who wanted to keep the Russian missiles.[17]

The result of negotiations with the Clinton administration found
Kazakistan gaining $310 million for dismantling its nuclear weapons.
President Nazarbaev used the occasion to enhance the international
position of the newly independent country. He pledged that "over the
next seven years, in accordance with the START (Strategic Arms Reduction Treaty) commitments, we're going to begin decommissioning
strategic weapons." In January 1994, he requested $1 billion in com-
pensation for Kazakistan's dismantled nuclear weapons. Russia will sell
the uranium from the warheads to an American firm.[18]

President Nazarbaev flew to the United Sates on 13 February 1994
for an official visit to enhance bilateral political and economic relations.
During this visit, the White House announced the decision to increase
U.S. aid to Kazakistan from $91 million to more than $311 million for
1994. In addition, President Clinton reaffirmed an earlier commitment
to allocate $85 million toward the cost of dismantling the nuclear
weapons inherited by Kazakistan after the Soviet Union broke up in
December 1991. Clinton claimed that there was no quid pro quo linking increased U.S. aid to preferences for American corporations, which
might be interested in developing Kazakistan's vast natural resources.[19]
Nazarbaev also met with U.S. economic and financial officials, the president of the World Bank, and the managing director of the International
Monetary Fund (IMF). In his meeting with American businessmen,
Nazarbaev highlighted his country's need for assistance in developing its
transportation system.

Security concerns have arisen from developments on the Tajik-Afghan border. Tuleutai Suleimenov expressed Kazak's official and serious concern about the conflict in Tajikistan and the tension surrounding the Tajik-Afghan border. He believes these pose a "real threat to the entire Central Asian region." He contends that stability can only be achieved by the adoption of multi- and bilateral agreements on preventive measures. Accordingly, Kazakhstan has taken a strong stand supporting the establishment of a long-term collective security system in Central Asia by initiating a meeting of the foreign ministers of the countries concerned with promoting interaction and confidence-building measures in the area.

In connection with the security and a number of armed conflicts in the region, in a nationwide address on 15 December 1999, Nazarbaev warned of the possibility of "spillover" from armed conflicts in neighboring countries. This will constitute a main challenge to the country in the next century. Further potential sources of dangers, he added, are politicoreligious extremism and drug trafficking. In order to increase security, government will expand security cooperation with Russia and China and among Kazkistan, Kyrgyzstan, and Tajikistan. He also identified the strong American political and commercial presence as a security source.[20]

On 7 December 1999, the U.S. ambassador, Richard Jones, at a press conference in Almaty, defined Kazak-American relations as "very important," adding that ties between the two countries are getting more "complicated." The Associated Press quoted Ambassador Jones as saying that "such issues as arms trade, democratic reforms and economic freedom in Kazakhstan [sic.] had to be taken into account by the Kazakh [sic.] politicians." He told the press that he had met with President Nazarbaev and Prime Minister Qasymzhomart Toqaev, and those issues were discussed. The ambassador also told the audience that U.S. military officials held talks with the Kazak defense minister and signed a program of "the U.S-Kazak military cooperation for 2000, and a joint peace keeping military maneuvers, 'Centrazbat-2000' will be held in Kazakistan during 2000."

ECONOMIC CONDITIONS

In 1993, Kazakhstan adopted its own national currency, the tenge. This change precipitated periods of national instability. The tenge, at its inception, was established at 4.68 to the American dollar. A year later, the currency was exchanged at 54 to the U.S. dollar. The tenge then fell another 117 points before the government stepped in and implemented programs to try to stabilize the currency at around 43 to the dollar. One of the main contributors to the instability of the economy was Kazakistan's decision to print bank notes in order to meet its financial obligations. By 1995, the country's economic situation had deteriorated sharply as had also happened with the other former Soviet republics following independence. The GDP fell to 55 percent of its 1991 levels before the downward trend halted between 1996 and 1998. Other problems were unbelievable rates of inflation (3,061 percent in 1992; 2,265 percent in 1993; and rates increasing 46 percent on a monthly basis from January through June 1994), a shortage of electricity and a lack of improvement in industrial production, while prices for industrial material continued to rise. The scarcity of food, customer goods, and other daily needs remains a serious problem for the country in addition to its nonpayment of debts. Decline in the grain harvest will seriously damage its grain export, which Kazakistan depends upon to pay for its electricity arrears that amounted to more than $7 million in 1995. Moreover, financial crises in Asia and Russia have had a direct effect on its economy, as well as on the loss in export earnings from depressed world oil and metal prices. Reports point out that the official government target of 3 percent GDP growth in 1998 is not likely to be met. In early July 1998, the head of Kazakistan Central Bank is quoted as saying that the rate of inflation for 1998 may fall to around 8 percent, against 11.2 percent in 1997. Reports estimated that 60 percent of the population of 16.8 million is officially classified as poor. Inflation and poverty continued to be problems faced by the government during 1999.[21]

Kazakistan continues in its attempt to attract investment. Its credit worthiness and investment potential are more favorable than is the case of other Soviet republics, because of Kazakistan's oil and mineral resources. The first oil in this country was found in September 1899 at the depth of forty meters (130 feet) at Karachungul in the west of the country. Because the area was remote, commercial production never got started. It was the small town of Dossor, fifty-five miles east of Aturau, where a gush of oil spewed out of a well. In 1911, oil production began in Kazakistan. During its peak production, in the 1940s, Dossor had more than five hundred wells. Only seventy remain, and production has fallen to around forty barrels a day.

Nevertheless, this country is the second largest oil producer among the former Soviet republics after Russia, producing over five hundred thousand barrels per day. It is eager to achieve its production potential of 3 million bpd. The country needs to resolve two major issues in order for it to further increase oil production. First, the dispute over ownership rights of the offshore needs to be resolved before development of the offshore potential in the Caspian Sea can take place. These are directly connected to the disagreement among the littoral states over the treatment of the Caspian Sea or Caspian Lake under international law. In 1997, Kazakistan signed a communiqué with Turkmenistan pledging to divide their sections of the Caspian Sea along median lines, and in July 1998, Kazakistan signed a bilateral agreement with Russia—not yet ratified—dividing the northern Caspian along median lines between them. Both of these interim agreements are in effect until the status of the Caspian Sea is settled between the littoral states. The second issue is connected to the possible increase in oil production and the selection of pipeline routes to transport the country's oil to the world markets.

An estimated half of all oil production comes from the three large onshore fields of Tengiz, Uzen, and Karachaganak. Oil and natural gas account for about a quarter of the country's export earnings and two-thirds of direct foreign investment. The direct foreign investment varies from year to year. On 9 December 1998, Shell, Chevron, and Mobil signed a new agreement with Kazakistan for oil exploration in the Caspian Sea. However, its landlocked geographical location requires that Kazakistan secure the agreement of other countries in order to acquire access to the international market. This presents an obvious obstacle to attracting trade. Kazakistan has found negotiations with Russia to be particularly problematic.

Kazakistan possesses up to 83 trillion cubic feet of natural gas. Most of the reserves are located in the Karachaganak field, which is an extension of Russia's Orenburg field. In 1997, an international consortium consisting of several companies from Italy, Russia, the United States and the United Kingdom signed a $7 billion agreement to develop the field for forty years, with a planned investment of $4 billion by 2006. Other significant gas producing areas of Kazakistan include the Tengiz, Zhanazhol, and Uritau fields.

Overall, Kazakistan is in a stronger position than the other former Soviet republics because of its well-developed industries, which were established back in the late nineteenth and early twentieth centuries. In addition, it possesses a relatively productive agricultural sector, despite its high vulnerability to variations in the weather. Grain is often lost to extreme climatic changes. All of the cotton and a third of the grain crops cultivated in the former Soviet Union are now grown in Kazakistan, Uzbekistan, and Turkmenistan. It also contains 90 percent of the former Soviet Union's chrome and much of its silver, tungsten, lead, zinc, copper, bauxite, iron ore, gold, and other minerals.[22] This country has a great potential for economic development and the modernization of its industries and resources. However, whether this potential is actualized will depend on the republic's ability to attract foreign investment and technology, especially from industrialized countries.

Addressing the subject of the development of natural resources, Nazarbaev says, "We've signed a contract with the French Oil Company ELF for exploring an extremely promising deposit and for producing oil." He adds, "The oil will be sent via pipeline through the former USSR, all the more so as oil production has declined and pipeline capacity is enormous. We're in the process of building a pipeline, which will have its terminus at Novorossiisk on the Black Sea. In this way, we'll have two oil routes for moving our oil."[23] The White House has been pressuring Kazakistan not to make any move toward the construction of a pipeline route through Iran. However, an alternative route, favored by many, would be a three-thousand-kilometer (two thousand-mile) pipeline to China. However, high construction costs make the feasibility of this project very doubtful, unless China decides to fund it unilaterally.

The British Gas Company and Agip of Italy have joined the ELF Acquitan agreement in order to exploit the Karachaganak gas fields. Chevron of America, as noted before, is developing the Tengiz oil fields and, along with six other oil companies, is exploring northeastern areas of the Caspian Sea. The natural resources of Kazakistan are attracting foreign investors in droves, so much so that the head of British Petroleum in this country calls it one of the "oiliest places in the world."[24] By increasing its market economy, if it were to be followed up, Kazakistan could lessen its dependency on Russia. It is also attempting to establish itself as a viable regional actor in the post–cold war international system. However, this task has been very difficult due to the landlocked nature of the country and the American policy of containing Iran and Iraq. The latter imposes an embargo on the pipeline route through Iran despite the fact that it is the shortest and least expensive way currently available to Kazakistan for the transport of oil.

In order to create a more enticing atmosphere for foreign investment, Kazakistan maintains an active and open foreign policy. In general, Kazakistan has already opened embassies in many countries throughout the world, including Russia, Uzbekistan, Kyrgyzstan, Turkey, the United States, China, Iran, Germany, France, Belgium, India, and Egypt. During the early November 1996 World Bank conference in Tokyo, donor countries agreed to grant Kazakistan a loan of $1.35 billion to assist the country with its balance of payments.

Kazakistan became a member of the World Bank in July 1992. This marked an attempt by the leaders of the country to seek aid in a transition process toward a market economy. These leaders realized the vast potential of their country, particularly, the availability of resource potential and numerous areas of arable land. A well-trained workforce, along with a relatively well developed and ever-increasing level of industry and natural resources presents the potential for long-term economic prosperity.

The outlook is grim for Kazakistan's economy for 2000. The large budget deficit will continue to be a problem. The Central Bank was able to protect the country against the fallout from the financial turmoil in Russia and to maintain a stable currency in 1998. However, the currency tenge, similar to the currency of other former Soviet republics, was devalued due to the pressure of Russian financial and political turmoil. Intervention by the central bank kept the currency remarkably stable before the presidential election in early January 1999. The budget for 2000 provides for expenditure of 404.8 billion tenge ($276 million) and revenues of 340.3 billion tenge; the deficit of 64.5 billion tenge equals 3 percent of GDP. During the deliberation of the budget, Prime Minister Qasymzhomart Tqaev noted that it might have to be amended to meet social requirements. But in order for the country to meet certain requirements set by the International Monetary Fund, the Kazak government may have to increase revenues through an effective tax collection system that may result in the bankruptcy of some industrial enterprises. In his economic program for the period 2000–2002, the prime minister said that by 2000, the government is aiming to increase GDP by 10 to 12 percent compared with 1999, to cut inflation to 4 to 5 percent, and reduce the budget deficit to a little over 1 percent of GDP. Unemployment is to be brought down from the current 13 percent to 8 percent. It should be noted that the country's GDP fell by more than 2 percent in 1998. Moreover, the economic recovery is also jeopardized by the negative balance of trade.

However, analysts speculate that it is likely for the currency to fall again. It is expected that there will not be enough money to even provide $900 million for pensioners, and the numerous difficulties faced by the government will make it hard to reduce unemployment. This problem will continue, because of low international oil, metal, and grain prices. The state-owned oil company registered losses for 1998. Therefore, Kazakistan would need to secure revenue to help a looming 1999 budget deficit of more than 3 percent of GDP. The president is offering a privatization program, which is expected to bring in 49 billion tenge ($582 million) in much needed revenue. The question still remains, whether or not Kazakistan is wise enough to sell its oil and gas industries at a time when world oil prices are so low?

CHAPTER 5

Uzbekistan

Uzbekistan is the only republic that shares borders with all the other Central Asian republics. Uzbekistan borders Kazakistan to the north and west, Afghanistan and Turkmenistan to the south, and Tajikistan and Kyrgyzstan to the east. Home to 23.6 million people, Uzbekistan is the most heavily populated republic. It is also the most ethnically diverse republic, consisting of 120 nationalities. All of the urban centers in the region are located in Uzbekistan. In fact, these cities have existed for thousands of years. The Persian and Islamic cultures, more than any others, have influenced this country, particularly its major urban areas.

BACKGROUND

The word *uzbek* is made up of two words *uz*, which denotes "self" or "personality" and *bek*, which literally means "strong." The Kyrgyz people refer to the Uzbeks as *Sart*, "old Iranians." The name Uzbek became official under the Soviet system in 1918. However, there was a Khan named Uzbek (1282–1342), who roamed with his people in present day Kazakistan. He is credited with a role in the conversion of his people, the *Golden Horde,* to Islam. During the fifteenth century, these people began to move south, and they established the khanate of Khiva, which lasted until 1920, Bukhara, and Kuhkand.

Khiva Khanate was notorious for its violent rulers and slave market. Cruelty was the dominant feature of the Central Asian khanates of Khiva, Bukhara, Kukand, and the local Turkman rulers. The latter were notorious slave owners and traders who attacked caravans and hauled young Russians, Persians, or any others they could find to the slave markets of the khanates. Among all the khanates, Khiva lasted the longest.

The Uzbek people are predominantly Turkic, with a significant mixture of Old Iranians, who had been the dominant population in the region. The Uzbeks are also connected to the various invading Turkic and Mongol elements that are located mainly in the valleys of the upper Syr-Daria (the district known as Ferghana Valley), the Zeravshan (Zarafshan), and the Amu-Daria. They formed the khanates of Khiva and Kokand and the Emirate of Bukhara. The Uzbeks were a nomadic people and the last of the numerous invaders in the fifteenth century to settle in and mingle with the indigenous population. Eventually, they were, to a large degree, assimilated. Yet their name remained attached to the indigenous Old Iranian, town-dwelling population of the region.

POLITICAL UNREST

Uzbekistan is representative of the Central Asian republics' search for their history and identity following the breakup of the Soviet Union. Intellectuals and other leaders of Uzbekistan are attempting to establish Uzbeki independence and revive its cultural and historical background. They are attempting to do this without fueling the existing ethnic and tribal rivalries.[1] In Tashkent, Uzbekistan's capital city, statues of Lenin and Marx were replaced by one of Tamerlane, and Lenin College became Timur College. This gives us a glimpse of the strength of the ethnic nationalism that persists among the Central Asian ethnic groups.

In Kyrgyzstan, the Oymag tribe of Osh is trying to clear the region of its Uzbek minority. Osh is located in the Ferghana Valley, adjacent to the border of Uzbekistan. This was the scene of a horrific organized massacre of Uzbek families that occurred in June 1990. An ethnic rivalry also exists amongst the Tajik population of the republic. Ironically, the name *Kyrgyz* means "forty tribes."

In general, the question of land distribution in Uzbekistan is the pivotal issue on which the country's future political stability and economic viability now rest. A senior official in the Interior Ministry of Uzbekistan recently stated that the Ferghana Valley is ready to explode at any time. Due to its strategic location, Ferghana Valley was once the political and religious center of Central Asia. However, the Communists, under "Stalin, divided the valley between the three newly created republics of Uzbekistan, Tajikistan and Kyrgzstan." Now, "with the battle lines of civil war in neighboring Tajikistan already drawn, Central Asia's next flash point is likely to be in Uzbekistan's Ferghana Valley, where a combination of looming economic collapse and persistent ethnic nationalism are threatening the survival of President Islam Karimov's government."[2]

President Karimov's aim, as he puts it, is to never allow his country to go the way of Tajikistan or Azerbaijan, where the Communists were forced out of power. He said in an interview that he could "feel the pressure being put on Uzbekistan, placed as it is in the front line . . . of terrorists, saboteurs, and brigands who are readying themselves in Iran and Afghanistan."[3] He was amazed that the West failed to support his efforts to combat Islamic radicalism. He understands that Uzbekistan alone cannot prevent the spread of Islamic radicalism. Thus, Karimov proposed at the 15 May 1992 summit in Tashkent that "a collective security pact" should be established, which would include Russia, the Central Asian republics, and Armenia.

In the latter part of 1997 and early 1998, Uzbekistan's government has quietly but aggressively used its iron-fist rule to crack down on the people it considers Muslim extremists. Parliament passed a law on 1 May 1998 that places restrictions on many religious organizations in the country. The "freedom of conscience" law requires all religious groups with over one hundred members to register with the government. The swift and deliberate actions taken by the government, which began at the end of November 1997, followed closely on the heels of the killings of at least nine police officers and government officials in the eastern town of Namangan. This has underscored the seriousness with which the government is treating those it considers to be extremists. Among those killed, according to Miasy Weicherding of Amnesty International, was the head of the traffic police. He was decapitated, and his head found pinned to a door. Weicherding added, "Since then, we have received reports that up to one hundred people were arbitrarily detained in Namangan."[4] However, it should be noted that this region of the country, similar to the southern towns of Osh and Jalalabad in Kyrgyzstan, are areas where drug trafficking is widespread and where people from all aspects of society are involved in drug trafficking. Sadly, this does not exclude the security forces.

These recent killings may be the result of a group rivalry. Assassinations, revenge killings, and counterrevenge murders are the characteristics of the drug trafficking culture. Nevertheless, the authoritarian government in Tashkent denies the existence of drug trafficking in the country. It has not been difficult to convince the regional and the international communities that Muslim extremists are responsible for the killings in Namangan. Because the people of the Ferghana Valley region are known to be practicing Muslims, the civil war in Tajikistan allows the government to make such an accusation. On 26 March 1998, President Islam Karimov lashed out at the Wahhabis and repeated his earlier claim, made on 17 February 1998, that Wahhabi militants receive training in Pakistan. He also blasted human rights organizations for complaining about the treatment of those arrested in Namangan in late 1997 for their alleged role in violence against the security forces. He added that the trials of those arrested would be open to journalists and observers from other countries.

On 16 February 1999, six bombs exploded. These explosions were followed by a gun battle in the capital city, Tashkent. One blast was inside government headquarters where Islam Karimov was to address the cabinet on the morning of 16 February 1999. A policeman reported that he heard gunfire and grenade concussions as the president's car approached the cabinet building. Russian television showed several wrecked vehicles next to deep craters and tall buildings with shattered windows. This was the first unprecedented act of violence in this country since its independence. Fifteen people were killed and more than 150 injured. The attack shattered the country's reputation as a safe, stable place. According to the residents of Tashkent, the bombing caused quite a scare in the country.

It is unclear as to whether or not the bombs were intended to assassinate the president, Islam Karimov, or whether a more general attack on the current government was planned. The officials were quick to blame Islamic militants for the act. Uzbekistan had expressed fear for a long time about the rise of Islamic fundamentalism, imported from neighboring Afghanistan, Pakistan, and Iran. Speaking during April 1999 in Washington, D.C., Karimov attributed the 1999 bombings and an attempt on his life as an expansion of religious fundamentalism in the region.

Islam Karimov connected these bombings to the Islamic groups in Tajikistan. Tajikistan was shaken by an attempted coup in November 1998, in which Uzbekistan was accused of supporting rebels. Russia, a very close ally of the regime in Tajikistan, would have no reason to restrain Dushanbeh from fomenting unrest in Uzbekistan. Karimov accused Russia of using the CIS collective security treaty to further its own ambitions and said repeatedly that Uzbekistan would withdraw from the treaty. That would be a major blow to Moscow's influence in Central Asia.

However, the Islamic militants were not the only ones who might take such an action against Islam Karimov's government. Other possible supporters of such an act include the disaffected Uzbek groups within the country. During 1998, Karimov sacked several government officials—the vice president, a number of provincial governors, "Vilayat Hakims," and other powerful people—of the different Uzbek tribes for alleged corruption. The bombing could have been the work of drug trafficking groups who are very active in the south and southeastern part of the country. Last, but not least, the bombing and attempted assassination could have also been the work of internal dissidents spurred by the worsening economy.

Islam Karimov, on 23 February, revealed the name of one of the primary suspects in the bombing and attempted assassination: Ulugbek Babajanov. Ulugbek Babajanov had visited the government headquarters six times before the bombings. Babajanov, who is still at large at the time of this writing, obtained permission, according to Karimov, to enter the government buildings from a deputy prime minister. Karimov added that the official was guilty of negligence and poor judgment rather than complicity in the attack. He said not only Wahhbis but also members of Hezbullah were involved in planning the attack. According to the Associated Press, Karimov said the attacks were planned in a foreign country.

Observers contend that Karimov used the bombings to crack down on religious groups because he considers them the last threat to his iron-fist rule over Uzbekistan. On 25 June 1999, Karimov told Uzbekistan's national news agency that the religious groups in question have intensified their activities in recent years, seeking especially to recruit sympathizers among the Uzbek population. There was widespread criticism of the court by human rights observers. They claimed biased procedures and shoddy legal practices. In particular, the human rights observers complained that six of the men were already in prison at the time of the bombing.

On 28 June 1999, the Uzbekistan Supreme Court sentenced six men to death for setting off six bombs in Tashkent, which killed sixteen people in February 1999. These were in addition to sentencing on a series of murders in the Ferghana Valley region. Twenty-two men were on trial in connection with the bombings and murders in the Ferghana Valley. In addition to handing down the death penalty to the six, who have since been executed, the court sentenced eight to twenty-year prison terms, while the other eight defendants received prison terms of between ten and eighteen years in a hard labor camp. According to reports, the state will confiscate the property of all twenty-two men. The relatives of the men were not allowed in the courtroom to hear the sentences and were told of the ruling by local journalists leaving the heavily guarded courthouse. Mohammad Solih, exiled chairman of the Erk opposition party, condemned the repressive policies implemented by President Islam Karimov over the past seven years in the name of "stability" with the tacit support of Russia and the West.[5] However, Karimov's tough stance against the suspected bombers is supported by a nation worried by the threat of the kind of violence that has left neighboring Tajikistan and Afghanistan in ruins.

Early in August 1999, more than three dozens armed Islamist militia crossed into southern Oblast of Osh and took a number of people hostage, including four Japanese mining engineers. Later in the week, militia numbers grew to several hundred. The majority of the armed Islamist militia are Uzbeks, like their leader, Juma Namangani, who fled to Tajikistan during the breakup of the Soviet Union. Their aim was to escape religious and political persecution. Juma Namangani is reported to have close ties with the Islamic Movement of Uzbekistan (IMU), a shadowy organization whose spiritual leader, Tahir Yoldosh, operates from a base in the Taliban-controlled part of Afghanistan.

In Tajikistan, Juma Namangani and his group fought alongside the Islamist opposition during the 1992–1997 civil war. After the UN-sponsored peace in Tajikistan gained roots and matured, the Tajik Islamists accepted shared positions in the government. A decision was made to isolate the Uzbek Islamist armed group and eventually force them out of the country. This happened in August of 1999. Consequently, the Uzbek Islamist militia crossed into Kyrgyzstan, with an alleged claim that they intend to move into Uzbekistan and establish an Islamic state in the Ferghana Valley, a territory that spreads into Uzbekistan, Tajikistan, and Kyrgyzstan. From there, they will carry out an armed struggle against the government in Uzbekistan.

In response to the taking of hostages in Kyrgyzstan, Islam Karimov on 7 September 1999 said that the act was "prepared long in advance and constitutes part of a major conspiracy orchestrated by Islamic terrorists who aim to establish an Islamic state in Central Asia. One cannot be complacent and disregard this threat." He characterized the armed group as "criminals" who "do not represent any country or political party."

It is reported that Karimov persuaded Russia not to disengage from Tajikistan, as it was tempted to do. Some people claim that Karimov helped to secure decisive assistance for the former Communists in Tajikistan, which enabled them to oust the coalition of Islamist Democrats. He permitted an Uzbek aircraft to be used for bombing the opposition forces. He noted that "if a few planes are taking part in wiping out brigands in Tajikistan, you must put the question to Yevgeny Saposhnikov, Commander-in-Chief of the CIS armed forces."[6] He also claimed that at the last CIS summit in Minsk, Russia, and Tajikistan's three Central Asian neighbors decided to send forces to Tajikistan in response to a call for help from the government in Dushanbeh.

Leaders of the five Central Asian republics met at Tashkent in early January 1993 and agreed to step up cooperation on regional security and to provide moral and humanitarian aid to war-torn Tajikistan. This was the second regional meeting of the leaders since the breakup of the Soviet Union. The first meeting had been held in early 1992 in Kazakistan's former capital city of Almaty.

POLITICAL DEVELOPMENTS

Uzbekistan held a parliamentary election on 5 December 1999. Five political parties participated, none of which were in opposition to Islam

Karimov's leadership. However, OSCE criticized the process as not being free and fair and accused the authorities of interfering with the nomination of candidates and ban on two opposition parties from the election process. Therefore, the election could not be considered democratic.

In its first presidential election held on 9 January 2000 (the 1996 election was canceled), Uzbeks reelected Islam Karimov, as expected, to a second term, with more than 90 percent of the vote. He has ruled the country since before independence. A Communist-style referendum in 1995 extended his term to 2000. The U.S. State Department criticized the presidential election and characterized it as neither free nor fair, as it did not offer Uzbeks true choice. However, the majority of the Uzbeks believe Islam Karimov is the best choice available despite the absence of democracy or a vital challenger. Even his nominal contender, Abdulhafiz Jalalov, who appeared in public, ultimately voted for the incumbent. On 17 December 1999, the British Broadcasting Corporation, World Services, conducted a nationwide poll, including six thousand people, in which President Islam Karimov was established as the most popular man in the country. Most of the respondents expressed their intention to vote for Karimov in the 9 January presidential election.[7]

Under Islam Karimov, the country has avoided the upheaval and violence experienced by other former Soviet republics. But this relative stability was achieved at a high cost. Opposition parties are banned, and dissidents are harassed, imprisoned, and forced to flee the country. The government's crackdown on Muslim extremists has resulted in the harassment and persecution of peaceful, practicing Muslims. The latter governmental action is helping opposition Muslim extremists of Uzbekistan to transform Islam, as a religion, into an alternative political means to generate momentary upheaval not only in this country but also within the region. Human rights groups characterize the regime as one of the worst violators of civil liberties and most repressive among the former Soviet republics.

ECONOMIC CONDITIONS

Uzbekistan's economy depends on its rich supply of gold, uranium, oil, natural gas, coal, silver, and copper for economic gains. Uzbekistan is ranked as one of the ten largest suppliers of natural gas in the world. In 1997, the deputy prime minister reported that oil production in the country had risen by 180 percent since the year of its declaration of independence. Many of the nation's economic hardships stem from a difficult business atmosphere. The European Bank for Reconstruction and Development (EBRD) criticized the nation's controls on outside investment in the area. Subsequently, this has turned away many Western investors from Uzbekistan. Furthermore, the government's failure to disassemble the collective farms has led to an increase in prices and massive food shortages. Many of the farms still operate as they did under Soviet rule, making the Communist farm manager wealthy, yet keeping the workers at a subsistence level. Although the government has allowed the farms to sell 50 percent of their vegetable harvests on the private market, this helps them less than one might initially suspect, since their collective farms are chiefly geared for cotton production. It will take time for farmers to diversify their products. Uzbekistan suffers from a monoculture of cotton. This monoculture was imposed on it by the Soviet Union and also arose from the export of its energy and raw materials. Fewer than 10 percent of its raw materials were processed in the republic, and the rest were shipped out north.[8]

Those running the collective farms are eager to begin working their own small plots of land, but the government has yet to allot many parcels of land to be distributed by the populace. Even if the government distributes more land, the farmers still face the problem of securing the needed supplies, as the prices for materials have increased tremendously due to high inflation and shortages.

Government officials in Uzbekistan maintain that there are too many people for each person to own his or her own land. Even if the land were available, it would be too expensive. Uzbekistan faces serious problems as the government fails to restructure farming to allow the workers to grow their own food. The government is setting up laws in an attempt to facilitate the transition to the private ownership of farmland. The World Bank has loaned Uzbekistan $28 million to encourage the continuation of the privatization process. Recent reports indicate that the International Finance Corporation will give Uzbekistan more then $60 million in credits for agricultural purchases to strengthen its economy. Uzbekistan has recently signed an agreement with Elf-Aquitaine of France and Chevron of the United States for the development of its oil fields. In his visit to China in November 1999, Karimov was able to secure a loan of $11 million. During his meeting with Chinese officials, Karimov called for expanded cooperation in the chemical, aircraft building, and light industry sectors. The annual trade between the two countries as of November 1999 was estimated at $830 million. Karimov called for the expansion of trade between Uzbekistan and China.[9]

Karimov has promised to liberalize the deteriorating economy by extending privatization, promoting small businesss, and by the end of

2000, freeing Uzbek currency, the som, which is traded over the official rate of exchange in the black market. These promises, if carried out, could attract foreign investment in the country. However, he is cognizant that these developments could undoubtedly encourage political and social unrest.

CHAPTER 6

Kyrgyzstan

Kyrgyzstan is the least known of the former Soviet republics. Its name is believed to stem from *kyrgyz*, which means "forty girls" or "forty tribes." No one knows for sure the source of the name *Kyrgyz*, even though there are several myths surrounding it. The Kyrgyz people divide themselves into two major branches known as Kanat, which literally means "Wing," as in bird, or in this case the Golden Eagle. The Solkanat (Left wing) and Ongkanat (Right wing) are divided into smaller clans and subclans. In such divisions, regional affiliation outweighs tribal loyalty. The country is divided into the northern regions of Chui, Issy-Kul, and Narin (meaning northeast) and Talas in the northwest. Southerners refer to the northerners as Arghalik, which literally means "Back." The country is also divided into the southern regions of Osh and Jalalabad. The Kyrgyz people refer to southerners as Itchkilik, which literally means "Stomach."

Talas is the home of the majority of the Solkanat. As the people from each region were ruled by different khanates, such as Kharazm and Kukand, they had different historical experiences. They cohabited with different ethnic groups, such as the Persians, Chinese, Tajiks, and Uzbeks.

The Kyrgyz people, who are closely related to the Kazaks in language, ethnic composition, social organization, and economic makeup, occupied the mountain districts of the Ala-To and Lake Issy-Kul. Before 1917, Russians referred to them as the "Kara-Qyrqyz" "Black Kyrgyz," to distinguish them from the misnamed Kazaks or Qazaqs.

The term *kyrgyz* is referred to in written sources dating as far back as the third century B.C. It is believed that the Kyrgyz originated from Mongolian Oirot (Kalia), Naiman and a number of ancient Central Asian people, who are currently living in the region. During the second and first centuries B.C., some of the Kyrgyz tribes set themselves free from the Hun (Hunnu) domination and moved to the Enisei "Yenisei" River (*Yeni-sei* means "The Mother River") and Lake Baikal (*Bai kol* means "Rich Lake"). In this region, they formed the first Kyrgyz Khanate, which stretched from the Yenisei River to the eastern slopes of the Tien-Shan Mountains. However, the khanate system was destroyed during the thirteenth century by Mongolian conquerors. A known Kyrgyz system was not to be established again until 31 August 1991, when the parliament proclaimed Kyrgyzstan an independent state. Kyrgyzstan shares borders with Kazakistan in the north, Uzbekistan to the west, Tajikistan and China to the south, and the province of Xinjiang to the east.

POLITICAL DEVELOPMENTS

The country's constitution was adopted in 1993, but President Akaev held a controversial referendum in February 1996, changing more than 50 percent of the original constitution. Under the 1993 Constitution, only Parliament had the right to change the constitution. The 1996 referendum gave the president the right to appoint most governmental officials, while the prime minister has to report to Parliament on activities of the government. Therefore, the 1996 referendum has ensured that the office of prime minister is a nominal rather than real office.

The new legislature of Kyrgyzstan met for the first time in March of 1995, preceeding Akaev's successful bid to amend the Constitution and create a bicameral legislative body. The lower house, the House of National Representatives, consisting of seventy members, was established along with the upper chamber, referred to as the Legislative House and was comprised of thirty-five members. In March of 1995, there were still fifteen seats that were unfilled. The seats were left unfilled because of a stipulation imposed by Akaev, which stated that no member of Parliament would be allowed to hold another political office. This left the new Parliament with many new faces in the political arena. However, only six members had previous experience in Parliament. There were raised concerns about the specific duties and limitations of the new body of the government. Not surprisingly, many of the early sessions consisted of debates over the exact duties of the legislature. Critics felt that with extensive concentration on the role of the legislature, other important issues would fall by the wayside, and Parliament would overwhelm itself.

The president, with the advice and consent of Parliament, has the ability to appoint judges. According to the Constitution, a judge must be between the ages of thirty-five and sixty-five, with some legal education and at least ten years of prior legal experience. Judges are appointed for unlimited tenures and can only be removed by Parliament.

In 1993, Apas Jumagulov was appointed prime minister. His tenure was marked by numerous allegations of corruption. Two years after his appointment, his son drowned mysteriously in Lake Issy-Kul. It was alleged that the younger Jumagulov was involved in illegal gas and cigarette smuggling in the region. On 13 and 20 March 1998, the Kyrgyz nightly newspaper *Vecherny Bishkek* reported that the elder Jumagulov was the founding member of an obscure Austrian company, which handles the sale of Kyrgyz gold. According to the newspaper, the company is estimated to make profits totaling $80 to 100 million over the next three years.[1]

On numerous occasions, Jumagulov expressed and promoted political and economic policies that were contrary to those championed by President Askar Akaev. Since 1992, the government has taken steps to stabilize the economy. In 1992, the inflation rate hovered at over 1,000 percent. The government's efforts decreased this rate to about 20 percent in 1997. During Jumagulov's tenure, the economic conditions of the Kyrgyz people had hardly improved, and inflation, budget deficits, and unemployment were the major features of the Kyrgyz economy. On 24 March 1998, Apas Jumagulov announced his resignation, which was immediately accepted by President Akaev. The president did not waste any time in appointing the head of the presidential administration, Kubanychbek Jumaliev, as acting prime minister. Within twenty-four hours after Apas Jumagulov's resignation as prime minister, Parliament approved Kubanychbek Jumaliev as the new prime minister.

POLITICAL TURMOIL

This tranquil republic was shaken in August 1999 when a group of armed militant Islamists entered the southern Kyrgyz region of Batken and took several hostages, including four Japanese geologists. The militants were later identified as followers of Uzbek Islamic leader Juma Namangani. The militants claimed that their aim is to establish an Islamic state in the Ferghana Valley, which spreads into the three adjacent countries. This was the second invasion by the militants. During the first incursion, a guard and an official were killed. On 29 August 1999, four residents of the Kara-Teyit village were killed during bombing by Uzbek warplanes.

During September, Kyrgyz Defense Minister Esen Topoev and Deputy Foreign Minister Asanbek Osmonaliev participated in an urgent meeting of CIS defense ministers in Moscow. This meeting was held to deal with two urgent items: the improvement of the collective defense system of the CIS and the situation in southern Kyrgyzstan. The hostages, including the four Japanese geologists were freed on 25 October 1999. Shortly after, Bishkek established several new border posts along the border with Tajikistan in the newly formed Batken region.

Kyrgyzstan is more vulnerable than the other adjacent countries because it is politically more open than the other two, and it lacks the military and economic wherewithal to deal with such problems if they were to persist. The author does not believe that the Kyrgyz people would welcome or support politco-Islamic aims to establish an Islamic state. The historical, social, political, and religious experiences of the Kyrgyz people are not in tune with such a worldview or acceptance of such a political system. However, deteriorating economic conditions of the country may become a source for opposition to the government and demand for major changes in the political and economic system of the country.

It should be noted that the southern Kyrgyz regions of Osh and Jalalabad have been identified as the center of the Islamic movement in Kyrgyzstan. During early January 2000, the Kyrgyz law enforcement authorities began a campaign of arresting a number of Islamic activists in the area. The region, abutting on Tjikistan and Uzbekistan, has a significant population of Uzbeks and those who have family connections with Uzbeks and Tajik people. Authorities accuse the detainees of belonging to a movement aimed at overthrowing the constitutional system and establishing an Islamic state in the Ferghana Valley.

ECONOMIC CONDITIONS

Kyrgyzstan's population of 4.6 million depends heavily on agriculture. Most of the working-age people are engaged in the agricultural sector of the economy. Only 1 million of those of working age are engaged outside of agriculture. Besides agriculture, Kyrgyzstan offers abundant hydroelectricity and assorted minerals, such as coal, gold, and uranium, but little else. Until the end of 1995, the country continued to struggle with a high rate of inflation and a negative gross domestic product (GDP). In 1996, it experienced its first minimal growth; estimated at 5 percent, even though the country's external debt continued to increase. Since 1996, the country has experienced a growth in its economy by 7 percent, which is partly due to the progress that has been made in the privatization of both agriculture and industry.

Kyrgyzstan was the first Central Asian country to move away from the ruble. Unfortunately, its currency, the som, has caused a great deal of trouble for the country. Uzbekistan, which once had been a major trading partner of Kyrgyzstan, responded to President Askar Akayev's announcement introducing the new currency by cutting off all major links with Kyrgyzstan. These links include telephone, gas, land, and air.

According to Khalid Bouzerda, member of the European Bank for

Reconstruction and Development, these actions make Kyrgyzstan the most advanced of the former Soviet republics in regards to its ability to convert itself into a market economy. Nevertheless, it should be noted that Kyrgyzstan's economy is so small that its attractiveness for European investment is limited.[2]

As poorly as the som initially was received, it does appear as though it will eventually come to be accepted, albeit with great caution. With financial help from the IMF and Japan, it is likely that the som will stabilize soon. This country is committed to the democratization of the political, social, and economic systems in the region. This has allowed it to attract limited investment from European Union member states, as well as from Japan. This may eventually present Kyrgyzstan with the opportunities needed to reduce its dependence on Russia.

The nation still depends on Russia for military assistance. Kyrgyzstan has ground forces but continues to look to Russia for its national security interests. Akaev signed a contract granting Kyrgyzstan favorable trading status with Russia, which ensures that Russian oil and other natural resources are delivered to Kyrgyzstan before they are sent to other countries. This agreement also made Russian the second official language in the country.

Tursunbek Chyngyshev, then Kyrgyzstan's prime minister, toured the European Union during February 1992 to enlist the assistance of private enterprise and, more importantly, the governments of the European Union countries to assist in the revival of the republic's economy. Chyngyshev's request had three main features. First, Kyrgyzstan would present these countries direct access to western China through the long common border shared by the two countries. Second, it would continue its dedication to a secular and open governmental system to prevent the spread of "Islamic radicalism" and "ethnic rivalry," which has brought massive upheaval and chaos to Tajikistan. The third and most important feature of Chyngyshev's appeal was Kyrgyzstan's goal of becoming a free market economy. Significantly, its central bank is already independent of both the government and parliament. Kyrgyzstan has sold off 11 percent of its state-owned enterprises (most of them small) and expects to sell off another 25 percent by 1993. Although such developments in the economic sector tend to evolve rather slowly, the government is promising to guarantee direct foreign investments and to allow unlimited repatriation of profits (including hard currency) by foreign firms.

Since 1994, the country has worked on creating a more open atmosphere for the privatization of business. With a lack of hard currency, the government issued coupons to certain individuals to allow them to buy state-owned enterprises and turn them into private companies. The implementation of this system has helped to increase the country's GDP slightly. The GDP growth rate was expected to be slightly over 3 percent, and the industrial output was expected to grow by over 3 percent for 1998.[3]

Despite these advances, 60 percent of the population still earns less than minimum wage, and 18 percent lives in "absolute poverty."[4] In order for a Kyrgyz to get a job, the government must invest in the rural infrastructure. In response to the economic situation, government officials have redrawn the social services and pension systems. National programs are being created to aid the Kyrgyz in their quest for a decent standard of living.

President Askar Akaev asked Moscow for some "unspecified special assistance." The most pressing problem faced by the republic is the need for hard currency to finance a balance-of-payments shortfall of about $400 million. Kyrgyzstan's foreign debt for 1999 was estimated at $1.27 billion, according to Prime Minister Amangeldy Miraliev. The debt substantially exceeded the country's 1999 GDP, which amounted to $978 million. Foreign debt service alone amounts to 40 percent of budgeted total expenditures for 2000. A major portion of the debt is owed to the international financial institutions, and the remaining, estimated during summer of 1999 as $132.8 million, is owed to the former Soviet republics. Failure to secure this sum may cause the International Monetary Fund (IMF) to reject the promised aid.

Kyrgyzstan, like the other Central Asian republics, faced a high rate of inflation with the introduction of its national currency. In 1995, when this author taught in Kyrgyzstan as a Fulbright scholar, the rate of exchange was about ten to twelve soms to the U.S. dollar. By August 1998, the rate had risen to twenty soms to the U.S. dollar. The rate of inflation for 1999 was 35 percent despite the attempt by the government to reduce it to 15 percent. Inflation remains a major problem for all of the former Soviet republics, in addition to a continuous negative foreign trade imbalance. The World Bank is particularly interested in helping Kyrgyzstan to lower its poverty rate, supporting its growing private sector, and promoting the effective management of its public finances. The International Development Association (IDA) has given the country money for many programs, such as the development of telecommunications. It has also aided in Kyrgyzstan's transition to a market economy and helped the country's small farmers with a credit program.

In fact, it was announced that on 25 January 1999, a visiting IMF delegation agreed to increase its aid to the country from $15 million to $28 million to cushion the impact of the 1998 Russian financial crisis. A European Commission representative also confirmed that the EU would grant Kyrgyzstan 1 million Euros ($1.56 million) in 1999 to help reform the country's health service.

President Askar Akaev met with acting Russian president Putin in Moscow on 24 January 2000 on the eve of the CIS summit. Akaev requested that repayment of Kyrgyzstan's large debt, estimated in summer of 1999 at $132.8 million, to Russia be rescheduled. However, the interest payment on the loan to Russia for 2000 will be very large for the country to meet.

Russia is not the only country to step in and assist Kyrgyzstan. China has also agreed to invest money in the nation. On 27 April 1998, Akaev met with Jiang Zemin, and the two signed a declaration of friendship to improve ties between the two nations. China has pledged to invest about 100 million yuan (approximately 8 million U.S. dollars) into factory production and another million yuan in the Kyrgyz health care system. Moreover, on 2 September 1999, Akaev met with a visiting U.S. delegation to discuss strengthening bilateral economic ties. At the meeting, it was disclosed that in the year 2000, Kyrgyzstan is expected to meet foreign debt repayments equal to 40 percent of the annual budget. The lion's share consists of a $130 million Russian loan. This means that the government would need to restructure its foreign loans. Because of the country's poor economic conditions, more than 3,000 ethnic Russians left Kyrgyzstan in the last few months of 1999. Russia's ambassador to Kyrgyzstan cited the reasons for this exodus as deteriorating economic conditions, the hostage taking in the southern region of the country in August-October 1999, and moves by the Kyrgyz leadership to officially popularize the use of Kyrgyz language in public life. In early 1990, an estimated 900,000 Russians lived in Kyrgyzstan. Today, that population has declined to approximately 650,000.[5]

CHAPTER 7

Tajikistan

Tajikistan declared its independence on 9 September 1991 and shortly thereafter became a member of the CIS. It shares borders with Uzbekistan, Kyrgyzstan, China, and Afghanistan. Seventy percent of the population resides in rural areas. Tajikistan is a small country, approximately the size of Wisconsin, and it is 93 percent mountainous terrain. Approximately 6.05 million people live in Tajikistan, which is large compared to the amount of arable land. It has the highest birthrate among the former Soviet republics. A significant number of the inhabitants reside in the western part of the country.

The Tajik people consist of surviving Iranian groups, who were the dominant population of the Central Asian region prior to the Moghul (Mongol) and Turkic invaders. Tajiks occupied the mountain areas of the Pamir and Ferghana Valley. Tajiks speak Persian (the language of Iranians), Dari (a Persian dialect), and Russian, which is the language spoken by most of the urban residents, government officials, bureaucrats, and business people. Ethnically, the population is composed of 62 percent Tajiks, 23 percent Uzbeks, 8 percent Russians, and a little more than 1 percent Tartars and Kyrgyz. Overall, the country encompasses nineteen different ethnic groups. However, this division is not limited to ethnicity, rather the Tajik themselves are divided into the Garmis (central), Kulabis (south central), and Khojandis (north).

POLITICAL DEVELOPMENTS

The parliamentary republic was established by the 1994 constitution that set up the new Parliament, the Majlis-i Oli. In February 1995, for the first time in the republic's short history, political parties nominated the candidates. The framework for this system calls for the head of state (the chairman of the Supreme Soviet of the Republic of Tajikistan), the legislature (the Majlis-i Oli), and the executive (the Council of Ministers) to run the state.

The government is highly restrictive and controls what the mass media is allowed to report to the population. However, the government provides for the freedom of religious worship, and women are allowed to participate in the electoral process. This is probably due to the fact that quotas in the Soviet system had mandated that a set number of women must hold positions in the government. However, since the breakup of the Soviet Union, the number of women in the government has decreased drastically.

On 6 November 1999, Imamali Rahmonov was reelected with 96 percent of the votes. The other 2 percent went to Davlat Usmon, who was running against Imamali Rahmonov. According to the official report, 98 percent of the country's 2.8 million electorate participated.

While Russian and CIS election observers said they registered no violation of voting procedures, the OSCE did not send observers and said that democratic conditions had not been created for a free and fair election. Opposition parties told the journalists on the following day that the outcome of the poll was rigged and that only 20 to 30 percent of voters had participated. The U.S. State Department voiced its dismay in connection with irregularities in the presidential election. However, on 8 November, the UN Security Council approved to extend for another six months the mandate of the UN Observer Mission in the country.[1] The UN observers will monitor preparations for the February parliamentary elections. There is a debate between the government and the United Tajik Opposition (UTO) concerning the configuration of the upper and lower houses, particularly the number of seats. The government proposed that the upper chamber have thirty-five deputies and the lower house fifty-five, while the opposition called for forty-five and ninety-one, respectively.[2] After a lengthy and arduous debate between government and opposition representatives, the two sides agreed on the number of deputies in each chamber. The lower house will consist of sixty-three seats and the upper chamber thirty-three, respectively. Rahmonov and opposition politicians viewed the completion of the draft of the election law as a foundation for a transition to a popular participation in the political process.

The leader of UTO, Abdulla Nuri, in his comments in connection with the November 6 presidential election, expressed UTO's delight that the process did not exacerbate the existing tensions in the country. Another member of the UTO leadership, Hoji Akbar Turajanzoda, first deputy premier, characterized the election as free and democratic, while Duvlat Usmon of the Islamic Renaissance Party, who failed to receive more than 2 percent of the votes, criticized the election.

Russia's Prime Minister Putin attended Imamali Rahmonov's official inauguration in Dushanbeh on 16 November 1999. During his visit, he held talks with Yahya Azimov, the Tajik president and prime minister, which focused on bilateral relations, the status of Russian troops in Tajikistan, and cooperation within CIS, among other regional issues.

Rahmonov told Putin that Tajikistan still regards Russia as a "strategic partner." Putin characterized the two countries' bilateral relations as "constructive" and added that the countries' mutual debt can be resolved without difficulty.[3]

POLITICAL AND SOCIAL TURMOIL

On the surface, life looks normal in the country. However, the country is now enmeshed in social and political turmoil. Tajikistan is known as one of the poorest republics of Central Asia. Pessimists fear the outbreak of an all-out civil war between regional clans would divide the richer, secular, industrial north from Dushanbeh and the poorer Islamic south. This might be prevented through serious negotiations between the contending groups and factions emphasizing tolerance and the accommodation of opposing views.

There is an unsubstantiated fear promoted by Moscow, Uzbekistan, and some in the United States that if Tajikistan's radical Islamists gain control of the government, then they will attempt to spread their influence to neighboring countries, specifically Kazakistan. This would allow them to access the vast natural resources and perhaps even nuclear weapons.[4] The Russian military has laid out such a scenario in an attempt to substantiate its claim that it needs to maintain a military presence in these republics since Russian security is jeopardized.

Part of the reason for the current strength of the Islamic religion in Tajikistan, even during Soviet rule, is that it is "the only ethnically Persian state of Central Asia, which is otherwise Turkic-speaking." As a result, Tajikistan looks more toward Iran and Afghanistan, where many ethnic Tajiks also live, than to modern and secular Turkey. Turkey is Washington's favored model for Central Asian development. Other Central Asian peoples, such as "the Kazaks and Kirghyz [sic.], mostly stemming from nomadic tribesman, tended not to build up urban centers for Islamic study."[5] In contrast, the Tajiks are proud of their centers.

The Islamists seem to be a strong force in the otherwise shallow opposition alliance that took over key government ministries in May 1998. To add to the confusion, there are splits between the Sunni Wahhabi fundamentalists and other Islamists who prefer the Ismaili's Shi'a model. Both groups share the same Persian language and literature. However, it must be highlighted, the Islamic groups are not unified or for that matter can easily merge into a single group because of religion. The numerous Islamic groups cannot easily claim to represent the population of Tajikistan or for that matter other former Soviet republics, as individually they each follow a particular Islamic school of thought, such as Wahhabi.

The recent campaign against Islamists has been successful, leaving the latter in retreat and disarray. Even if an Islamic republic were to be established in this ethnically mixed, Soviet-educated population of over 6 million people, it is unlikely to be in the rigid Iranian mold or Saudi Arabia's Wahhabi mold. Most of the Tajiks and other Central Asian Muslims could be characterized as followers of the Sufi worldview. Sufism is a mystic Islamic sect that pays very close attention to philosophical discourse and poetry, while other existing Islamic sects concentrate on the Quran and the Hadeeth. Wahhabi Islamic school of thought outright rejects the Sufi school of thought, which is widely accepted by the educated Muslims in the regions under study and in Iran. Sufiism's strong use of philosophical poetry and mysticism allows for an individual to accept and practice that without interfering or contradicting the modern with the Western political, economic, social orientation. Sunnis have been very active in reestablishing themselves with financial help from outside the region. In the midst of such activities, Wahhabis who have never been in this part of the Islamic world are particularly interested in establishing themselves with the available funds from the Saudi ministry of religion, as well as from some well-endowed citizens of the country. For starters, Tajik women do not wear a black veil commonly used by the women in Saudi Arabia, Islamic Republic of Iran, or for that matter any other Islamic societies. They prefer, particularly in the rural areas, colorful yellow, red, green, and white national dresses. Women in the urban area dress in Western style, as one would see in any parts of the former Soviet republics.

On 27 June 1997, at a ceremony in Moscow, Tajik President Imamali Rahmonov, the head of the Tajik opposition, and the National Reconciliation Council leader, Sayed Abdulllo Nuro (Nuri), signed an agreement ending five years of war. The other Islamic opposition leader, Akbar Turajannzoda, has taken over as the republic's first deputy prime minister. The 1997 peace agreement has proved to be observed by all political rivals. Despite the peace agreement of 1997, there have been frequent clashes between government forces and rebels. Tajikistan will probably remain vulnerable to the outburst of violence and instability for some time to come. An attack in 1997 was one of the most violent attacks since the government, and the Muslim opposition in this country ended a five-year civil war in the summer of that year.

Growing animosity by Islamic groups, democratic movements toward the Communist regime, and the outbreak of civil war have caused many Russians to emigrate. In addition, many Uzbek minorities fled to the northern part of Tajikistan. This migration is detrimental to the republic's industry and diminishes its medical capabilities and health services.

According to the director of the Institute of Economics, another Tajik major problem is the border dispute with Uzbekistan. "Central Asia's two main Persian-speaking cities, Samarkand (Samangun) and Bukhara, were included in Uzbekistan, leaving the Tajiks with the back-water town of Dushanbeh as their capital." There is also disagreement between the republics of Kyrgyzstan and Tajikistan over the placement of their common border.[6]

Despite its domestic problems, in March 1998, Tajikistan became a member of the Central Asian Customs Union. Kazakistan, Kyrgyzstan, and Uzbekistan founded this organization shortly after achieving independence. During their meeting on 26 March 1998 in Tashkent, the heads of states of Tajikistan and the republics that were founding members of the Central Asian Custom Union agreed to form a regional hydroelectric energy system. They also agreed to cooperate with each other in regards to the establishment of a regional securities market. Islam Karimov of Uzbekistan said that the entry of Tajikistan into the union makes the country eligible to receive firmly committed assistance from other member states. During the meeting, Nursultan Nazarbaev of Kazakistan reminded the others that the member states would remain members of the CIS. Tajik president Imamali Rahmonov attended the CIS summit in Moscow on 24 January 2000, during which he met with acting President Putin and discussed economic and military-technical cooperation with Russia. Included in the discussion was the situation in Afghanistan, and the threat posed by armed militant groups in the region.

ECONOMIC CONDITIONS

With the breakup of the Soviet Union, Tajikistan's government has been faced with a declining economy. The civil war has severely damaged the infrastructure of the economy and has been the cause of food shortages due to the processing of raw materials and production limitations on industry and agriculture. Moreover, Tajikistan's economy hinders several building projects that would increase the productivity of the state, including a hydroelectric plant.

Tajikistan has one of the lowest standards of living among any of the former Soviet republics. Cotton and aluminum productions are the major components to their economic base. Hydroelectric resources and minerals are also important to the country, but it lacks the capability to process these raw materials. Silk, fruits, and vegetables are Tajikistan's primary agricultural products. The country is highly dependent on agriculture and forestry, with about half of the population cultivating only

7 percent of the total land mass. Tajikistan takes advantage of its inexpensive supply of water to irrigate crops. Approximately 20 percent of the population is employed in industry and construction. The country has a great potential to develop gold and silver if the industry responsible for processing these raw materials can be developed.

According to the State Statistics Agency, Tajikistan's foreign trade for the first half of 1998 decreased by 12 percent in comparison with the same period for 1997. This totaled an estimated $660 million. For the same period, the imports ($262.1 million) exceeded the country's exports ($225.9 million). The imbalance of payments was caused by a decline in cotton fiber export by 23 percent, aluminum and its byproducts by 11 percent, canned vegetable products by 52 percent, alcohol and soft beverages by 8 percent, leather and animal hides by 60 percent and silk by 81 percent. During the same period, importation of the following goods increased: oil products by 29 percent, baked products by 53 percent, alcohol and soft drinks by 22 percent, chemical products by 18 percent, and vehicles by 3 percent.

On 1 December 1999, President Imamali Rahmonov signed two decrees regarding the expansion of "the process of democratization of socio-political life" in the country and on "measures for the further development and enhancing the effectiveness of economic reforms." The first decree announced an intention to guarantee political pluralism and the free participation of all political parties in elections and in the state administration. The other directs the government to take steps to improve the investment climate and to draft legislation for state treasury and national security to develop measures to protect the most vulnerable group of the population.[7]

Tajikistan was the last republic to adopt an independent currency, the Samani. The new currency which is equal to 1,000 Tajik ruble was introduced on 30 October 2000. There are some indications in the financial sectors and the industrial sectors that the country is moving towards a market economy.

The director of the IMF second European Department, John Odling-Smee, held talks on 4 November with President Imamali Rahmonov on the possibility of further support for the economy of Tajikistan. Rahmonov said the support is needed to reduce Tajikistan's budget deficit and to help it with the balance of payments.

CHAPTER 8

Turkmenistan

Even before 27 October 1991, Turkmenistan was not an independent nation in the modern sense of the word. It was for centuries a loose confederation of nomadic clans who lived the traditional nomadic lifestyle and roamed around, never establishing a national state. These nomadic clans were often divided among the Iranian Empire, the Khanate of Khiva and the emirate of Bukhara. They inhabited the desert steppe region between the Syr-Daria River and the Caspian Sea. Like the Kazaks and the Kyrgyz, their social organization was primarily by family and clan. Most of the Turkmen were engaged in a pastoral economy and lifestyle, except for the farmers, who resided in Marv (Mary) and Tajan.

Present day Turkmenistan is surrounded by the Caspian Sea to the west, Kazakistan and Uzbekistan to the north, Amu-Daria and Tajikistan to the east, and to the south by Iran and Afghanistan. Since the independence of Turkmenistan, many streets, buildings, and government positions have been renamed from Russian to Turkman. Tribalism remains one of the dominant strains of the republic, which tends to hamper economic and political development and becomes a source of conflict. The written language has been another source of controversy in the country. For years, the standard Turkman has been written in a Cyrillic script, but in 1996, the president issued a statement declaring that, henceforth, the script would come from a Latin base and would go into effect on 1 January 2000.

POLITICAL DEVELOPMENTS

The 1992 constitution declares the government of Turkmenistan to be a secular democracy; however, the iron-fist rule of a personality cult and a single party system of government run the country. The Constitution declares Turkmenistan to be a presidential republic, therefore giving Niyazov the power to make all major decisions. It remains a one-party state with the Communist Party type structure dominating the government. The Constitution also establishes the judiciary as an independent institution, but in reality it is beholden and subordinate to the president.

Turkmenistan has three branches of government, the executive (the presidency and the Cabinet of Ministers), the legislative (the National Assembly), and the judiciary, (the Supreme Court, and the Supreme Economic Court). In addition, the Halk (Khalq) Maslahaty (Consultory) (People's Assembly) is an influential advisory board in addition to sixty other elected members and local government officials. As it stands today, the president has most of the power within the government. President Saparmurat Niyazov makes the policies, appoints officials, and has the ability to select which legislation is proposed in the People's Assembly.

Among the Central Asian republics, Turkmenistan seems to be the most stable country. Niyazov has managed to contain any significant political opposition in the country, including challenges from the established Islamic religion. On 15 January 1994, an estimated 99.9 percent of the nearly 2 million electorates voted in a referendum to extend Niyazov's presidency to the year 2001.[1]

Islam, possibly Sufiism, is gaining popularity throughout the region. Niyazov has even embraced it himself and has increased the public role of religious elders in establishing and supervising the social norms of the Turkmen people. Still, the executive branch of government maintains considerable control over religious activities within the country. All religions are required to register with the government, even though there is supposed to be freedom of religion in Turkmenistan. The government strictly regulates political and civil liberties, as well as the media.

President Saparmurat Niyazov visited the United States to present a speech sponsored by the Eurasia Group and the Council on Foreign Relations. He used this platform to express his reservations over the impatient manner with which officials from the United States have encouraged the implementation of their democratic views. His speech highlighted the problems the post-Soviet republics are experiencing in grappling with those issues which either directly run against, or at least are not wholly compatible with, the interests of the Western countries. He suggested that in order for the former Soviet republics to complete their transitions to democratic political systems, it is imperative that the Western countries look at the political, economic, and social conditions of these new republics.

Contradictions in speeches and the actions of the heads of these republics are numerous and clearly indicate that it would take these countries many years to allow for the establishment of democracy and popular mass participation in the political lives. On 27 October 1999, in a speech marking the anniversary of the country's 1991 declaration of independence, President Niyazov vowed that the upcoming 12 December parliamentary elections would be free and democratic and that anyone may run as candidate and have access to state television to present their election platforms. He promised similar policy for the presidential elections due in 2002. However, in early November 1999, the Central Election Commission, following a presidential decision, announced that all candidates must be registered as independent, because Niyazov believes that Turkmenistan will not be ready for a multiparty political system for at least a decade. Interestingly, a day before, Turkmenistan's Parliament approved an amendment to the country's Constitution allowing incumbent President Saparmurat Niyazov to remain president for an unlimited period. On 29 December 1999, Niyazov said that no alternatives to the ruling Democratic Party, which remains the sole political party for some time to come, exists.[2]

ECONOMIC CONDITIONS

Niyazov has been the sole economic planner for the country since it achieved independence in 1991. In 1996, Niyazov presented what was known as the "year of fundamental reform," but during the same year, grain and cotton production fell two-thirds short of the government's targets. In 1997, Niyazov's economic program of "one thousand days," called for boosting the GDP by 60 percent before year 2000 and eliminating demand for import goods in favor of the domestically produced ones. However, by the end of the first year of the plan, Turkmenistan's GDP fell by a sixth and has remained stagnate ever since, while the country's dependence on imports has remained large and is growing by the year.

During 1999, Niyazov introduced an eleven-year economic plan, similar to those of the Soviet era, in which he speculated that Turkmenistan will increase production of cotton and wheat fourfold, natural gas exports fivefold, and oil production by sevenfold. The plan called for making water, salt, gas, and electricity available for the people free of charge. The plan further claimed that the country's standard of living should triple or quadruple by 2010, restoring it to what it was under the Soviet rule. The feasibility of achieving such a plan in light of the country's economic reality is undoubtedly wishful thinking. Similar to all other republics, rural Turkmenistan has not seen any results of economic prosperity!

In fact, Turkmenistan is the least developed of the former Soviet republics. Turkmenistan introduced the manat as the country's currency on 1 November 1993. As of March 1998, the GOTX Statistics and Economic Forecasting Committee recorded that the average salary of a Turkmen was 255,000 manats per month (approximately $49.03).

While state intervention is on the decline, for the most part, the economy is still centrally planned.

Similar to other former Soviet republics, inflation has been and continues to be a problem for Turkmenistan. Inflation has declined significantly since peaking at nearly 10,000 percent in 1993. It dropped to 84 percent in 1997.[3] Inflation for 1999 was estimated at 40 percent, double the rate for 1998. Government will maintain the existing tight monetary policy for some years. The aim is to reduce annual inflation to a single digit number by the year 2005 and a lower-level single digit by 2010, making the manat fully convertible. However, the draft budget for 2000 presented on 23 November 1999 reveals the existence of a significant budget deficit.

The country's major products are natural gas, cotton, wool, grapes, and vegetable oil. It has the fourth largest natural gas reserve in the world, which generates a large amount of the country's revenue. Economic reform is slowly moving along, but 80 percent of its oil, natural gas, minerals, and agriculture are still under state ownership. Agriculture accounts for about half of the GDP, as well as around 40 percent of Turkmenistan's total employment. The government is striving to become self-sufficient in food supplies, and it has invested large amounts of money into purchasing equipment to meet this goal.

The area where Turkmenistan is located is self-sufficient in energy, containing a bountiful supply of natural gas. Turkmenistan, which is the world's third largest producer of natural gas, produced about 86 billion cubic meters in 1990. About 8 billion cubic meters of natural gas are allocated for domestic use. Turkmenistan's reserves are estimated at about 13 trillion cubic meters of gas in its Sovietabad field.

However, its gas production plummeted from 86 billion cubic meters to 17 billion in 1997. At the beginning of 1994, a dispute with the Russian giant company Gazprom resulted in the company's refusal to allow Turkmenistan to use its gas pipeline to ship gas to Europe. A visit by Russian officials to Ashqabad in 1998 failed to resolve the dispute. Also in 1997, the government of Turkmenistan halted gas exports to Armenia, Georgia, and Ukraine because those countries had built up large arrears to it for earlier deliveries.

Since natural gas makes up two-thirds of both the GDP and exports in 1994, this decline in production has had serious consequences for the country's economy. Turkmenistan faces a substantial trade deficit as a result. Moreover, this has resulted in more than 25 percent of the GDP in 1997. However, it is expecting to have a positive real GDP growth rate between 2 and 5 percent in 1998. This follows real declines of more than 7 percent in 1995, 4 percent in 1996, and 25 percent in 1997.

Similar to Kazakistan and Azerbaijan, Turkmenistan's oil production declined during the early 1990s. Since 1995, there has been a steady, even though small, increase in production of oil. Oil production, for 1997, increased to 128,000 bpd, up from 88,000 bpd in 1996 and 130,000 bpd in the first six months of 1998. Turkmenistan, in June 1998, established the country's first national oil company in Turkmenneft, the Turkmen National Oil Company (TNOC). Immediately after, President Niyazov set out a program for the development of the country's oil export strategy, pipeline use, and construction. This also includes the marketing of oil projects in the next few years. Similar to all other former Soviet republics, one of the main obstacles curtailing the development of its oil industry is the lack of export routes.

Most of Turkmenistan's resources are shipped to Russia. A new gas pipeline was recently constructed, which passes through Iran. During July 1998, Turkmenistan signed two protocols with Iran in 1998. One called for continuation and expansion of political cooperation between the two countries, and the other called for stepping up the surveys for the building of a reservoir dam over the Harirood River. This represents a compromise in the U.S. policy of preventing foreign investment in Iran. In fact, because of various business reasons, the U.S. administration, the defender of capitalism and free trade, ought to ease sanctions on Iran, particularly in connection with the pipeline. Numerous U.S. corporations want to see the sanctions lifted so that more of the resources of Azerbaijan, Kazakistan, and Turkmenistan could be transported via Iran, since this is the most direct and the cheapest available route. On 26 July 1997, the White House decided not to oppose a $1.6 billion natural gas pipeline from Turkmenistan across Iran and Turkey, to Europe. The White House decided not to challenge the Western European countries eager to invest in Iran and Central Asia. (They are especially interested in investing in energy projects.) The United States Export-Import Bank is going to loan Turkmenistan $96 million to help modernize the country's pipelines.

Therefore, Turkmenistan began to develop alternative export routes in order to increase its natural gas export in addition to oil. In late 1997, Turkmenistan and Iran opened a 124–mile pipeline linking the Korpedzhe gas field in the western part of the country to the Iranian town of Kurt-kui. In March 1998, the U.K.'s Monument Oil (the operator of the Burun offshore oil field) reached an agreement with the National Iranian Oil Company (NIOC) to swap oil. The oil from the Burun oil field will be used in the northern region of Iran, and in return, Iran will sell a similar quantity of oil in the Persian Gulf at the international market price. The shipping of oil from the Turkmen oil field to the Iranian Caspian port of Neka began in July 1998.

On 20 October 1999, President Niyazov met with the Iranian foreign minister, Kamal Kharazi, who headed a delegation from several different ministries. They discussed plans for cooperation on the extraction of gas from the Caspian Sea basin and possible export of natural gas to Turkey via Iran.[4] Two weeks earlier, the Turkish energy minister had paid a visit to Ashqabad, during which Niyazov had informed him about the upcoming meeting with the Iranian delegation. An agreement was signed between Iran and Turkmenistan on the construction of a $167 million dam and reservoir for irrigation purposes on the Tajan River, which makes up the border between the countries. As of this writing, Iran imports approximately 2 billion cubic meters of gas via the Korpdez-Kurtkui pipline in payment for Iranian infrastructure construction. Tehran expressed its preparedness to import 8 to 10 billion cubic meters.

Another pipeline route proposal is the one from Turkmenistan to Pakistan through Afghanistan. In July 1997, officials from Turkmenistan and Pakistan and representatives from Unocal and Saudi Arabia's Delta Oil signed an agreement to build this pipeline. The approximate cost of this pipeline, which is estimated at one thousand miles, will be between $2 billion and $2.7 billion. It has the capacity to carry approximately 700 billion cubic feet from Turkmenistan's Doulatabad gas field to the Pakistan city of Multan. Construction was scheduled to begin in 1998. However, because of the inability of one of the partners to secure funding and the continuing civil war in Afghanistan, on 22 August 1998, Unocal announced the suspension of the project.

PART III

Neighboring Influences

CHAPTER 9

Contending Regional States

GENERAL EVALUATION

Several countries have waged a quiet struggle for power and influence in the former Soviet republics of Azerbaijan, Kazakistan, Kyrgyzstan, Tajikistan, Turkmenistan, and Uzbekistan. The extent of their influence will depend mostly on the needs and aspirations of the newly independent republics in the post–cold war international system. Close attention will be paid to the influences of Iran, Saudi Arabia, and Turkey due to their geographic proximity and power. The contending countries' capacities to influence the former Soviet republics must be understood as a function of relationships at two levels: the state and the regional.

THE STATE LEVEL

Iran is located nearest to the landlocked republics and has the advantage of offering them access to the outside world via the Persian Gulf or the Gulf of Oman. Turkey shares an eleven-kilometer common border with the enclave of Nakhjevan, which is populated by more than three hundred thousand Azeris, who are mostly active in agriculture. Turkey aspires to secure land access to the Central Asian republics through Nakhjevan.

Since September 1991, Iran and Turkey have been struggling to attract these newly independent countries, which remain reluctant to accept the overtures. In contrast, the former republics are very eager to attract investment and technology from the West and Far East because of the great need of these landlocked republics for both short-term and long-term investment if they are to achieve complete independence and enhance their living standards.

Turkey has already extended about $700 million in credits, with the major portion going to Uzbekistan. Pakistan has granted $60 million in credits to five of the republics, and Iran has sold each of the Central Asian republics oil products and gas on deferred payments

THE REGIONAL LEVEL

Several regional organizations have been formed and have met with varying levels of success.

Commonwealth of Independent States

The Commonwealth of Independent States (CIS), whose member states were to develop strong economic, strategic, and eventually political ties with Moscow, was established as part of Russia's foreign policy to retain influence in the region. However, it is evident that Moscow's policy regarding the CIS encountered difficulties in practice, as policies that were appropriate for one state were profoundly inappropriate for others.[1]

Andrei Kozyrev emphasized the importance of raising the status of the CIS to that of a "full-fledged regional organization," and he saw that Russia brought this about during its chairmanship of the CIS, which ran through June of 1994. Kozyrev linked CIS development to the codification of a system that aimed to protect the rights of ethnic Russians and to proposals designed to ensure international support for Russian peace-keeping efforts.[2]

During a visit to Moscow on 29 March 1994, Nursultan Nazarbaev repeated his proposal, which he had made in London only days earlier. He proposed that the member states of the CIS should form a Eurasian Union. The union Nazarbaev called for would allegedly possess structures to aid in the coordination of the economic, military, and foreign policies of its members. Nazarbaev intimated that if other CIS members would not join the union, then Kazakistan and Russia could unite on their own. Although Nazarbaev denies it, some fear his proposal was an attempt to resurrect the former Soviet Union.[3] On 17 September 1997, Islam Karimov pointed out that some people in Moscow who influence Uzbek-Russian relations have not "renounced the imperial vision with regard to former USSR republics." He argued that he wanted relations developed "on an equal basis." However, the relations in the CIS were being developed according to Russia's desire.[4]

Andrei Kozyrev stated that during the CIS foreign ministers' meeting in Moscow on 16 March 1994, the council discussed ways to protect "the outer borders" of the CIS. He noted that there is full consensus among the various ministers for the CIS to gain the status of an international organization. In a partial reversal of this claim, Defense Minister Grochev suggested, in a meeting that same month with German Foreign Minister Klaus Kinkel, that Russia would withdraw troops from the Baltic States by 13 August 1994, which Russia did. He also indicated that the CSCE should be the "main peacemaking organization" in Europe.[5]

The leaders of the former Soviet republics are well aware of their proximity to Russian military power. They also know about Russia's contacts with the restive ethnic minorities, and they realize that Moscow's threshold of tolerance for true independence is low to non-existent. As matter of fact, the CIS member states, since the creation of CIS in 1991, have not fulfilled any of the goals that were established for the organization. The failure has been due to the sharp economic differences, conditions, and approaches and the member states' fear of Moscow's aim to reestablish the old Soviet Empire under the new "political system." Therefore, it has remained an ineffective regional organization, except for some Russian military troop deployments in the conflict areas. But it should be noted that the CIS member states owe Russia billions of dollars for energy supplies and needed raw material.

Despite the reluctance of the heads of CIS member states, on 25 January 2000, they attended the organizational summit at the Kremlin with the aim to help settle disputes that have undermined the republics. The heads of states unanimously elected Valadimir Putin, acting Russian president, as (largely ceremonial) chairman of the CIS heads of state council. This act was an affirmation of their support for his candidacy in the 26 March 2000 presidential poll. Putin held several meetings with the heads of the member countries. During the summit, Putin declared that Russia would not attempt to dominate the CIS or revive the Soviet Union and called for close cooperation among the member states to resolve conflicts in the Caucasus as well as other places. He met with the presidents of Armenia and Azerbaijan and discussed their nations' conflict over the disputed enclave of Nagorno-Karabagh. Putin met with the Georgian president Eduard Shevardnadze, former Soviet foreign minister under Gorbachev, together with the heads of Armenia and Azerbaijan, to discuss regional security in the Caucasus.

Economic Cooperation Organization

In early February 1993, Central Asian foreign and economic ministers arrived at Quetta in Baluchistan, a province of Pakistan, with maps and feasibility reports to discuss how to open routes to the Persian Gulf and the Gulf of Oman. The Economic Cooperation Organization (ECO) members in the Quetta Conference produced an ambitious plan, dubbed the "Quetta Plan of Action for the ECO," which aimed to create a new regional economic bloc in the center of Asia by the end of this century. The plan called for building roads, setting up rail and air links, and developing ports so that trucks and trains can "travel from one end of the region to the other" by the year 2000. Air links and an ECO airline would connect the capital cities of member states, and a transport company would eventually be built. Tariffs, customs duties, visas, and other restrictions on the free flow of people and goods would be uniformly regulated and eventually abolished. The ECO Trade and Development Bank opened for business in the summer of 1993, when the ECO summit was convened in Istanbul, Turkey. Oil and gas pipelines and a power transmission system are to be constructed across the region and beyond to expedite the energy trade.

Although the plan dealt with everything from agriculture to industry to tourism and training, there was little indication as to where the funding for such an ambitious plan would come from. Still, officials of the member countries were optimistic about securing the necessary funding. For example, Shahriyar Khan, the foreign minister of Pakistan, the host country for the ECO summit, noted, "We are at the starting point of a new era in this region. The funds will be forthcoming once the world sees the economic potential that can be harnessed here.[6]

In the West, however, little attention has been paid to ECO, as the nature of political, economic, and social development of the member states are so diverse and limited that it would make it very difficult if not impossible to bring about an integration on the European model. It is not unusual to hear contending views that tend to use the EU as a model to emulate by other regional states, even those of the developing countries. However, the major factors that facilitate regional integration are the economic financial strength or credibility of the member states, or at least a few of them, in addition to democracy. The ECO's member states lack the aforementioned strength to carry out such a task. This is especially necessary if they are to remain tranquil and survive in the modern age. Thus, the Western experts are not wrong for not paying any serious attention to ECO's activities.

The former Soviet republics joined ECO, so it would serve their needs, specifically to offer access to the international market for the energy-producing republics. However, this particular need has not been realized due especially to U.S. foreign policy, which has been aimed at keeping both Russia and Iran out of the pipeline route.[7]

Although ECO is an economic organization, the political issues concerning Afghanistan and Tajikistan dominated the conference. Particularly disconcerting are the wars and unrest in both republics, which have forced the Central Asian republics to close their borders with Afghanistan to prevent the spread of "Islamic radicalism" and the shipment of arms into Tajikistan by Afghan Mujahideen. S. Karman Gozhan, Kazakistan's deputy foreign minister, expressed the concerns of the Central Asian countries as follows: "The fundamentalists [sic.]

should learn a lesson from Tajikistan. We will reject cooperation with any country, whether Iran, Saudi Arabia or Afghanistan if it exports fundamentalism [sic.] along with its goods."

After the first blast of Muslim radicalism in 1983, the Beirut bombing, and the ongoing military campaign of the Soviet Union in Afghanistan, U.S. authorities conceived a plan to make Moscow pay a dear price for its intervention in Afghanistan. The plan, developed and put into effect jointly by the CIA, the director of the Saudi Intelligence Department, Prince Turki bin Faisal (who is still in office), and Pakistan's Inter-Services Intelligence Directorate (ISI), established and recruited the Muslim radicals who apparently opposed the "godless" Soviet Communist troops. However, the plan, at the same time, intended to mobilize the Sunni Islamists against the Iranian Shia's. The Islamist radicals were encouraged to call for the full application of Sharia' (Islamic law), while they would not promote Islamic "revolution." This was compatible with the Saudi rulers and the Pakistani military rulers who were anxious to strengthen their Islamic credentials *vis-à-vis* Khomaini's regime.

The recruiters gave the job to the Akhwan ul-Muslimeen (Muslim Brothers) and the Pakistani Jama'at-i Islami (Islamic Party), who supported the Pakistani military ruler Zia ul-Haq from 1977 through 1988. The recruitment of thousands of radical Muslim Brothers was coordinated by Osama bin Ladin. Most of these recruiters included those who were politically active against their own governments or political systems where they resided; for example, the Israeli occupied territories. The relation between the Muslim radicals, known as "Afghans," changed radically after the withdrawal of the Soviet Union from Afghanistan, the Persian Gulf War (1990–91), and the collapse of the Soviet Union in 1991, when the radicals found themselves to be of no use to U.S. officials. The Muslim radicals turned against U.S. officials, accusing them of waging war on the "Muslim world." However, Pakistan remained actively involved with Osama bin Ladin and created the Taliban group, and Washington followed the path of Pakistan and supported the Taliban up to some time in 1996. But by 1997, Washington changed its approach to the Taliban, when the latter group gave refuge to Osama bin Ladin.[8]

The early August 1998 bombing of the American embassies in Kenya and Tanzania, which have been attributed to the Islamic radical leader Osama bin Ladin, who resides in Afghanistan, will hinder further the political position of the Afghanistan Taliban leaders. These bombings have uncovered the existence of a menace of the U.S. creation with the direct involvement of Pakistani intelligence services. Osama bin Ladin, Saudi heir to a large business enterprise, has become an anti-

American rallying personality, particularly among the Islamist groups. He was one of the heroes of the Afghan guerrilla war against the Soviet invading army. He was a fighter, financier, and recruiting officer with the backing of the CIA, Pakistan, and the Saudi ruling royal family. During 1996, bin Ladin began to redirect his Islamic "fundamentalism" against U.S. interests, particularly in the Middle East. Evidence of these could be seen in the continuing armed Islamic groups in Algeria, Egypt, Israel-occupied territories, Gaza and the West Bank, the United States (the New York City bombing traced to Pakistan), and the Khobar U.S. military barrack in Saudi Arabia. Recent arrests in the United States, Uganda, Kenya, Tanzania, and Germany are linked to Osama bin Ladin. If true, this strongly supports the existence of a widespread and well-organized network that is aimed to carry out similar actions.

These bombings should be viewed in context with the recent military victories of Taliban militia forces in the northern part of Afghanistan. The Soviet army was defeated in Afghanistan by Mujahideen groups in the 1980s. These groups were armed and financed by the United States and Pakistan. Once they had won the war, the various warrior groups, mostly Islamic fundamentalists, began fighting with each other. The fighting caused immense suffering for the Afghani people and devastation and destruction to whatever was left in the towns and villages. By fighting, not only did they weaken themselves but they also paved the way for the Taliban, as a substitute to the groups in Kabul, to be organized, financed, and supported by non-Afghanis. This funding is believed to have come from Pakistan's former interior minister, Nasrullah Babaar, the man Iran and numerous Western governments believe fathered the Taliban movement along with the CIA and Saudi Arabia. Evidence strongly suggests that the Taliban militia is among the most retrograde of Islamists. Washington was convinced that the Taliban was the only group that could restore order in the country. This was likely to play a key role in the export of oil and natural gas from the Central Asian republics. This scenario was, and continues to be, compatible with the U.S. policy of isolation in Iran and continuation of its embargo against Tehran. The rift between Tehran and Kabul has further deepened, especially in light of the arrest and later killing of nine Iranian diplomats who were stationed in Mazareh-i Sharif. A minor gas pipeline from Turkmenistan to Turkey may be part of the U.S. policy to keep Iran out of consideration for any pipeline route.

The leaders of the Central Asian republics are concerned about the possibility of the spread of Islamic radicalism into the region, but they also realize that the beleaguered economies of these republics are in need of aid from Muslim neighbors.

A widespread fear for the future dominates these republics, which have remained authoritarian and traditional, allowing the existing leaders to maintain and even increase their power through the use of "referenda." The referenda remains a tool used by those in power to sidestep presidential elections. In these referenda, the presidents have received more than 99 percent of the voters' support.

Among the three contending countries, Iran and Turkey are still struggling to find a practical form for their particular versions of democracy. However, none of the governments of these contending countries can be classified as strictly democratic. The concepts of 'equality' and 'democracy' are highly ambiguous. Perhaps the best description of their meanings is contained in Alexis de Tocqueville's remark that democracy involves "the equal right of all at birth to liberty." He further observed that the two fundamental principles of democracy are "freedom and equality."[9]

The meaning of democracy, as it has been developed in the industrialized capitalist nations, depends on a dominant middle class and the general narrowness of the gap between the rich and the poor. This interpretation must not be strictly applied to the former Soviet republics. They lack the philosophical and material experiences of the Western democracies. The recent developments that brought about the collapse of the Communist governments in the Soviet Union and in Eastern Europe point toward the strong need for democracy in the material, as well as political, aspects of these republics.

The leaders of the landlocked Central Asian republics are committed to setting up trade routes to the open sea, especially to the Persian Gulf or the Gulf of Oman. The possibility also exists to set up a trade route to the Black Sea. Competition among Iran, Pakistan, and Turkey for trading privileges with the Central Asian republics is fierce. Secular Turkey holds its attractions for Central Asian leaders, while Iran has an optimal geographical location *vis-à-vis* the republics. However, Iran's Islamic regime, with its domestic instability and weak economy, provokes serious concerns among the leaders of the former Soviet republics. At the Quetta meeting, Iranian Foreign Minister Ali Akbar Valayati, who is well aware of the Central Asian reluctance toward the Islamic regime, tried to assuage the concerns. Government in Tehran under President Khatami continued to alleviate the fear of these republics about the spread of Islamic worldviews with the aim of establishing such a political system.[10]

Meanwhile, Pakistan does not possess any geographical, political, or social attractiveness for the Central Asian countries. The recent (1998) nuclear testing competition between Pakistan and India has forced the former to pay closer attention to its relations with the latter and to devote special attention to the issue of Kashmir. Moreover, Pakistan's direct involvement and support for the Islamic regime in Kabul has diminished its role in the region.

Despite the ECO's plan for economic development and interlinking, it must deal with issues such as "Islamic radicalism," the civil war in Afghanistan, unrest in Tajikistan, and Azerbaijan's conflict with Armenia over Nagorno Karabagh. This also encompasses the conflict between Georgian rule and the Abkhazians and South Ossetian. It will also have to deal with the Kurdish conflicts in Iran and Turkey, which may, at least temporarily, diminish its effectiveness as an economic organization.

THE ISLAMIC REPUBLIC OF IRAN (IRI)

The founding fathers of the Islamic Republic contended that the aim of the 1979 revolution and the establishment of the IRI were to improve the life of the *mustaza'feen* ("downtrodden") and to liberate the people from the tyranny of the dictatorship. However, the growing *aloonaks* "slums" surrounding the cities and the towns are the characteristics of many places since 1979. In the slums of Tehran, Shiraz, Ahvaz, Tabriz, Mashhad, Arak, and other towns, groups of unemployed men stand idly around the main intersections, while children play in the dirt between piles of garbage, *Joob* "open sewage" and dust. Many, if not most, of the residents of these slums are part-time or daily *Amaleh* "laborer" and wage earners, if they are lucky. Their fate is determined day to day on whether they can afford to buy a loaf of bread.

Since the 1979 revolution, wages have risen by about 25 percent, but they do not compensate for an official inflation rate of more than 30 percent. The actual rate of inflation is somewhere between 50 and 60 percent. Iranian currency has lost much of its value since the establishment of the new regime, which precipitated an increase in capital flight, starting as far back as late 1978 and continuing to this day. Consequently, the black-market exchange rate between the U.S. dollar and the rial, the currency of Iran, has been many times higher than the official rate.

Although Iran is a fertile agrarian country, it currently cannot feed itself without imports. The government now spends approximately $4 billion annually to import foodstuffs. According to Dr. Ali Ahoomanesh, the country's vice minister of agriculture, Iran's food imports for 1989 cost $1.9 billion. This has more than doubled in nine years. If agricultural production were to remain at its present level, while the population continues to grow at the current birth rate of 3.9 percent, Ahoomanesh estimates that Iran's imports by the year 1999 will reach $10 billion. In other words, as Ahoomanesh notes, the revenue from oil will be used to import foodstuffs.[11]

This is problematic because with the continued decline in oil revenues due to lower prices, the Islamic Republic may not be able to afford high levels of imports. The oil revenues generated by the 2.5 million bpd from 21 March 1992 through 20 March 1993 was estimated at $19.79 billion plus another $4.25 billion from exports of natural gas and other products. Iran's oil revenue in 1979, when its population was 37 million, amounted to about $18 billion. For 1992, its oil revenue was approximately $19.79 billion, while its population at the time stood close to 59 million. At present, 20 percent of its population is below five years of age, with 45 percent of Iranians not yet fifteen. About 56 percent of the population resides in urban areas. According to a report by the Bank-e Markazi-i Iran (Central Bank of Iran), the per capita income of the population since the establishment of the Islamic Republic (1979) declined 56 percent since 1979, while during the same period, the population grew by twenty million. The drastic decline in per capita income has had a dramatic and negative impact on the standard of living and will probably continue to do so for some time to come. Iran's economy is growing weaker by the day.

The price of oil continues to plummet. Oil dropped to ten dollars in December, the lowest in the past twenty-five years. Oil revenues dropped from an estimated $20 billion in 1986 to about $10 billion in 1998. The annual budget for 1998 was based on the speculation that the oil revenue would remain at least at the level of 1997. The Islamic Republic's annual budget for 1999–2000 has been cut drastically due to the plummeting oil prices ($10.82 as of January 21, 1999). The projected oil revenue for the year of 1378 (starting 2 March 1999) is estimated at $12.084 billion, which includes $1.472 billion from export of oil products and liquefied gas.[12] The budget deficit for 1998–99 (21 March 1998–20 March 1999) is estimated at more than $6 billion. The Islamic Republic has been forced to postpone payment on its foreign debts. The government did not make a payment in September toward the $5.9 billion it owed in 1998 to Germany, Italy, and Japan. Repayment of this debt package had already been rescheduled once in 1993.

During 1990 and 1991, the Islamic Republic accrued about $12 billion in short-term foreign trade debt despite drawing from its foreign reserve to pay for its imports. In 1991, civilian imports totaled $21 billion, with an additional $6 billion worth of military imports coming from Russia. The Bank-e Markazi-i Iran reported that the government had signed agreements for foreign loans in the amount of $10.6 billion by March 1992, when in fact it had secured only $1.5 billion. For a recent five-year plan (1990–94), an official estimate concluded that it needed more than $26 billion. In contrast, experts estimated correctly that the Islamic Republic actually required about $40 billion in order to meet its needs.[13]

The Islamic Republic, even under the "Moderate" Rafsanjani, failed to attract foreign investment, which the country still needs badly.[14] Persisting political, economic, and social crises overwhelm the Islamic Republic. Thus, Iran remains a high-risk country for investment, even with the election of Mohammad Khatami, who is characterized as a "reformist," in part because he promises to make the regime more relaxed and to elevate the status and role of women in the country.

Iran's GNP for 1987 was $86.4 billion, and its per capita GDP was $3,300. However, the per capita income in 1989 was only 40 percent of what it was in 1979. Therefore, many of the people are becoming increasingly poorer, and their purchasing power is much lower than officials there claim it to be. Shortages of food, pharmaceutical products, and other essentials, along with the high inflation rate and widespread black market activities make life in Iran difficult. The gap between the rich and the poor is much wider today than it was in 1979, and the poor *mustaza'feen* (downtrodden), in whose name the Islamic Republic claimed its legitimacy, have become poorer. The social, economic, and political deprivations of the poor have increased tremendously, especially when compared with the privileges of the Iranian rich (*mustakbareen*). Rafsanjani was quoted as saying that 20 percent of the population controls 50 percent of the country's wealth. A closer examination of the economic and social conditions of the people reveals that only 10 percent of Iranians control more than 75 percent of the wealth. Government officials acknowledge that more than 22.5 million Iranians, out of approximately 70 million, live below the poverty level. It should be noted that the poverty level in a country such as Iran is not comparable to that of Western industrialized countries.[15]

Since the inception of the IRI, inflation has increased continuously, at an annual average rate of 25 to 35 percent. During the last year of the Iran-Iraq war (1988), the Iranian population increased by more than 3 percent, while the country's GDP for the same year was negative, and the inflation rate was officially reported at more than 28 percent.

The government's lack of economic planning and the resulting uncontrollable inflation have placed real estate out of the reach of a large number of Iranians, especially the poor. The price of real estate in Tehran between 1990 and 1991, for example, rose from 30 to 66 percent. This caused a large increase in the price of rented properties.[16] Most Iranians are tightly squeezed for money and very desperate to find housing. Iranian newspapers, such as *Kayhan International,* and government officials in their public speeches generally use the future tense when addressing economic problems and talk of the revitalization of the stagnant economy. Subsidization has been, and continues to be, one of the major policies used by the IRI to deal with economic, social, and political problems.

The cost of the eight-year war between Iran and Iraq was estimated by the United Nations to have cost about $1 trillion.[17] Iran desperately needs foreign investment and assistance. Some ten thousand Iranian towns and villages, including crucial oil installations, were damaged or destroyed during the war with Iraq. Power stations, agriculture, and roads require large infusions of investment. However, the instability of the IRI and the maze of political and regulative obstacles has strongly diminished the likelihood that investors will invest in long-term projects. For that matter, in most sectors of the economy, except for oil and natural gas, the country has been deprived access to badly needed hard currency. Moreover, the internal problems and the lack of understanding of the economics, especially that of the market system, and the forces involved and its principles thwarted efforts to privatize the economy. The state owns approximately 80 percent of the country's economy.[18]

Economy remains the main problem for the Islamic Republic. In 1989, the Iranian rate of inflation was about 50 percent, and from 1991 through 1992, it fluctuated between 50 and 60 percent, with unemployment estimated at more than 25 percent. Oil exports are the source of 85 percent of the country's main source of hard currency earnings. For 1998, the country faced a revenue shortfall of $6 billion, or one-third of the government's budget. Similar to his predecessors, President Mohammed Khatami promises to boost non-oil exports, but both manufacturing and agriculture are in trouble, partially because of the government's interference. Carpet exports, the second source of hard currency earnings, suffer from excessive regulation. In 1994, revenues from those exports were $2 billion, and for 1998, estimates indicate it will not even reach $1 billion. Most of this income has been spent on reestablishing a defense system and purchasing the large quantity of food imports needed for its quickly growing population, which at present is reaching the 70 million mark. Iran's population is projected to surpass 100 million by the year 2010.

Almost a year after becoming president, Mohammed Khatami concluded that the economy is in poor condition and needs structural reforms. The internal political battle among those in power, especially Mohammed Khatami and his opponents, is so time consuming that it will be difficult, if not impossible, to tackle the economy. The conservative wing of the Islamic regime in Iran is in coalition with merchants. Commonly known as *bazaaris*, these merchants are funded by the *bunyads*, semigovernmental foundations. In some cases, the *bunyads* have expanded into financial, industrial, and import-export empires. The latter development has created a closed economic system that will make it impossible to attract investment into certain sectors of the economy. The data is making it impossible to ignore, but political wrangling continues. On 2 August 1998, Khatami called for comprehensive economic reforms: "Our economy is chronically ill. It will not be cured unless we make fundamental changes." Khatami admits that his plan "may be words on paper." "The economy is our Achilles heel," says Ali Shams Ardekani, general secretary of the Chamber of Commerce, Industry, and Mines. "There's too much political maneuvering at the expense of the economy. The population and the government are aware of the problem, but, as the Iranian proverb goes, fish look for each other in water—in other words, everyone is worried, but nobody takes the problem seriously." "You just need to look at the statistics to understand the gravity of the problem," Ardekani says. "The population growth rate has been very high over the past twenty years—about 3.7 percent a year. Those born in the seventies and eighties are now coming on to the labor market." However, the expansion of the *bunyads* activities and their direct involvement in many sectors of economy weaken the position of the president.[19]

Successive governments promised economic changes but never delivered. The main challenge to the IRI is to create more jobs for the rapidly growing number of unemployed young people. An estimated 1 million youngsters join the workforce annually. The official unemployment rate for 1998 is reported at 11 percent. This rate is believed to be much higher.

All of the above factors have further weakened the Islamic regime in Tehran. The country's underdevelopment has been exacerbated, and it has made Iran even more dependent on international investment and foreign economic and technological assistance, which are not generally forthcoming. Although Iran has tremendous economic potential, it is handicapped by human rights abuses and the lack of a skilled, professional workforce. This is mainly due to the brain drain of the past ten years, serious image problems, and the absence of political stability. Therefore, the country's future economic prospects are not encouraging. If the government is incapable of remedying the country's economic problems, this could easily weaken the system and in turn force the regime to become more intolerant to any criticism. This would cause the government to lash back in a stronger manner, as it becomes vulnerable to be undermined by widespread discontent. The government has been able to delay such a development, in particular among the poor people, through its subsidizing policies, costing an estimated $11 billion a year. These subsidies control more than 80 percent of the economy. The gas prices in Iran are less than what it costs to produce gas. However, Iran still produces leaded gasoline, which has made the air pollution intolerable for the residents of Tehran. The inflation rate continues to grow; the currency continues to depreciate; and the production at factories has ground to a halt.[20]

The declining living standards will have a serious impact on the attempt to rebuild the country after eight years of war with Iraq. The future looks bleak for many Iranians, and, not surprisingly, there is growing discontent with the regime. The widespread unrest and frequent demonstrations in various cities throughout the country show no signs of abating anytime soon.

The riots and demonstrations in May and June 1992, in several major cities, such as Arak, Tehran, Khoramabad, Shiraz, and Mashhad (Toos), involved two thousand to four thousand demonstrators. These demonstrations revealed a mood of growing discontent. In the city of Mashhad, an estimated four thousand demonstrators set fire to cars and municipal buildings, while the police surrendered their weapons to the crowd. The riot in Mashhad was characterized as a highly organized demonstration against the system. The Islamic Republic response was instant. It sentenced four people in Mashhad to death by hanging on 10 June and four in Shiraz on 11 June. Five others were also condemned to death and faced the same punishment. These violent urban demonstrations were not exclusively political, and they occurred where poverty and housing shortages were widespread. Interestingly, Ayatollah Ali Khameneh'i, the country's spiritual leader, characterized the riots in a speech to Parliament as the work of "bullies," "ruffians," and "riff-raff," who should be dealt with in a revolutionary way, that is, punished harshly. In a sense, they should be pulled up and thrown away "like weeds."[21] A few weeks later, executions were carried out in the cities where the riots took place.

A widespread demonstration rocked the country, which caught the theocratic rulers in Tehran by surprise during the second week of July 1999. However, the July 1999 student demonstration, which lasted for six days and was held in a number of cities, was of a different nature and makeup. It is the first time that the security and police forces of the Islamic Republic have taken on a group as articulate, well connected, and organized as the country's university students.

Iranian university students have previously showed their muscles when, in the late 1970s, their widespread demonstrations inside the country and their well-organized and energetic Iranian student organizations outside Iran brought down the Shah's regime. In the 1970s, Iran's student movements, a majority of which were Communist rather than Islamist, were well organized both inside and outside the country.

The current student movements are active only inside the country. However, the current university student body, numbering over 1 million, seems to have a well-organized structure. Yet they lack a well-articulated objective and unanimity of purpose. Student demonstrations have been held in other university campuses in Birjand, Isfahan, Hamadan, Kashan, Korramabad, Mashhad, Orumiyeh, Rasht, Tabriz, Yazd, and Zanjan.

The week of demonstrations began after the closure of the "liberal" Salam newspaper on 7 July 1999 and the introduction of new restrictive legislation to curb the country's "progressive" press. The Salam newspaper was shut down, allegedly for publishing a sensitive classified document revealing the role of government in the assassination of several Iranian intellectuals during 1998 and the role of intelligence and security forces in curbing the press.

On Thursday night of 9 July, hardline Baseej (Islamic militia with a membership of 2 to 3 million, armed and trained by the Revolutionary Guards, "Sepah") and Ansar-e Hezbullah, "Supporters of the Party of God" (vigilantes backed by police and security forces who enjoy the support of the clerical regime) assaulted students who were holding a peaceful demonstration in the Tehran University dormitory compound against the measures taken by the Islamic Republic. By the following morning, 9 July, the paramilitary forces and religious vigilantes who were trucked in by the security forces attacked the students' dormitories. The assault, according to the officials, resulted in the death of two people and a large number of injured and arrested students.

The demonstrations continued for several days, during which the students' demands changed dramatically. The students demonstrated and chanted against the institution of the supreme leader, Ayatollah Khameneh'i, and demanded that he relinquish his control of the military and security forces. By 14 July, the regime was so shaken that an organized rally in support of the Islamic Republic became necessary. Hundreds of thousands of Tehran residents were bussed in, and people were given time off to attend the rally addressed by the cleric speakers. The Islamic Republic government controlled television networks and repeatedly broadcast the officially organized rally. The television interrupted its normal programming to appeal for tranquility and to warn of a plot to destabilize the country. A senior cleric told the crowd that those arrested for sabotage and destroying state property during the protest would face the death penalty. The remarks were greeted with chants of approval and shouts of, "Death to counter-revolutionaries." Defense Minister Ali Shamkhani told the crowd that order would be restored "at all costs."

The shaken Islamic Republic pulled out all of the stops when it mobilized further support for its existence and political, social, and economic behavior and to diminish the significance of the discontent. Tehran's Friday prayers of 30 July were led by the "Supreme Leader," Ali Khameneh'i, who accused the CIA of responsibility for the riots by saying, "The head of the Central Intelligence Agency had predicted last year that 1999 will be a year of some unexpected events in Iran which is unprecedented in the last twenty years history of the Islamic Revolution." Ali Khameneh'i pointed out that "This, in fact, shows that the U.S. agency was fully aware of the behind the scene moves inciting the insurgencies." He also highlighted that "foreign news agencies have in the past been arranging interviews with individuals that tended to portray that people were very discontented with the Islamic sovereign state," and "U.S., Zionist and British propaganda machinery have been aiming their psychological warfare such as spreading rumors, distortion of news and misinformation campaigns against the Islamic Republic of Iran."[22] So, similar to any dictator—throughout the underdeveloped world—he went on to blame the outside world for the riots—granted, some outside elements may be happy to fuel discontent, if possible—rather than accept any fault in the regime's political, economic, and social performance since its inception.

Ali Khameneh'i attended an orchestrated gathering of several thousand members of Baseej—code-named Imam's Devotees—in the north of Tehran on Thursday and Friday morning before the regular Friday prayer. In this gathering, in addition to Khameneh'i, the commander of the Revolutionary Guards, Major General Rahim Safavi, also addressed the members of the Baseej. This so-called maneuver had started in northeast Tehran on Wednesday, 28 July. General Safavi praised the institution of Baseej and said it is a great asset for the nation and government of the Islamic Republic.

It is appropriate to explain for the reader that the genesis of the Baseej and its subsequent development into an arm of the Islamic Republic has been to control the behavior of the citizens. In many instances, the Baseej is used to intimidate those whom the regime views as not towing the line or those whose activities tend to question the essence of the Islamic system. This organization's direct attack on the university dormitories and subsequent demonstration of support for the Islamic Republic are evidences of their role in the society.

The Baseej came into being by war volunteers during the Iraq-Iran war from 1980 to 1988. However, after the war, it became a more structured and organized institution with the blessing and support of the authorities in the government and other powerful clerical elite. Baseej served to act as a "guardian of public morals." In other words, the organization became a semisocial police force. The latter role is modeled after the Saudi Arabian "moral" police force Jama al-Amr bel-Ma'roof wa Nahi an-Monker (the Organization or Society for Decent Persuasion and Prevention of Indecent Behavior).

Public discontent sometimes takes the form of terrorist action against the officials. Highly organized attackers tried to assassinate Mohsen Rafiqdoost, a powerful Iranian official, on 14 September 1998 in Tehran. A bombing outside a downtown courthouse in Tehran, including the assassination of the former prison director Assadollah Lajevardi and his brother in August 1998, are further indications of the persisting opposition toward and disappointment in the regime. Mohsen Rafiqdoost is a leading conservative member of the IRI's political power establishment. Rafiqdoost now serves as director of the Foundation of the Downtrodden and Sacrificers (Bunyad-e Mustaza'feen Va Jonbazan), which controls most hotels and hundreds of other enterprises. The foundation has billions of dollars of assets.

During November and December of 1998, several dissident writers and opposition leaders were found mysteriously stabbed to death. The opposition leader Dariush Farouhar and his wife, Parvaneh, were killed in a gruesome fashion; their bodies were discovered on 21 November 1998. This killing took place while their house was under twenty-four-hour police surveillance. During the first two weeks of December, the bodies of three missing dissident writers—Javad Sharif, Mohammad Mokhtari, and Jafar Pouyandeh—were found. Relatives of the victims reported that they bore the marks of strangulation. None of their personal possessions, a watch, a gold ring, and wallet with money, was missing. It is worth noting that before the killings, several warnings were issued to the critics of the Islamic Republic. At the same time, the regime closed down the newspapers. These killings were a sign of the insecurity that would present opportunities for the regime to clamp down any discontent, particularly in the economic sector. However, the government claims that the killings are the work of rogue elements who have connections with U.S. and Israeli intelligence communities.

Since the inception of the Islamic Republic, riots and demonstrations have erupted more frequently in Iran and have involved a greater number of people and increased damage. Many Iranians resent the ruling clerics and the imposed "Islamic Values." Feelings of abhorrence are particularly strong among the youth.[23] Dissatisfaction with the political, social, and economic systems, as well as the institution of "Velayat-i Faqih" (religious jurisprudent) were expressed in the presidential election of 1997, when a majority of the people, more than 70 percent, voted against the conservative wing of the Islamic ruling theocratic elite in favor of Mohammad Khatami, a "reformist" Shi'ite cleric. Nonetheless, the conservative wing maintained its majority in the Majlis (Parliament). There are now three centers of power in Iran: former President

Ali Akbar Hashemi Rafsanjani, who still maintains an office in the first floor of the presidential office building, and Ayatollah Khamaneh'i, the regime's spiritual leader and favorite of the conservatives, and, last, the new president and his "reformist" camp.

For many years, the Islamic Republic rejected the report that there has been significant use of narcotics by the Iranians, particularly the youth. It is true that drug traffickers have used the country for many years. Since 1994, the authorities have stepped up their battle against well-organized and well-armed smugglers, who transport much of the world's illegal supply of opium, heroin, and hashish through Iran to markets both in Iran and in the West from Pakistan and Afghanistan. Twenty years of civil war in Afghanistan have made the country a haven for opium producers and for drug traffickers linked to various armed tribal factions.

The authorities in Tehran are slowly discovering that there is a lucrative narcotic market in Iran. Therefore, as was claimed by the authorities, not all the narcotics that enter Iran leave for markets in the West. The United Nations' drug control office in the country reported a growing demand for opium—a traditional choice of narcotic along with hashish—and heroin within Iran. The widespread use is prevalent, particularly among the 70 percent or so of the population under the age of thirty who are frustrated by the Islamic regime's strict social codes and high unemployment rate. The official estimate identifies more than a million—unofficial statistics are much higher—Iranians may be addicts.

Another problem facing the Islamic Republic is the continued ethnic unrest in the major cities of Shiraz, Mashhad, Arak, and Tabriz. The Kurds and other ethnic groups are no more satisfied with the Islamic Republic than they were under the Shah's rule. They continue to rebel and to attack the government forces. They are sometimes used as agents for manipulation by external forces unfriendly to Iran.

In foreign affairs, the Islamic Republic has been isolated, with a few exceptions, since the 1979 revolution. Shortly after leaving office, former President Rafsanjani came out in favor of the normalization of relations with Europe and even hinted at the possibility of formal talks with the United States. In the early 1990s, the Islamic Republic of Iran entered into negotiations on behalf of the United States with the pro-Iranian Shi'ites holding American hostages in Lebanon. It is believed that Iran did this in order to improve its relations with the United States and, more important, so that an Iranian request for an International Monetary Fund loan would not be rejected. Certain overtures have been made by Khatami and the White House to mend relations. However, relations are still uncertain, limited to a very small number of tourists visiting each country respectively.

Iranian relations with the former Soviet Union continued to improve after the ayatollah's death. Negotiations between the two countries resulted in Soviet offers of military aid and a $15 billion economic development program. The promised financial assistance never arrived, because of the disintegration of the Soviet Union. Since the USSR's collapse, the IRI has moved steadily toward Russia and continues to do so, while distancing itself from the Islamic issues in the region. However, Tehran's overture was not taken too seriously by Russia at the beginning, as its Islamic revolutionary posture was viewed by the Russians to be the foundation of Iran's theocratic oligarchic rule and a diversionary strategy to maintain an iron-fist rule for the sake of its survival.

However, relations between the two countries became stronger, and Russia came around to refer to Iran as its strategic partner. In response to U.S. criticism of Russian assistance to Iran, during March 1999, Yevgeny Adamov, Russia's atomic energy industry minister said, "Russia would continue its commercial nuclear cooperation with Iran, especially its program to help Iran complete two large reactors at Bushehr, one which was damaged in the Iran-Iraq war." On 14 January 2000, Russia's defense minister, Igor Serveyev, met with a top Iranian parliamentary security official and pledged to maintain Moscow's military ties with Tehran. He stated, "Russia intends to maintain the dynamics of its bilateral ties with Iran in the military, military-technical, scientific-technical and energy fields." Reports further asserted, "In addition to nuclear assistance, the United States believes that Russian companies and other organizations have provided Tehran with critical technology related to the development of ballistic missiles that could carry nuclear weapons."

During the 1990s, U.S. officials accused the Russians of assisting Iran to acquire a nuclear weapons system and to develop long-range missiles. On 25 October 1999, the *Times* reported, "Russian and Iranian shipping companies are suspected of using the Caspian Sea as a smuggling route for delivering prohibited parts for Tehran's missile and non-conventional weapons programmes." The report further quotes the Western and Middle Eastern intelligence that the sea is also used to smuggle banned equipment from Europe.

Houman A. Sadri contends that the Iranian foreign policy goals toward the Central Asian and Caspian Sea regions follow several principles:

1. An anti-hegemonic stand;

2. Opposition to the presence of foreign forces;

3. Non-intervention by states from outside the region on regional affairs;

4. De-militarization of the Caspian Sea;

5. Peaceful settlement of disputes;

6. Regional cooperation (on commercial, legal, political and security issues)

7. Necessity of access to international market, for all countries in the region;

8. Encouraging the role of the industrialized states to promote economic growth;

9. Protecting the region's fragile environment.

Sadri concludes with the following observation:

> In sum, contrary to its negative image in America, Iranian foreign policy has a constructive, cooperative, and crucial role in the region, especially for the integration process—the author means the future prospect of ECO. Former Foreign Minister Velayati has often high-lighted this by emphasizing Tehran's constructive role in decreasing the level of regional tension via encouraging and facilitating peaceful settlement of disputes between opposing sides in the Afghanistan and Tajikistan civil wars, the Georgian crisis, and the Nagorno Karabakh (sic.) conflict.[24]

However, shortly after the disintegration of the Soviet Union, Iran took several steps to break itself from the isolation. Iran and Turkmenistan signed an agreement on 25 August 1992 to build a pipeline for shipping Central Asian natural gas to Europe via Turkey. This particular pipeline received tacit approval from the White House, as it did not consider the pipeline covered under the U.S. embargo against Tehran. On 24 October 1992, IRI Broadcasting began the short-wave transmission of an Uzbek and Tajik language program and planned to add Azeri and Kyrgyz language programs as part of its policy to expand its influence in the region.

The Iranian Oil Ministry is working toward the installation of a second, larger-diameter oil pipeline in late 1998 or early 1999. This follows the government's decision to tender for the $400 million construction of the first 392–kilometer oil pipeline from Neka on the Caspian Sea to Tehran. The first pipeline (32 inches in diameter) will carry 370,000 bpd of Caspian Sea oil to Tehran and Tabriz refineries, and the second, which will run from the border of either Turkmenistan or Azerbaijan, will have a capacity of 400,000 bpd to carry to the Arak and Isfahan refineries. This plan is related to the previously announced plan to carry 800,000 bpd of Caspian Sea crude oil for use in the northern part of the country, in exchange for the same amount of oil that will be exported from the Persian Gulf ports. This plan will provide for the use of up to 800,000 bpd of crude oil from Azerbaijan, Turkmenistan, and Kazakistan. A test carried out in 1997 showed that Iranian refineries can handle crude oil from Azerbaijan, Kazakistan, and Turkmenistan. The decision regarding whether the pipeline will run from Azerbaijan's or Turkmenistan's border depends on the ongoing negotiations between the countries. Of course, President Saparmurat Niyazov of Turkmenistan has made no secret of his desire to establish the Caspian port of Tukmenbashi as a gateway for receiving and transporting Kazak and Turkmen oil via the second projected oil pipeline to Iran.

THE KINGDOM OF SAUDI ARABIA

Saudi Arabia has a tribal autocracy system, which attempts to function as a modern state. The country is governed and its financial activities are dealt with as a family affair. Thousands of male members of the royal house of Ibn-Saud dominate the political system and process of this country. At the head of the ruling family is King Fahd. Crown Prince Abdullah bin Abd al-Aziz al-Saud, who is Fahd's half-brother and the commander of the National Guard, also wields considerable power. King Fahd's brother, Prince Sultan bin Abd al-Aziz al-Saud, the minister of defense and aviation, is also part of the ruling family, as are the king's other two brothers, Prince Nayef Abd al-Aziz al-Saud, the minister of the interior; and Prince Salman Abd al-Aziz al-Saud, the governor of Riyadh. The country's foreign minister, Prince Saud al-Faisal bin Abd al-Aziz al-Saud, and the Saudi ambassador to the United States, Prince Bandar bin Sultan bin Abd al-Aziz al-Saud, are the sons of Prince Abdullah. It is clear that political nepotism makes it very difficult, if not impossible, to draw a distinction between the royal house of Saud and Saudi Arabia.

Saudi's tribal Islamic system is not conducive to the adoption of a constitution, because it claims the Qur'an and the Sunna serve as the basis for many legal decisions in domestic affairs. The Saudi king is an absolute monarch who rules by decree, appointing and dismissing ministers, most of whom are members of the Saudi ruling family. Political parties are absolutely banned, and the news and information media are thoroughly controlled by the government. The king appoints and dismisses members of a religious entity known as the "Supreme Authority of Senior Scholars," the highest religious body in the kingdom. In October 1992, King Fahd quietly removed seven of these high-ranking religious figures after they failed to support his government against criticism he received regarding the Saudi policy in the Persian Gulf and toward the United States. This body of scholars expresses opinions (mostly in support of government policy) on all matters of law that affect business, religious practices, and policy. For example, in 1979, when radicals seized the holy sites of Mecca and called for the overthrow of the Saudi family, a Fetwa (religious decree) of the Supreme Authority was required before force could be used to dislodge them. The king also consulted the group before inviting in American troops after the Iraqi invasion of Kuwait in 1990.[25]

Defenders of the Saudi ruling family contend that "Islam" or "the country" guarantees individual freedom and that broad consultation between the ruling royal family and the ruled takes place through regularly held *diwans* (public audiences), also referred to as *majlis* (an open meeting), at which any citizen, at least in theory, may air views and grievances. Saudi officials identify the public meetings as indicative of the Saudi leaders' accessibility to the people. Citizens cannot, however, legally express their views or grievances through any other political or social means. Even when *diwans* are held, grievances are expressed in an individual basis, either orally, directed to the king, or in a written petition form. Therefore, the system lacks avenues for the public to participate in the political process.

The house of Saudi uses two major tools at its disposal to deal with the ruled. First is the Wahhabi version of Islam upon which the ruling family lays its claim. Even though the Shia' community of the country does not adhere to the Wahhabi version of Islam, they are targets of its worldviews and rulings, through the regime. Second is the vast oil wealth at the disposal of the rulers that provides them with the tools to connect the ruled to the state. The Saudi government offers the ruled a lavish welfare service, education, and material wellbeing, in return for a complete surrender of political participation. However, the second factor can become compromised whenever either the international oil market faces a slump or the regime gets involved in a venture such as the Persian Gulf War, rampant purchases of armaments, or lavish family spendings, which drain the wealth.

Although the Saudi government is a monarchy, without a legislature or organized political opposition, most domestic and foreign policy decisions are not made by the king alone but by the leading members of the Saudi royal family. These decisions are usually made after the royal family arrives at some sort of consensus. In addition to Saudi Arabia's elite decision makers, the Council of Ministers was established by the monarchy in 1953 to make it possible for the Saudi bureaucracy to advise Saudi leaders on domestic and foreign policy issues. Members of this council are appointed by the king and include Saudi princes, religious leaders, and high-level bureaucrats. Not surprisingly, the most important ministerial positions, namely, in the ministries of Defense, Interior, and Foreign Affairs, are held by the leading members of the royal family.

On 8 November 1990, King Fahd announced that the long-promised Majlis al-Showra (Consultative Council) would be set up shortly, Insha-allah (God-willing), to help him run the country. Although the proposed consultative counsel is trumpeted by the ruling family as a "historic new step," it is nothing more than a formalization of the existing structure of the fifty or so members of the inner circle appointed by the king. There is no evidence of plans for elections anytime soon in Saudi Arabia, and it may be less likely that any political parties will come into existence. The appointed consultative council members are empowered to advise the nine provincial governors, as well as each member of the ruling al-Saud family. Saudi citizens have seen such arrangements before, usually when the ruling Saudi family has found itself in political difficulty.

A similar proposal was first made in 1962, three kings ago, with the Saudi ruling family being threatened by the radical regimes in Egypt and Syria, most especially by Jemal Abdul Nasser of Egypt, who backed the anti-Saudi faction in the civil war in neighboring Yemen. Overtures directed at greater citizen involvement were twice made and forgotten by King Khalid, first in 1979, after the seizure of the Grand Mosque in Mecca by Islamic militants, and again in 1980, when Ayatollah Khomaini of Iran called for the overthrow of the Saudi regime and riots erupted among the Shia' population of the eastern province. Such overtures, offered during times of difficulty, have become standard political gimmicks of the Saudi regime. For example, to minimize the criticism directed toward the royal family and especially the king, since 1988, the government has referred to the Saudi king as "The Custodian of the Two Holy mosques."[26]

It is quite possible that Saudi Arabia's war with Iraq, spearheaded by the United States, was a calculated strategy to provide the royal family a mandate that it had previously lacked. Since the invasion of Kuwait, the royal family and the Saudi government have become more ambitious in their foreign policy goals, and they have overcome their reluctance to be seen as close allies of the United States. This newly acquired confidence hinges on the reliability of the United States as an ally of the Saudi government, especially in times of dire need. Will the United States always be there for Saudi Arabia, or does it depend on which particular administration is in power at any given time? Is a close alliance with Saudi Arabia truly part of a genuine American commitment in the Persian Gulf in the post–cold war international system? Or do American administrations view the alliance as important merely in light of particular circumstances, which are likely to change in the future?

A clear example of the Saudis' newly found assertiveness was the scrapping of the Damascus Declaration in August 1992. The Damascus Declaration, which was supposed to provide the foundation for a new security arrangement in the Gulf region under the aegis of Syria and Egypt, has remained a dead letter. Of course, it has been reported that its failure was due to pressure from Iran. Bitter about this turn of events, Egypt pulled its troops out of the Persian Gulf region, and no one believes that the Damascus Declaration can be revived successfully.[27] Rejecting the declaration allowed the Saudis to support the United States, the United Kingdom, and France's imposition of an "air exclusion zone" in the southern part of Iraq. In addition, the Saudis allowed the British fighter planes the use of the Dharan air base.

It is worth noting that Saudi Arabia's security depends on three independent military and security entities. The Ministry of Defense and Aviation is responsible for meeting external conventional military attacks. The National Guard provides internal security and protects vital installations such as the oil fields and the refineries. It also serves as a backup to the Ministry of Defense in providing external security. The Ministry of the Interior is responsible for internal security, such as police functions and paramilitary frontier guard elements, which involves both internal and external security. Despite these three independent military and security entities, when faced with domestic crises or war, Saudi Arabia has shown that it is incapable of defending itself. Deficiencies in the Saudi military were evident in the Grand Mosque takeover in 1979, when a group of Islamic radicals took over the Mosque. After a long, bloody standoff, French special forces intervened to flush them out. Other examples are throughout the Iran-Iraq war, during the invasion of Kuwait, and in the Persian Gulf War against Iraq.

Saudi Arabia's foreign policy has traditionally favored the West, particularly the United States, along with its Arab neighbors. Its objectives are based upon the most fundamental foreign policy objective of all states, that is, maintaining and enhancing the security of its physical territory and its inhabitants from external aggression. From the Saudis' point of view, peace and stability in the Persian Gulf region are of the utmost importance for the creation of an environment in which the Saudi kingdom may exist and prosper. A regional military balance of power is considered by the Saudis to be perhaps the most favorable means for achieving peace, stability, and security in the region. However, since Saudi Arabia is a relatively weak military power, especially in comparison to Iran, which is the strongest Persian Gulf country, the Saudis are unable to unilaterally produce or promote a regional balance-of-power structure.

To be sure, by providing substantial sums of foreign economic aid, when the country's economic wherewithal would allow, the Saudis can influence, to some degree, the regional military balance of power, but they cannot fundamentally alter it. After all, the Saudis' economic power has not provided them with a defense system capable of repelling potential attacks by Iran or Iraq. Economic wealth is not sufficient compensation for military weakness. To bolster their security and compensate for their military inadequacies, the Saudis have traditionally relied primarily upon two security resources: first, their influence, which stems from their prominent role within the region; second, an informal alliance with the United States.

The Saudi government continues to rely on the United States for vital technical assistance, while the U.S. depends on Saudi Arabia for oil. American administrations have long urged the Saudi royal family to serve as a bulwark for Middle East stability, to restrain radical influences, and to press other Arab governments to negotiate with Israel. Nevertheless, as noted above, the Saudi military alone is not capable of defending Saudi Arabia, much less specific U.S. interests in the region, as was shown in the Iraqi invasion of Kuwait. For years, Saudis had resisted American pressure to allow U.S. troops on its grounds, but they resist no longer. The invasion of Kuwait, the perceived threat of an Iraqi invasion of Saudi Arabia, and increased pressure from the United States have forced the Saudis to open their naval bases and airport installations to American military forces. Thus, the Iraqi invasion of Kuwait presented the Americans with an opportunity to enter Saudi Arabia and to intervene militarily in the region, thereby effectuating a dramatic shift in Saudi foreign policy.

After Iraq invaded Kuwait, the Saudis struggled to become leaders in the Persian Gulf region through their attempts to unify the regional states in opposition to Iran and Iraq. In addition to its informal military alliance with the United States, Saudi Arabia has established the Gulf Cooperation Council (GCC), a de facto military alliance, with five other Persian Gulf Arab states: the United Arab Emirates, Qatar, Bahrain, Oman, and Kuwait. Despite its success with the GCC, Saudi Arabia's relations with Jordan and the PLO have reached a new low because the Jordanians and the PLO supported Saddam Hussein's regime while simultaneously opposing the invasion of Kuwait.

There is a need to understand the methods and policies the Saudi government uses to maintain its rule and promote its foreign policy objectives. Since 1979, Saudi Arabia has had to face many difficult challenges to its security and well-being. These challenges were more or less successfully managed through the Saudis' manipulation of particular internal and external factors that have played a role in determining their foreign policy over the last twenty years.

Saudi Arabia's economy was completely transformed in 1948, with the discovery of the massive Ghawar oil field, which is the largest proven accumulation of petroleum on earth.[28] Since that time, Saudi Arabia, like the rest of the Persian Gulf states, has relied heavily on oil for its continued prosperity. In fact, oil is the Saudi's main source of foreign exchange. Although the Saudis, and other oil-producing countries have experienced drops in oil revenues due to overproduction and a decline in demand and price, they continue to amass billions of dollars from the production and sale of crude oil.[29] A large part of these revenues has been used to modernize the Saudi economy and military. In 1983, about 89 percent of government revenues came from oil. Since then, this figure has dropped, but it still represents a majority of total revenues.

The Saudis have the capability of producing 10 million barrels of oil per day, and their oil reserves are expected to last another ninety years. The production of vast quantities of crude oil increased Saudi revenues from $1.2 billion in 1970 to $22.6 billion in 1974. However, this increase did not continue to be so dramatic. For example, the oil revenue for 1987 was $17.39 billion, which had increased to $20.27 billion by 1990.[30] As a result of the oil windfall, the government was able to begin pursuing various development plans. However, persistent low oil prices worldwide also means that the Saudis are strapped for cash needed to invest in their various development plans, specifically in their energy sector. Moreover, Saudi Arabia faces increasing competition in the U.S. oil market from Mexico, Canada, and Venezuela. Therefore, it would need to get closer to the United States, especially with the American oil firms that will give Saudis a large market share. Saudis are well aware of the fact that the competition for investment in the oil sector worldwide is increasing with the entry of Azerbaijan, Turkmenistan, and Kazakistan into the oil market.

Saudi Arabia did build up substantial foreign assets during this period, growing from $4.3 billion in 1973 to more than $120 billion in 1982. These assets, along with Saudi diversification and development programs, have protected the country from many of the economic problems faced by other states in the region.

After 1981, oil production in Saudi Arabia diminished significantly, dropping from 10 million bpd in 1980 to about 2.5 million bpd in 1985. This reduction in production, caused primarily by a fall in Western demand, affected all sectors of the Saudi economy. As a result, the Saudi government has been forced to operate with a government deficit ever since. In order to cover this deficit, Saudi Arabia has drawn on its substantial financial reserves, depleting them from roughly $114 billion in 1985 to about $75 billion in 1989. After the Persian Gulf War, Saudi

Arabia's foreign reserves were depleted, and it was forced to borrow from international financial institutions. The accrued debt in 1998 was very substantial, even though most of its debts are domestic.

Saudi Arabia, the largest of the oil-producing OPEC member states, became a major player in oil price control through production. In the 1980s, at the behest of the U.S. government, production was lowered to prevent a sharp decline in oil prices in 1990, and production was later increased to control rises in oil prices. Oil analysts have long suspected that the United States, the world's premier oil consumer, and Saudi Arabia, the world's largest producer and exporter, have had at least an informal agreement about an acceptable range for oil prices. The countries involved always deny such allegations. Not only does Saudi Arabia have the largest reserves—more than 260 billion barrels—but the cost of extracting oil in this country is among the lowest anywhere. In 1998, it produced 8 million barrels a day, making it the world's largest producer.[31]

The Saudi economy, despite the oil glut and the low prices of 1990, is improving. Due to the Saudi government's five-year development plans, first instituted in 1970, Saudi Arabia has greatly diversified its economy and improved its ability to produce products other than oil. A recent plan (1985–1990) dealt primarily with improving its utilization of present resources, expanding non-oil industries, promoting private business, and reducing foreign labor by increasing training opportunities for the indigenous workforce. The latter is a difficult task for the country. The Kingdom has been a major importer of foreign workers. According to the 1992 census, the country had 4 million foreign workers, compared with its population of 12 million. However, official statistics reveal that the foreign workers currently constitute 80 percent of the economically active population of the country. More than 2 million new foreign workers registered in the country between 1991 and 1995. Although the Saudi economy is improving, the invasion of Kuwait and its aftermath turned out to be very costly for the Persian Gulf Arab states, especially for Saudi Arabia and Kuwait. The capital flight, which began on the eve of the invasion, in August 1991, continues to weaken the economic systems of Kuwait and Saudi Arabia,[32] even in 1998, almost seven years later.

The Saudis learned quite some time ago the importance of diversifying their limited economy in order to bolster their infrastructure against downturns in the oil market. Official acknowledgment of the need to increase the number and variety of sources of national income and to strengthen the Saudi infrastructure can be found as early as 1970, in Saudi Arabia's First Five-Year Plan. This plan set forth industrial diversification as one of its chief goals. The Saudi economy and infrastructure have been successfully modernized in a number of key areas.[33] The modernization has come about through the importation of large quantities of agricultural machinery and materials, the building of roads, electric generators, airstrips, and seaports, the establishment of modern communications systems, and the development and expansion of a whole variety of new industries and businesses.

In the second half of 1991, 150 industrial licenses were issued involving a combined investment of $1.6 billion. The Saudi government claims that the non-oil gross domestic product grew at approximately 111.8 percent in 1990 and 7.2 percent in 1991, compared with a mere 2.7 percent in 1989. According to official figures, the total GDP has recovered since its decline in the 1980s, when it fell from Saudi rials of SR377.7 ($100.7) billion in 1983 to SR271.1 ($73.3) billion in 1986, before bouncing back to SR423.2 ($112.9) billion in 1991. Despite this recovery, officials readily acknowledge that "it is too early to say that the economy could be run without government spending. Things like government loans and encouragement of the private sector will be needed for some time to come. Innovative ideas to stimulate the economy must be provided from both sides."[34]

Mohammed al-Ali Abu al-Khail, Saudi Arabia's minister of finance and national economy, said in a recent meeting in Jeddah that one of the principal tenets of the Saudi economic policy is to provide support to the country's private sector. He said that SR52 ($13.86) billion was allocated in the 1992 state budget for a variety of projects directed toward the health and growth of private business. He noted that from 1990 through 1991 the private sector had an average annual growth rate of 8.2 percent, and he explained that in 1970, the private sector had accounted for some 32 percent of the national economy, but by 1990, that figure had increased to 51 percent. It continues to grow, albeit at slower pace, in 1998.

Abdul Aziz al-Shaikh said that the government allocated SR7.99 ($2.13) billion in the 1992 budget to assist the economy and the agricultural sector. In addition, a further SR4.636 ($1.236) billion has been set aside for developmental funds, which provide soft loans to citizens, including farmers. The minister noted that financial assistance provided by various government agencies to assist the economy was estimated at SR75.43 ($20.11) billion between 1973 and 1988. Land under cultivation increased from a total of 150,000 hectares (1 hectar = 2.471 acres) in 1975 to over 1.12 (2.747 million acres) million hectares in 1989, and government agencies continue to enlarge the size of arable land.

Minister al-Shaikh pointed out that governmental subsidies to farmers have been instrumental in increasing agricultural production. He said such subsidies totaled SR7.95 ($2.12) billion in 1991. The attempt to make Saudi Arabia's desert agriculture self-sufficient through the use of high technology has not been a cheap endeavor, but it has been largely successful. Wheat production rose from only 3,000 tons in 1975 to 3.5 million tons in 1991. Saudi Arabia exported 5.79 million tons of wheat from 1988 through 1990, with 400,000 tons of such export going to the other five GCC (Gulf Cooperation Council) member states.

The Saudi royal family has helped to secure governmental funding for the agricultural sector. Prince Abdullah al-Faisal is the major shareholder of the Saudi Arabian Agriculture and Dairy Company (SAADC), and other family members own five large farms. Government price controls, which apply to almost all agricultural products, enable consumers to more easily purchase Saudi agricultural products. The government's financial generosity is estimated by the Economist Intelligence Unit to have amounted to some SR20 ($4.3) billion between 1975 and 1987.[35]

In Saudi Arabia, where foreign workers in 1999 were almost as numerous as the indigenous population, unemployment continued an upward climb. The makeup of the foreign workforce has been changing. North Americans, Europeans, and, to a lesser extent, other Arabs are being replaced by Asians, who work for lower wages. Among Arabs, the number of Lebanese, Palestinians, and Syrians is being cut back for political reasons. The regime views these Arabs as potentially threatening to the political and social stability of the system, due to their educational backgrounds and social and political orientations, which differ greatly from those of the Saudi people.[36]

The major barrier to Saudi Arabia's 1991–95 development plan was the cost the Saudis incurred from the Persian Gulf War, which totaled somewhere between $60 to $65 billion, or more than half the kingdom's annual income. The largest outpouring of funds went to the United States, which had been promised and received $13.5 billion for the first quarter of 1991 alone. The Saudis entered the international financial market to borrow money to pay their debts.[37]

According to Edward Cody and Steven Mufson, there is an agreement between analysts in Saudi Arabia and those in the United States that the early 1990s borrowing was not indicative of the long-term liquidity problems for Saudi Arabia. According to Sharief Ghalili, who specializes in Africa and the Middle East and is affiliated with the Institute of International Finance: "There is a potential for borrowing by Saudis," but he adds that Saudi Arabia's international reserve holdings "have tended to be invested in highly liquid assets, such as U.S. government securities." Such holdings make it unlikely that the kingdom would need to borrow a substantial amount of money in the future because of liquidity problems. Saudi government's foreign reserves at the end of 1989, was approximately between $60–$70 billion, and the royal family's foreign holdings may amount to additional tens of billions of dollars. Of the government's foreign reserve holdings at the time, it is believed that the government's overseas liquid assets are estimated between $25–$30 billion.[38]

A number of Saudi companies in the past few years have been rapidly expanding their activities in Azerbaijan, Kazakistan, and some of the former Soviet republics. Nimir Petroleum Company, a privately owned company, along with Delta Oil, is currently operating in Kazakistan, Azerbaijan, and Russia. The Dabagh Group, through its subsidiary, Red Sea Housing Services, has undertaken joint ventures with Kazakistan Caspishelf, Kazak Gas, and has also been involved in the country's hotel, airline, and telecommunications sector since 1993.

Nowadays, we hear that all the militant Islamists in the former Soviet republics, particularly in the Caucasus and Central Asia, are in some way connected to the austere and traditional Wahhabi Islamic worldview. Even though this author does not adhere to such a commonly held view, I accept that the majority of these militants share a common religious view, which they use to express their grievances, which are rooted in that specific land. Militancy is different from one place to the other. However, it is appropriate for this writing to elaborate on the manner by which Wahhabis have entered the former Soviet Union and how the term *Wahhabi* became the coin phrase to refer to all militant Islamists.

In the 1980s, when the Soviet Union under Gorbachev introduced Glasnost (political opening or liberalization), among the numerous changes were the liberalization of its policies toward religion. The latter allowed for repossession of the mosques and to planning new mosques, particularly in Central Asia. It should be noted that, even during the strict Soviet Union rule, a small number of old Muslims from these republics made pilgrimages to Mecca, known in Islam as Hajj. These individuals and those who followed them had the chance to meet other Muslims and specifically Saudis during pilgrimage. Therefore, the Saudis, with available funds, arrived in the Central Asian republics in the late 1980s and began to fund reconstruction and the building of the new mosques. In addition to the private Saudi citizens, the Saudi Ministry of Religious Guidance representatives were involved in these activities. However, these activities did not go beyond mosque buildings, but it is not unreasonable to assume that they had established strong links with some of the religious figures. This is the eve of the Islamic Republic of Iran under Ayatollah Khomaini's rhetorical encouragement of the spread of Islam, particulary the Shia' branch of Islam. Ironically, the leadership in Moscow and other republics, along with the media, began using *Wahhabi* as a term to refer to the fear of the spread of militant

Islam because of the regime in Tehran. The Soviet invasion of Afghanistan and the subsequent war against the militant Islamists in Afghanistan who received financial and arms supports from Saudi Arabia, Pakistan, and the United States confirmed the existing common view that militant Islamic groups somehow are all connected to *Wahhabism*. Interestingly, this Islamic school of thought has become synonymous with international terrorism.

With their considerable financial wealth, whenever they could, the Saudis have also attempted to enhance the security of their kingdom through the modernization of their armed forces. Yet even after making a great many military purchases, which have led to an extensive modernization of the Saudi armed forces, Saudi Arabia has remained a relatively weak military power, still depending on other countries such as the United States to bolster its defenses. In compensating for its military weakness, the Saudi government has had to rely on its own foreign and domestic policy-making abilities to enhance the security of the kingdom.

THE REPUBLIC OF TURKEY

The Turkish people are still struggling with the legacy of nation building. The people are struggling with an often incompatible and sometimes volatile mix of European aspirations, mostly in the urban areas of the country—Istanbul, Ankara and Ezmir—and the Islamic traditions, which dominate the culture.

The military and other Western-oriented Turks see the future of the country as being inevitably linked to Europe. But the same military generals and their backers fail to realize that Western orientation is not simply a desire. Rather, it requires a democratic worldview that is grounded on tolerance for opposing views and policies. The Welfare Party government and Istanbul's mayor, Recep Tayyip Erdogan, were ousted on the grounds that their activities or political orientation are against those of the founder of Turkey, Mustafa Kemal. Both of these individuals were elected by their constituents, but the military took it upon itself to orchestrate their forced departure. He has been banned from politics for life, and at time of this writing, the mayor is awaiting a ten-month jail sentence. His crime was reciting the following poem: "Minarets are our bayonets, domes our helmets; mosques our barracks, believers our soldiers," which judges characterized as "inciting hatred based on religious differences." The military in the past used to roll out tanks and other military hardware to show its disapproval of government officials. The military has now decided to carry out its military coups from behind the scenes, as it would be too embarrassing to do so openly in the post–cold war environment, where numerous former dictatorships have given in to the will of people. The West, the United States in particular, ignored the military's abuse of power during the cold war, when the military carried out numerous coups and took power.

The same Turkish military, which sees itself as the custodian of Ataturkism, along with other security forces and authorities have been involved in a continuous misuse of power, torture, and other abuses against the Kurdish people. This has contributed to the recent rise in force within Islamic groups. In the past ten years, thousands of Kurdish people have been killed by the direct military campaign under the guise of national security. Therefore, the Turkish polity will continue to deal with the status quo because of direct military intervention in politics. Moreover, the Turkish military and the political elite somehow have begun to emulate the Israelis in regards to the Kurdish issue and its relations with Syria. However, Turks fail to realize that they are not Jews and, therefore, would not enjoy the support of the United States. At the same time, they are Turks and maintain a nondemocratic system. Consequently, the country will continue to suffer from the absence of democracy, the paramount feature of Western political systems, that the Turkish military and other Turks aspire to join, or claim to have the orientation. The recent development in the United Kingdom, Chile, and Spain in regards to General Augusto Pinochet is a warning to all those who have been instrumental in the abuse of power and the use of torture and murder of the opposition in order to maintain the status quo. In case of Turkey, those who were and are members of the National Security Council need to be cognizant of the new development in regards to the crimes categorized as "crime[s] against humanity."[39]

Turkey is handicapped by several major internal difficulties. One is its economic condition, which is rather weak, with high unemployment, continuing massive inflation, a large public debt, external debts, and the allegation of widespread corruption. The second difficulty is the ongoing challenge Turkey faces from Islamic forces, in particular the Islamic Rifah (Welfare) Party and the heavy-handed means employed by government forces to crack down on the PKK for the violent acts it has committed in the southeast region of the country. The third difficulty is the ongoing struggle between the military and the political parties, especially those that do not call for the military's involvement in the political affairs of the country. The Welfare Party was forced out of office by military generals in 1998, but the party has since reemerged under a new name, the Fazilat (Virtue) Party.

In June 1997, the Turkish generals forced the Islamic Rifah government out of office and set up a coalition government to replace it. The coalition government collapsed on 25 November 1998, as a result of

Parliament, which voted three hundred fourteen to two hundred fourteen to dissolve the government of Mesut Yilmaz and his Motherland Party in partnership with Bulent Ecevit, leader of the Democratic Left. Yilmaz was accused of involvement in a businessman's attempt to acquire a state-owned bank, and in return, the businessman would help Yilmaz in an election scheduled for April 1999. Mesut Yilmaz denied the allegation, claiming he was a victim of conspiracy to thwart his campaign against the country's Mafia.[40] The arrest of a most wanted fugitive, Alaattin Cakici, in August 1998 in France, introduced new evidence in a long-running investigation of ties among politicians, gangsters, and police officers. At the time of his arrest, he was carrying three Turkish passports under various names. According to reports in the Turkish press, cassette tapes found in the fugitive's possession revealed that Cakici had been in touch with cabinet ministers and other senior officials in the previous ten years when the Turkish police and Interpol were supposedly seeking him. Turkish press published photographs of Cakici with a former director of the Milli Istihbarat Teskilati (MIT) "National Intelligence Agency." The Turkish press links this man to various political killings, as well as to such crimes as extortion, heroin smuggling, organizing a failed coup in 1994 against President Haidar Aliev of Azerbaijan, and numerous other criminal acts.

The taped conversations implied that a former interior minister warned Cakici about attempts to capture him. These conversations appear to be in reference to Prime Minister Mesut Yilmaz (head of the Anavatan Partisi "Motherland Party"; ANAP) and a fugitive who claimed that he had spoken to Yilmaz "at least ten times" in the previous ten years. However, Mesut Yilmaz broke off contact after he became prime minister. One minister was forced to resign after a tape surfaced that proved the minister had assisted Cakici to evade capture. This tape was a recording of the crime boss's conversations with Korkmaz Yigit, a Turkish construction magnate. The construction magnate suddenly expanded his holdings with the purchase of the Turkish Bank of Commerce "Turk Ticarat Bankasi" from the government for an estimated $600 million.[41]

Interestingly enough, the Islamic "Virtue" Party maintains 144 majority seats. The second highest number of seats, 135, belongs to the Motherland Party. These are out of the 550-seat Parliament. However, President Suleyman Demirel instead asked Bulent Ecevit from the Democratic Left, with 61 seats, to form a government, because he is well aware of the reaction of the Turkish general to the formation of a new government by Recai Kutan, leader of the Virtue Party. In early January 1999, the Turkish military issued two statements underlining its opposition to the Virtue Party. The first one asserted, "A new war of national liberation must be launched with determination against Islamic activism that threatens the Republic." The other statement said, "Our democracy will be strengthened if political formations that will destroy democracy by abolishing secularism are banned. No democracy should be obliged to allow a political formation that uses democratic means to destroy it."[42] In mid-June 1988, Turkey's military dismissed more than a hundred officers for having ties with Islamist groups, and concurrently, it issued a statement characterizing the Islamist party and organizations as a "domestic threat." In January 1998, the Turkish Constitutional Court (the country's highest court) ruled to shut down the Welfare Party, subsequently reconstituted as the Virtue Party. The party has begun to change its image in order to fend off attacks by secularists and military generals who still see it as a threat to the state. In 1998, the Virtue Party recruited Nazli Ilicak (Ilijak), a well-known Turkish journalist, along with several other women. Ilicak rejects being labeled as an Islamist and contends that the Virtue Party does not aim to establish a religious state and further notes that her party supports the establishment of a secular democracy similar to those in Western countries. She accepts that Turkey's Islamists made mistakes in the past and that they should now make every effort to persuade secularists that they have no intention of overthrowing the present regime in Turkey or imposing religious principles.[43] Nevertheless, the present political system in Turkey does everything to prevent this party from gaining any significant role in the political life of the country. Thus, contrary to the views expressed in the West, Turkey could not be a good model for the former Soviet republics to emulate.

Nevertheless, government officials are making skillful use of promises to the secular power elite of Azerbaijan and Central Asian republics. Turkey has offered to help them link up with Western civilization, while simultaneously pledging to the West that it will serve as a bulwark against Islamic fundamentalism. Meanwhile, the voice for a single homeland, which never existed, for all Turkic-speaking people has been quietly revived, and "Pan-Turanism" (*Turancilik*) may, in the mind of some, have a role to play in this grandiose plan.

Ankara's government elite views its linguistic and "cultural" leadership of all Turkic-speaking people as inevitable. Most of Ankara's activities have been limited to the cultural sector, as it has already promised to supply "brother nations" with books, films, typewriters, and printing presses to disseminate the Latin script, in the event that the Turkish-speaking republics would return to the Latin alphabet from the Cyrillic. In its drive for influence in the former Soviet republics, Turkey's Cultural Ministry is banking on Project Turksat, a communication satellite designed to broadcast Turkish TV, which began operations in the summer of 1993, as well as certain construction projects such as the airport in Ashqabad, Turkmenistan. The Turkish-Canadian Company Netas has already begun converting Azerbaijan's telephone network to the digital system, and its negotiations with the Central Asian republics are proceeding as expected. The escalating violence in the Transcaucacus, specifically the Armenian-Azerbaijani conflict over Nagorno Karabagh, has turned out to be too difficult and complicated for Turkey to handle. There are those who argue that the turmoil may strengthen Turkey's Westernization, but this is yet to come true.

It is possible that Ankara may see itself as the Nasserite of the Turkic-speaking people, and thus aspire to establish Turanistan or Turkistan. However, Ankara needs to realize that Arab nationalism (Qawamiya al-Arabia) has never achieved a monolithic legitimacy. Whatever level it has reached, its failures have tended to be more pronounced than its achievements. Arab nationalism emerged in the context of the Arab-Israeli conflict and struggle against colonialism, and the idea of Turan is not new. A sociologist, Ziya Gokalp, ironically a Kurd, put forward in the beginning of the twentieth century the concept of a "vast and eternal homeland" called "Turan" for all Turkish peoples, which would stretch from China across southern Asiatic Russia to the Adriatic Sea. Gokalp touted the racial and historic superiority of all Turkish-speaking peoples and promoted the "great goal" of their unification under Turkish leadership.

Mustafa Kemal "Ataturk," the founder of the modern state of Turkey, adopted Gokalp's doctrine as part of his philosophy, which later became known as "Kemalism" or "Ataturkism" (Ataturkculuk). But Ataturk realized that Gokalp's aspiration was too grand to achieve in the face of the pronounced ethnic diversity of the Turkish-speaking people and that geographic factors did not favor Gokalp's goal. Turkey has never shared a common border with any of the Turkish-speaking peoples, aside from the small, autonomous enclave of Nakhjavan in Azerbaijan. Ataturk, therefore, decided to abandon the grand scheme of supporting irredentist movements among the 20 million Turkish-speaking Muslims in the Soviet Union in favor of rescuing the newly established Republic of Turkey. In fact, of all the nationalist movements in the twentieth century, that of Turkey had the distinction of being sober-minded and restrained. Since its establishment in 1923, Turkey's official document notes that it "has consistently pursued a foreign policy aimed at international peace based on the principle of 'peace at home and peace in the world,' laid down by the Republic's founding father and first President, Mustafa Kemal (Ataturk)."[44]

During January 1992, Ankara announced that it was opening a diplomatic mission, its first organized "embassy" in the Azerbaijani capital of Baku. Altan Karamanoglu, the new Turkish ambassador, was housed in an inexpensive hotel to convey a diplomatic message from Ankara to the region. The message is that through skillful diplomacy and a common language, the Turkish government has to move quickly to compete with wealthy Saudi Arabia and "fundamentalist" Iran.

In the days of the cold war, from Harry S. Truman to the Reagan doctrine, it was believed in Ankara, Washington, and the NATO member states that Turkey's value was primarily of a geostrategic nature, since Turkey was the only NATO member country to share a long border with the Soviet Union. The Turkish government was also viewed as an anti-Communist stronghold, due in part to its militaristic orientation, repeated *coup d'etat*, and repressive system and laws.[45] In fact, anti-Communism was the historic basis for Turkey's place in the Western alliance. Consequently, Ankara was able to count on generous financial aid and political concessions from the United States and other NATO allies.

The collapse of the Soviet Union and Communist regimes in Eastern Europe ended the cold war. It is very likely that the development of a "partnership"[46] between the United States and Russia in the aftermath of the Persian Gulf War and the recent nuclear agreements signed by these countries will diminish the geostrategic importance of Turkey. As a result, Turkey will probably be placed on the periphery of a "United Europe." Members of Turkey's ruling elite has indefinitely postponed their application for full membership into the European Union because they expected that their country would not be accepted as a member of the European Union, and indeed it was not.

Meanwhile, Washington persists in promoting the concept of a non-secular Turkish model to be emulated by the former Soviet Muslim republics. Turkey is thereby encouraged to see its future more in the Caucasus and Central Asian regions than with the West. Such encouragement is especially welcome to Turkey at a time when its strategic importance to NATO is diminishing rapidly in the post–cold war environment. Still, Turkey lacks the resources to be competitive in Central Asia, where capital and technology are the major needs.

The United States and other Western countries do not back their encouragement with financial support, which Turkey desperately needs to raise its standard of living and to become a vital force in the Central Asian region. Taking matters into its own hands on 3 February 1992, Turkey invited representatives from nine nations to meet in Turkey to form the Black Sea Economic Cooperation Association (BSECA). While this organization was not established explicitly to rival the economic power of the European Union, it brings Turkey a step closer to attaining its goal of reestablishing itself as an important bridge to the Western world.[47]

According to Fikret Ertan, editor of the daily *Zaman*, a pro-Islamic publication, Turkey cannot break off its relations with the West for two important reasons. First, approximately 60 percent of Turkey's trade is with the West, and second, turning its back on the West might jeopardize Turkey's relations with the former Soviet Muslim republics. Seventy years of Soviet rule in the republics has produced a power elite that is strictly nonreligious and very interested in, almost to the point of being obsessed with, the accomplishments of the West. Most of those in influential positions in the republics are more interested in the scientific, economic, and managerial achievements of the West than they are in religious discussions with the governments in Ankara, Tehran, or Riyadh.

Turkey imports a major portion of its oil from Saudi Arabia and Libya. Its oil imports increased by 8.8 percent in the first ten months of 1992. The Turkish state-owned petroleum company, the Turkiye Petrolleri Anonim Ortakligi (TPAO) appealed to Western countries on 2 April 1993 for funds so that it could better compete with Western companies in the search for oil in Kazakistan. In a statement issued by the Petroleum Geologists Association (PGA), which is affiliated with the TPAO, PGA general manager Okan Ozdemir is quoted as saying, "This is an historic opportunity for Turkey." He also told Ercan Ersoy of the Reuters news agency that "we need $800 million in the next four years, and $200 million of it very urgently. . . . It's clear that our budget cannot meet what is needed in a year."

Turkey was unable to attract investment for its peace pipeline because it could not convince its target market, Western countries, to go along with it. These countries were not persuaded that Turkey could carry out the project. Had President Ozal's peace pipeline plan come to fruition, Turkey would likely have alleviated some of its economic woes. The pipeline was intended to pump 6 million cubic meters of water a day to Syria, Jordan, and a number of Persian Gulf states. The would-be-recipient states rejected the pipeline due to its estimated cost of $20 billion and because it would make them more dependent on Turkey. Although experts speculate that the water needs of these countries are likely to increase by 150 percent over the next twenty-five years, in addition to their industrial and agricultural needs, the Persian Gulf Arab states are unwilling to commit funds to and rely upon a country such as Turkey. Qatar signed an agreement with Iran for a supply of water from the Karun River and is expected to pay $13 billion for the project.

Thirty-six percent of Turkey's population is under the age of fourteen, and the country's population is growing by 2 percent a year. Squatter towns (*gecekondu*), or literally "night settlements," which are characteristic of underdevelopment, have mushroomed around Turkey's large industrial cities. The urban population of Turkey has increased dramatically since the 1950s, and Istanbul's population has practically doubled every fifteen years for the last fifty years. Its estimated population, should its growth trend continue, may be as high as 10 million by the close of this century.[48] The appearance of *gecekondus* followed closely on the heels of the Menderes governments program of rural regeneration in the 1950s, which produced a large rural labor surplus. By the 1970s, these squatter towns accounted for up to 60 percent of the population of cities such as Istanbul. These *gecekondus* pose serious problems for the major industrial cities in Turkey.

In October 1992, consumer prices increased by about 8 percent, which is an annual increase of approximately 70 percent. These price increases in consumer goods indicate that Ankara has been unsuccessful in its attempt to curb inflation. The annual inflation rate for 1993 was around 70 percent.[49] The rate of inflation remained very high in 1998, due chiefly to the massive public debt, part of which was incurred to finance state-controlled industries that were losing money. The budget deficit in the first quarter of 1993 ballooned up to $3.2 billion, which was more than half of the government's total deficit target for 1993. Turkey's external debt remains very high. To service that debt in 1989, Ankara paid close to $7 billion. In 1997, while its total export was reported at $26 billion, the country's import was at $46 billion, adding $20 billion to Turkey's negative balance of trade. In fact, the country's external public debt for the third quarter of 1997 was reported at $81.2 billion.[50]

Until the summer of 1998, the country had enjoyed three years of steady growth, and Yilmaz's anti-inflation policies brought inflation down from 91 percent in December 1997 to 67 percent in 1998—policies had received praise from the International Monetary Fund and attracted foreign investors. But Russia's economic problems had already begun to erode Turkey's sound economic base. The September and October Russian financial collapse and the free fall of the ruble sent shock waves through Turkey. Turkey's official trade with Russia declined 15 percent in the first half of the 1998. Turkey's trade deficit grew to $7.5 billion during the same period.

Construction of the vast Ataturk Dam, one of fifteen dams involved in the Anatolia Project (known as GAP, the Turkish acronym for the Southeast of the country), started on 25 July 1992, and has cost $9.3 billion so far. The project will eventually cost approximately $23 billion. Funding for the project came along entirely out of Turkey's own depleted coffers. The project is a massive scheme of fifteen dams that, by the year 2013, will distribute the waters of the Euphrates and the Tagris to irrigate some 2 million hectares (5 million acres) of farmland throughout the eastern part of the country.[51]

President Turgut Ozal, who died on 17 April 1993, shortly after returning from a long trip to the Central Asian republics, attempted to secure credible regional and international roles for Turkey, on the eve of the collapse of the Soviet Union and the outbreak of war in the Persian Gulf. He and other Turkish leaders hoped that through a common language and historical ties to the former Soviet republics, Turkey would become a major player in the republics. Among other benefits, Turkey would stave off regional violence in the Transcaucasus by encouraging and promoting secularism and encourage foreign investment and serving as a force against Islamic radicalism. As a major player in the republics, Ankara would also encourage and promote secularism and foreign investment and would serve as a force against Islamic radicalism. Turkish officials "take considerable pains to deny any hostility toward either neighbor, insisting that in the case of Russia 'we want the same thing in the Caucasus and Central Asia—stability.'" Such policy, officials contend, manifested itself in high-level contacts, such as Ozal's trip to Moscow in March 1991, the first visit by a Turkish president in twenty-two years. Ozal's policy toward the former Soviet republics was supported by the United States, but the latter country failed to give him the financial support that Turkey desperately needed and still needs for its domestic development programs and for the expansion of its trade and commerce with the new republics. President Ozal was trying, mainly unsuccessfully, to establish a vast network of highways, railroads, oil and gas pipelines, and telecommunications systems, as well as trade and cultural links that would bind the former Soviet republics to Turkey. The Turkish leaders later discovered that many of the republics are not receptive to their overtures. The infrastructures of these republics, after seventy years of the Soviet system's incompetence, are simply too devastated to be rebuilt with limited Turkish resources. In 1993, Turkey granted $1.1 billion in credits to the former Soviet republics and negotiated with Kazakistan to extend an oil pipeline from Baku to the Turkish port of Iskenderun. However, Turkey's former prime minister Demirel, who is now president, was unwilling to take part in Ozal's empire building.[52]

The forced departure of Azerbaijan's former president, Abolfazl Elchibey (died in 2000), who was openly anti-Russia and pro-Turkey, dashed the aspirations of Ankara. Elchibey's departure hindered plans for the oil pipeline and other linkage projects, which Turkey wanted to establish with its Central Asian Turkish cousins. Haidar Aliev may move Azerbaijan closer to Russia, where he has numerous former Communist colleagues who continue to run the Russian government.

Shortly before his death, Ozal had begun a break with the past by taking steps toward the democratization of Turkey, increasing the power of the citizenry rather than that of the military through the establishment of a "political elite tutored in republican virtue." But his conversion came too late, and "his era may be known, not for economic reforms, but for tolerance of pay-off and corruption." His critics note that he "allowed the police and security forces to disregard human rights."[53] An Amnesty International report charged that the government failed to protect human rights and that political killings and torture still continue today.[54] At a meeting on 12 December 1997 in Luxembourg, the European Union approved eleven countries for possible membership but rejected Turkey's decade-old request. Referring to Turkey's campaign against its Kurdish minority, Luxembourg's prime minister, Claude Junker, host of the summit, said, "It cannot be that a country where torture is still practiced has a place at the European Union table." Two days later, the prime minister of Turkey, Yilmaz, accused the EU of erecting "a new, cultural Berlin wall" and added, "We will have no political dialogue with the European Union anymore."[55]

In June, at the EU summit in Cardiff, England, the United Kingdom and France tried to heal the wounds of Luxembourg by calling for more positive relations with Turkey. Turkey responded once again in an exaggerated accusatory tone. Deputy Prime Minister Bulent Ecevit described the action as "a disgrace," "a slap in the face," "prejudice," and "a blunder." This clearly indicates that Turkish officials are inclined to overlook the fact that their country has simply failed to meet the political and economic criteria necessary for membership.[56]

It is important to acknowledge that Ozal's influence was crucial in whatever improvements did occur. He was recognized as having been instrumental in moderating PKK activities in the southeast and expanding the limited rights of PKK members in Turkish society. After Ozal's death, the government began brutal attacks on the PKK, and conflict flared up. At the end of June, the cease-fire, which had been declared unilaterally by the PKK in February 1993, was broken. By the end of July, at least two hundred members of the PKK had been killed by Turkish soldiers, and the PKK fighters have been killing large numbers of civilians and Turkish soldiers ever since.

Disgusted by the brutality of Turkey's military actions against the Kurds, former Secretary of State Warren Christopher sought a solution to the conflict. He was influenced by information disseminated by the State Department's 1992 Global Human Rights Report, which disclosed that political murders and other killings had increased. This report also documented cases of rape, torture, disappearances, and denials of fair trials to political opponents. Secretary Christopher offered economic and political incentives to Turkey if it were to stop infringing on human rights. He also stated that while the U.S. does not consider Turkey as a gross violator of human rights, the government's behavior must be "factored" into the consideration to extend economic and political assistance to Turkey. Shortly thereafter, American officials announced that the U.S. would provide Turkey with $336 million worth of aircraft and military equipment, because "Turkey lives in a rough neighborhood."[57]

Abdullah Ocalan (Ojalan), the leader of the PKK, announced in March 1993 that he would no longer seek to establish an independent Kurdish state and that he would settle for an arrangement allowing Turkey's 12 million Kurds to be part of a unified and democratic Turkey. Such an arrangement would require an amendment to the Turkish Constitution. To assuage Ocalan (Ojalan), Turkey would also have to allow the Kurds to use the Kurdish language in schools and to conduct broadcasting activities in Kurdish as well. To illustrate the "one step forward, two steps backward" nature of relations between the Turkish government and the Kurds, on 15 July 1993, Turkey's Constitutional Court outlawed a hitherto legal Kurdish party, the People's Labor Party, eighteen members of which were serving in Parliament.

On 16 February 1999, the Turkish commandos flew into Nairobi, Kenya, and arrested Abdullah Ocalan the leader of PKK, who is currently in prison in Turkey. This has been one of the objectives of the Ankara for the past few years. Therefore, it is appropriate to present a brief historical background of the PKK and its leader. In 1970, Ocalan, along with other Kurds from the southeast, founded Turkey's Kurdish organization then known as the Democratic Association of Patriotic Higher Educationalists. However, shortly after, the name of the organization went through several changes, it was the Revolutionaries of Kurdistan—as a consequence of the spread of Marxism among them—and ultimately the Kurdistan Workers' Party. The leadership later escaped to Lebanon's Bekaa (Beqaa) Valley, and later moved to Syria. Ocalan has been on the run since he became the leader of the PKK, albeit living in Syria for some time. However, Turkish sabre rattling in October 1998 forced Syria to expel Ocalan. However, his arrest has placed Turkey once again in an odd position, when it comes to the fair trial of a Kurdish leader, specifically one who is characterized by the government of Turkey as a "terrorist."[58]

After his departure from Syria, Ocalan went to Russia, then Italy, where he was arrested. Two court cases and two rescinded arrest warrants later, he set off for a new refuge, while being chased by the media and by Turkish secret services. With Russia, the Netherlands, Switzerland, and Germany all unwilling to give him refuge, Ocalan found himself on a plane above Europe with nowhere to land. The Greek authorities allowed his plane to refuel in Corfu before smuggling him into Nairobi, Kenya.

TURKEY AND THE PIPELINES

Turkey, as noted before, is one of the countries that compete for the pipeline route from the Caspian and the Central Asian regions. This country is making every effort possible for a Western route pipeline proposal, that would carry oil from Azerbaijan's offshore oil fields through Azerbaijan and Georgia and then across Turkey to the Mediterranean port of Ceyhan (Jaihan). The proposed pipeline would cost an estimated $3 to $4 billion, at a capacity of eight hundred thousand barrels per day. It would cost $2.80 per barrel to ship oil from the Caspian via Ceyhan to ports in Italy. A study asserts that Azerbaijan and the oil consortium AIOC—BP, Amoco Corporation, Exxon Corporation, Pennzoil, Unocal Corporation, Ramco Plc, Norway's Statoil, Itochu Corporation of Japan, Russia's LUKoil, the Turkish Petroleum Corporation, and Delta International of Saudi Arabia—could lose $1 billion a year by opting for a Western route.[59]

Under the agreement with Azerbaijan, AIOC was to announce its routing decision by the end of October 1998. Yet the agreement was signed in late 1999 by Azerbaijan, Georgia, and Turkey to build the Baku-Ceyhan pipeline. AIOC and the countries involved are still negotiating all the concerned issues. Moreover, test wells in the Caspian produced gas rather than oil. But as early as April 1998, AIOC made a new pipeline route proposal for "early oil"—short-term—from Caspian offshore oil fields. These would run from Baku to the Georgian Black Sea port of Supsa to western markets, which will be sufficient for Azeri's current oil production of three hundred thousand barrels per day. This pipeline is currently under construction. However, AIOC must still decide on an export route for the greater volumes—two million barrels per day or more—of oil production expected to become available from fields in Kazakistan, Turkmenistan, and Azerbaijan in the early twenty-first century.

In addition to oil, there are similar concerns about natural gas pipeline routes from Kazakistan, Turkmenistan, and Uzbekistan, which are located further away from the Western markets. The distance from potential markets and the relative lack of infrastructure to export the gas have become major concerns of these three countries.

PART IV

Looking Ahead

CHAPTER 10

The Future

The collapse of the Soviet Union has resulted in the establishment of several independent republics. Most of these republics have not had any previous experience ruling themselves. If they had lived under any form of governing system, it was a traditional khanate, emirate system, which co-existed throughout most of the twentieth century with the centrally controlled Communist government. The emergence of these newly independent republics has presented opportunities for Iran, Saudi Arabia, Turkey, and China to develop economic inroads into and to influence these republics. These opportunities may be attributed chiefly to the historical, religious, cultural, and linguistic connections that exist between many of the nations in the region. The three contending countries have had varying degrees of success in gaining access to the republics.

The political, social, and literary elite in these former Soviet republics may find common ground with Turkey and other Muslim countries. It is appropriate to note that, when it comes to the subject of Islamic militants and their activities in the regions, there are misconceptions in this regard. Moreover, there are numerous Islamic militant groups throughout the world and particularly the regions in this study. It is erroneous to either contend or assume that Islam as a religion is a unifying force in these regions or throughout the Islamic world. The doors of these republics could be opened for capital inflow that exists in a limited sum in the contending states. The invasion of Kuwait and its aftermath have cost the Persian Gulf Arab states, particularly Saudi Arabia and Kuwait, large sums of money. The former Soviet republics, in particular, want access to capital, technology, computers, and the economic and managerial know-how that would enable them to alleviate their poverty and raise their standard of living.

Shaikh Saleh Kemal, the chairman of the Jeddah-based Saudi conglomerate Dallah al-Baraka, has claimed that his group reached an agreement with Russia and signed an accord with former Vice President Aleksander Rutskoi during a 1993 visit to Moscow. This agreement will set up a joint company to increase the capability of Russian military industries to manufacture civilian goods. The group also negotiated the possibility of opening a bank in Moscow. Dallah al-Baraka plans to earmark special investment funds for Uzbekistan, Kazakistan, and Turkmenistan.[1] However, the group has not yet taken any concrete steps. It has not set up the joint company or provided special investment funds for these Central Asian republics.

Iran's newly established EPB (Export Promotion Bank) has the potential to penetrate the former Soviet republics, but Iran is handicapped by its lack of capital and political instability. Nevertheless, it has been able to grant Turkmenistan $50 million for purchasing Iranian exports, such as automobiles, medicine, food, and machinery. It plans to extend similar export credits to other former Soviet republics.

At the encouragement of the U.S. administration, due to its rivalry with Iran, historical animosity, and unresolved disputes with Armenia, President Suleyman Demirel visited Georgia in early January 2000. In his meeting with the Georgian president, he proposed a Caucasus security system, but in fact, the pact is intended to help countries in the Caucasus to resist or become a wall against the Russian power. This security system, interestingly enough, is proposed by a NATO member state, which will bring NATO directly in a confrontational posture toward Russia. Such a view has already been aired by Valadimir Putin, the acting president of Russia in his meeting with Georgia's president on 25 January 2000, during the CIS summit in Moscow.

The fall of the Soviet Union and the emergence of the newly independent republics have presented opportunities for study and speculation regarding their current and potential positions and conditions as "independent" nation-states.

RUSSIA AND THE FORMER SOVIET REPUBLICS

This study has presented a brief exploration of the political, social, and economic conditions of these republics. It has highlighted their relations with the new Russia, their immediate region, and the international system in general. Without the inclusion of the foreign policy goals and behavior of Russia in this study as a major external factor, the analysis would be incomplete.

Recent publications have presented several scenarios concerning the future of Russia and its implications for the former Soviet republics, to which Moscow refers as "near abroad." These studies point to the possibility of the democratization of Russia or to the expansion of its assertive foreign policy and the threat of further upheaval in the country. Moscow intends the "near abroad" (*blizaeshii zarubezh*) policy to maintain a monopoly interest over the former Soviet republics, which are regarded as nonforeign countries. Former Russian Foreign Minister

Andrei Kozyrev during 1994 sketched Russia's overall foreign policy agenda. Highlighting Russia's prioritization of its relations with the Former Soviet Republics, he stressed, "Russia sees the emergence of new threats to our interests, above all those of instability and armed conflicts across the whole space of the former USSR." Kozyrev reported that at times Russia has found it necessary to advance its interests in the world "in a tough manner," but he assured his audience that Russia's approach in the future would always remain within the bounds of international law. In March 1994, Kozyrev indicated that the Russian Pacific Fleet must expand its presence in order to "show the world at large that Russia is not a weak power." This reassertion of military strength comes at the time of the apparent decline in Russian naval combat capabilities. However, Prime Minister Putin became very assertive in Russia's policy toward the Caucasus. Putin became active president of Russia on 1 January 2000, when he visited Russian troops in Chechnia.[2]

Several high-ranking officials and military officers opposed legislation to cut Russia's arms procurement budget. The opposition warned that not only would the cuts affect 15 to 20 million Russian employees but also they might gravely endanger national security. Russia decided to maintain the previous year's arms budget, but the decision is not necessarily binding for the government. Kozyrev also stated that Western forces should not join in peacekeeping efforts in Georgia. These statements indicate a gradual rebuilding of Russia's military power base.[3]

Russia is once again pushing its sphere of influence right up to the borders of Iran and Turkey. On 3 February 1994, Boris Yeltsin signed a treaty with Georgian leader Eduard Shevardnadze, confirming Georgia's reentry into the CIS and shoring up "Russia's sphere of influence." The treaty gives Moscow the right to establish military bases in Georgia, to station some five thousand border troops at five military bases and ports on Georgia's border with Turkey, and to train and arm the Georgian military. Russia is seeking a similar agreement with Azerbaijan, which would enable Moscow to formally extend its military presence all the way to the borders of Iran and Turkey.

In a recent interview with the *Washington Post*, Eduard Shevardnadze, in reference to the role of Moscow in the region, noted, "In Russia, the forces trying to pull society back into the past—they haven't been overcome. It's a very diverse society, with genuine democrats. But there is also a very powerful force that thinks in imperial terms and has not taken off the agenda the restoration of the Soviet Union." He asserts, "Russians were behind the attempts on [Shevardnadze's] life. They are still harboring the main organizers, and preparing new plans. Russia has backed separatists in Georgia's northwest corner who are trying to secede. And you mustn't think these are weak groups. They have serious funding."

In October 1993, during the civil war, Russia presented Tiblisi with a choice of joining CIS or watching Georgia fall apart. Russian troops were instrumental in the defeat of Zyiad Gamsakhurdia in November 1993. Russian Defense Minister General Pavel Grachev had made it clear during his visit to Tiblisi that he wanted to establish military bases throughout the Transcaucasus.[4] In fact, on 14 March 1994, Russian Commander Andrei Nikolaev signed an agreement in Tiblisi under which Georgian conscripts and volunteers served in Russian border forces on the Georgian-Turkish border. The next day, Russia signed a similar agreement with Armenia. A Russian commander described the agreement as creating a legal basis for military cooperation between Armenia and Russia. It should be noted that Eduard Shevardnadze has always defied expectations. At the age of seventy-two and deeply engaged in his country's presidency, he is trying to build an independent and unified Georgia in the turbulent region of the Caucasus. As the foreign minister of the Soviet Union, he helped Mikhail Gorbachev to dismantle the Warsaw Pact and free the states of Eastern Europe to pursue their own destinies. Since the collapse of the Soviet Union, Georgia has been involved in a civil war that has devastated the country. Warlords carved up territories, the economy went to waste, and guns were the only law. In fact, in some areas outside of Tiblisi, lawlessness still rules. Shevardnadze, similar to other former Soviet republic leaders in the Caucasus and Central Asia, has taken steps to establish democratic institutions. But the viability of these institutions rest on a single leader. When he departs, those institutions that were built from the top down will cease to exist as they lack popular support, because of the absence of public participation during their development. In the past three years, the economy has grown. The growth should be viewed within the context of the nonexistence of a functioning economy. Therefore, any minimal change is undoubtedly accepted as growth. It should be noted that Georgia has been gradually moving out of Moscow's shadow and has sought to develop economic and political ties with the West. Shevardnadze has even said that Georgia plans to apply for NATO membership in 2005.[5]

In April 1997, Russia and Belarus signed a treaty to unify their monetary systems. According to the agreement, Belarus will forfeit to the Russian Central Bank its right to control any monetary supply. Russia will also receive a free lease on military bases inside Belarus. For its part, Russia will supply Belarus with cheaper gas and oil, minus transit fees, and lift all customs and tariffs. Russia will also exchange its rubles for Belarus' rubles, at a cost of billions of dollars to Russia. Although the treaty still needs to be ratified by the parliaments of these countries, it already has Belarus' experts fearing a new kind of Russian hegemony.

Alezander Lukashenka, the Belarusian president, was elected chairman of the Supreme State Council of the Union of Belarus and Russia on 26 January 2000, the day on which the treaty of the union went into effect. "The treaty meets not only the national interests of our two countries, our two states, but also embodies the aspiration of Russians and Belarusians to live and work together for the common good," Putin said during a televised ceremony. The treaty, signed by Yeltsin and Lukashenko in December 1999, envisages by 2005 harmonized national legislation, uniform customs, tax, defense, and border policy, common securities and a single currency. But Russia and Belarus remain separate nation-states at the United Nations and other international organizations.[6]

When Kozyrev met with the CSCE high commissioner for national minorities, Max von der Stoel, later that month, he took a noticeably stronger stand. Kozyrev made it clear that Russia would not cease urging the Baltic countries to protect the rights of Russian-speaking citizens, who constitute a distinct minority in those states. He stated that it depends entirely on Estonia whether they will agree to a withdrawal of troops. He also called for an accord with Latvia establishing a "new standard of relations" between the two countries. Almost every high-ranking official in Moscow agrees that Russia has the right and duty to protect the interests of ethnic Russians in the former Soviet republics. In January 1994, the Russian foreign minister announced that "one of Moscow's main strategic interests" is to meet this responsibility.[7]

In April 1994, Azerbaijan dismissed the rumor that it would withdraw from CIS in order to protest Russian plans for deployment of peacekeeping forces in Nagorno-Karabagh and for the closure of the Azerbaijani-Iranian border. Azerbaijan has been negotiating with Russia on the renewal of a leasing contract for the Gabala radar station. Azerbaijan's show of support for the CIS was taken a step further than one by Armenia and Georgia, who consented to the continued presence of Russian military bases within their countries.[8]

While negotiating with Russia, Azerbaijan has successfully resisted Russian bullying. Unlike the Baltic nations (Estonia, Latvia, and Lithuania), it is the only former Soviet republic with no Russian troops on its territory. In April of 1997, leaked reports to the Russian press revealed clandestine arms shipments from Moscow to Armenia between 1994 and 1996, which illuminate the Russian role in the Azerbaijani-Armenian conflict over Nagorno Karabagh. The arms shipments included eighty-four T-72 tanks, fifty infantry fighting vehicles, and missile complexes that can carry conventional, chemical, or nuclear warheads. The cost of the arms shipments is estimated at $1 billion dollars. According to the Russian press, in mid-March, Russian Defense Minister Igor

Rodionov confirmed the transfer of arms to Armenia.[9]

Since Russian troops intervened in the bloody Tajik civil war in late 1992, Russia has maintained a predominant role in Tajikistan. The headquarters of Russia's 201st Division, which is located in the heart of the capital city of Dushanbeh, Tajikistan, consists of about twenty thousand soldiers, which includes border troops. Russians view themselves as the defenders of the relative peace and tranquility enjoyed by the Tajik population. "We need to bring peace and stability back to this region so people can toil peacefully," says Colonel General Valery Patrikeyev, the Russian Commander of the 201st Division. Colonel Ivan Malevich, spokesman for the CIS command, adds, "One has to be a realist. If the border troops and the peacekeeping forces withdraw, it will mean a second round of civil war." More revealing, however, is the observation of the commander of the border troops, Colonel Yevgeny Merkulov, who declares, "We are here because the interests of Russia are above everything, in light, of course, of the interests of Tajikistan."[10]

Others see the troops as part of Russia's assertive policy to reestablish its imperial aspirations. In October 1993, the Russian forces were reorganized as "peacekeeping forces." The CIS includes small contingents of Uzbek, Kyrgyz, and Kazak troops, so this would not be viewed as a solely Russian venture. On 12 August 1998, Taliban militia forces expanded their control and captured the town of Hairaton, which lies on the southern bank of the Amu Daria River across from the Uzbekistan border. President Imamali Rahmonov of Tajikistan in connection to the development in Afghanistan called on the CIS member states to take all necessary measures to strengthen security along the border with Afghanistan.

During his April 1999 visit to Moscow, Tajikistan President Imamali Rahmanov reported that he and Boris Yeltsin tentatively agreed to allow Russia to establish a military base in Tajikistan, where Russia maintains a large number of military forces. The agreement would allow Russia to have a direct role in the security and military developments in the region. Tajik officials pointed out that such a military base would help provide increased stability for the country, which borders Afghanistan to the south, where anti-Tajik government forces are based.[11]

Russian Foreign Minister Yevgenii Primakove, in a speech on the two hundredth anniversary of the birth of Alexander Gorchakov, who was responsible for rebuilding Russia's power and influence after the Crimean War (1853–56), characterized Gorchakov as a model for Russia's gains since the collapse of the Soviet Union. Primakove presented five lessons from Gorchakov's foreign policy approach. This speech is undoubtedly intended to gloss over the weak and chaotic predicament the Russian people are in now that the Soviet Union has disintegrated. The lessons of the Crimean War are argued by Primakove as a guide for Moscow's actions today:

1. Russia, even when weakened by defeat, can pursue an active foreign policy. (Primakove notes that his predecessor showed that Russia has no other choice.)
2. Russian foreign policy must not be unidirectional or limited to a region. Rather, it must seek to be active globally.
3. Russia has always had "enough strength" to play a leading role in the world.
4. Gorchakov understood that Russia could always exploit the resentment many smaller powers inevitably feel vis-à-vis larger ones. In this way, Russia can rebuild and then expand its own influence.
5. Gorchakov's policy and actions provide one negative lesson. His predecessor's maneuvering among the great powers of Europe is now "out of date." Instead, Moscow must seek constructive partnerships with all countries rather than seeking some "mobile" or permanent coalition.

During September 1998, Primakove was appointed prime minister of Russia. He was relieved of his post in August of 1999 and was replaced by Valadimir V. Putin. It should be noted that U.S. government officials had a difficult time dealing with the new prime minister and subsequently dealt with Yeltsin. However, Boris Yeltsin, at the eve of the new year (31 December 1999), shocked the world and unexpectedly announced his immediate resignation, a move that was unpredictable and inconsistent but shrewd, classic Yeltsin behavior. He handed over the presidency of Russia to Putin, effective 1 January 2000.

On his second day as acting president, Putin visited with Russian troops fighting in Chechnia. His visit clearly was a sign of Putin's close association with the war in Chechnia. Since Putin—a largely unknown former member of the KGB—became the prime minister in August 1999, his visibility and popularity soared with the conduct of the war in Chechnia. Putin's visit to the war zone presented Russians a different image of their leadership from an inconsistent, unpredictable role "to an active and vital one." In a special document, "Russia at the Turn of the Millennium," published on a Kremlin internet site (*www.pravitelstvo. gov.ru/english/statVP engl1.html*), Putin said it would be a mistake for Russia not to recognize communism's accomplishments. "But it would be an even bigger mistake not to realize the outrageous price our country and its people had to pay for that Bolshevik experiment." He went on to say, "Russia needs a strong state power and must have it," but he added that a strong state means "a law-based, workable federative state." Putin backed up his call for reform with "sobering statistics: even if Russia's per-person domestic product were to rise by 8 percent per year for the next 15 years, the nation would still only reach the level of present day Portugal. Achieving the level of Britain or France would require a 10 percent annual growth rate—and even then, Britain or France would have to stand still."

It should be noted that Primakove never expressed ambitions to succeed Yeltsin. Primakove began to reassert Russian influence when he became the foreign minister in 1995. His actions are presented in the context of establishing a "multipolar" international system. On 10 September 1998, he laid out his ambitions to rebuild Russia's global role, amidst the economic and financial turmoil. "There have been those who believe that Russia today is incapable of pursuing an active foreign policy. They argue that Russia must first get out of its economic crisis. . . . Events show that without Russia's active participation . . . it is difficult if not impossible, to resolve world tasks." He lobbied against the expansion of NATO into Poland, Hungry, and the Czech Republic but acquiesced after negotiating a special relationship with the alliance designed to allow Russia to express its views in NATO affairs. Primakove persistently opposes the use of force by NATO to pressure Yugoslavia to end its antiseparatist war in the Serbian province of Kosovo. He denied repeatedly the complaints from the United States and Israel that Russia has supplied Iran with technology useful in building medium- and long-range missiles. A veteran of the KGB secret police, he headed the foreign branch of Russian intelligence from 1991 to 1996. He also has experience in the Arab world, where he was a correspondent for Pravda and covered the 1967 war between Israel and its Arab neighbors.[12]

While Russia is expanding itself in these areas, it still suffers from internal turmoil. President Yeltsin has been under attack recently by hard-liners in Parliament. Vladmir Isakov, head of the State Duma's Committee on Constitutional and Legal Reform, has proposed that in presidential elections, the national election system should be replaced by a joint meeting of the two chambers of the Federal Assembly. In addition, Deputy Yurii Vlasov has openly denounced Yeltsin as a leader. Vlasov argues that Yeltsin has exhausted himself and should therefore be replaced by a more energetic leader. Viktor Ilyokhin, the head of the State Duma's Security Committee, charged Yeltsin with committing an illegal act when the latter proposed that the Federal Counter-Intelligence Agency (FCIA) be transformed into a presidential agency.

On 14 March 1994, Defense Minister Grachev canceled a planned inspection of the St. Petersburg military district. At that time, both President Yeltsin and Chief of General Staff Kolesnikov were out of Moscow, and Grachev claimed that the cancellation ensured the control of Russian strategic nuclear forces. This suggests that either the Russian control system is not as reliable as once thought or that Grachev does not trust his subordinates.

Russia's ambition in the former Soviet republics should be viewed within the context of the country's economic deterioration, especially during 1994, 1995, and 1998. The Minister of Education has warned that steep falls in production, investment, and tax revenues will create a greater risk for a "social explosion." Recorded production fell by 25 percent in the first quarter of 1994, compared with the same period in 1993, and by 29 percent between April 1993 and April 1994. The economic problems faced by Russia since the collapse of the Soviet Union have been enormous and will continue unless it will take firm and constructive steps to deal with them. The gross domestic product has dropped by 50 percent, the average life span has fallen two and a half years, the birthrate has dropped by one-third, and the mortality rate has risen by one-quarter. The deaths exceed births by about 700,000 a year—all just since 1990. Inflation, while down from the three-digit rate of the early 1990s, is expected to be more than 30 percent in 2000. Nearly one-third of the population live under the official subsistence level—a bare thirty-six dollars a month. Economic problems are present in the armed forces as well. Once, this country had a strong and vital military; now the soldiers involved in the war in Chechnia face food shortages.

The devastating economic collapse of 1999, which wiped out many Russians' savings for the second time in a decade, turned out to be a blessing for Russia's exports. The event caused a large depreciation in the value of the ruble, making the exchange rate favorable to Russian exports and domestic production, but at the same time, making the price of imports dearer. The latter caused growth in the Russian economy in 1999 and an expectation that it will grow again in 2000. Yeltsin's decision to privatize state industries hastily through a voucher program devised by American economists proved to be a clear avenue to corruption. The majority of Russia's population had no experience with stock certificates, much less in participation in corporate governance. Subsequently, entire companies and even industries were snapped up and their assets looted by "crooked factory management, mobsters and tycoons; workers were left holding the empty bag." According to President Putin, "Investment has dwindled: only 4.5 percent of the nation's industrial equipment was less than five years old in 1998, compared with nearly 30 percent in 1990. Except in the electricity and raw material industries, individual productivity is one quarter of that in the United States."[13] Decline in the economic output continued to cause social and political problems for the country well into the late 1990s.

The recent reentry of Georgia into the CIS and the enlargement of the Russian military presence at the former Soviet borders are evidence of Russia's active and assertive position. Moreover, some of Russia's political and military activities, such as its involvement in the Armenian-Azerbaijani war, the Abkhazian revolt and the Tajik civil war are a clear indication of the inevitability of Russia's access to the domestic, regional, and international politics and trade of the former Soviet Muslim republics.

Moscow repeatedly voices certain major concerns, including the following: the protection of the rights of Russian minorities in the former Soviet republics, the issue of duel citizenship, the threat of Islamic radicalism, the security of the borders of the former Soviet Union presented as the current borders of Russia, and last, the future role of the CIS.

The former Soviet republics of Azerbaijan and Central Asia are generally less developed than those republics located in the Western region. These former Muslim republics face many difficulties, which will prolong their dependency on Russia. This dependency ranges from access to capital and technology to difficulties in maintaining their present energy sources, which requires a large amount of capital. Satisfying industrial and consumer needs is also a major concern. Ultimately, they would need to attain these national goals of self-identity and national sovereignty. However, poor economic condition and performance of these republics makes it ever more difficult to deal with the economic, social, and political problems in the countries. Therefore, so far, independence has not translated into prosperity for these countries, but in fact had negative economic consequences. In addition, former Communist leaders and the elite rule almost all of these republics, as is the case now in Russia. Almost all of the presidents of these republics have been in office since the collapse of the Soviet Union. The iron-fist rule and no toleration for opposition or criticism are characteristic of most of these nations. Haidar Aliev of Azerbaijan, Nursultan Nazarbaev of Kazakistan, Saparmurat Niyazov and Islam Karimov of Uzbekistan, all former Communists (see: Appendix I), will do anything, as information from the recent elections in Uzbekistan and Kazakistan attests, to maintain their hold on power. Securing their rule keeps these leaders and elite close to Russia if not completely dependent on it. Domestic issues such as ethnic rivalries and adverse economic conditions continue to place a heavy burden on these governments. The republics cannot cope with these problems on their own. They seem to be compelled to ask for military and security assistance from their former ruler, Russia.

Moreover, the leaders of the former Soviet republics and the contending states of Iran and Turkey have apparently come to believe and present a notion to the outside world that the electoral system is the sole indication of democracy, or at least ought to be viewed as a commitment to establish democracy because the ruling elite controls electoral systems in these countries. In Iran, for example, no one can be a candidate for office without direct officially scrutiny—to classify the possible candidate as a good or true Muslim—by an entity established by the ruling elite to perpetuate the political system. Even in some cases, such as Turkey, the military changes the "democratically" elected administration.

This analysis of the former Soviet republics has been offered with the intention of helping the reader understand the political and economic trends in the region.

NOTES

INTRODUCTION

1. This legal term is adopted from the phrase "State Succession," Gerhard von Glhan, *Law among Nations*, 6th ed., New York, NY: Macmillan Publishing Company, 1992, p. 114.

2. *New York Times*, 20 March 1999; *Christian Science Monitor*, 11 August 1999.

3. Nozar Alaolmolki, "American Geostrategic Interests in Transcaucasian Region," paper presented at a panel sponsored by the American Foreign Policy Institute, U.S. Congress Office Building, Washington, DC, 24 June 1997. *Christian Science Monitor*, 30 July, 11 August 1998; *Economist*, 18 July 1998; *New York Times*, 20 March and 15 August 1999; and *Agence France-Presse* (hereafter *AFP*), 22 August 1999. Quoted in *Christian Science Monitor*, 17 August 1999. In 1998, 33 million people had incomes below six dollars a month, the official poverty level, according to the Russian government. As of this writing, 55 million people live in poverty, according to government statistics *New York Times*, 23 August 1999.

4. East Turkistan, a formerly independent (1944–1949) nation, was annexed by the People's Republic of China in 1949. Interestingly enough, the Chinese named the territory "Xinjiang," which means "New Frontier." It is inhabited mainly by Ughurs (8 million out of the 20 million), and other non-Chinese are Tajik, Kyrgyz, Kazak, and Dungan. These people culturally are Muslim. There have been occasional violent attacks against the police authorities and pro-Chinese Muslim clergies, in Kashgar and *Urumqi* (*Urumchi*).

5. The Shanghai Five got its name for its first summit in Shanghai, China, in April 1996, where the five countries penned a historic treaty to demilitarize their common border. *AFP*, 22 August 1999, *The Washington Post*, 26 August 1999. They held another summit on 7 July 2000 in Tajikistan. For the first time, Uzbekistan's president, Islam Karimov, attended the meeting. RFE/RL, 26/27 August 1999 and 7 July 2000.

6. *Economist*, 27 June 1998.

7. Prime Minister Li Peng visited the Central Asian republics (except Tajikistan) with an aim of promoting Beijing's political, commercial interests and border agreement with its newly independent Western neighbors. Besides trade, China hopes to secure help from these republics in controlling the Ughir, Tajik, Kygyz, Kazak, and Uzbek separatists in the Chinese province of Xinjiang. *Financial Times*, 19, 26, 29 April 1994; Paul George, Commentary, 73, A Canadian Security Intelligence Service publication, 25 June 1999; *Los Angeles Times*, 10 October 1997 and 17 October 1998; *Manchester Guardian Weekly*, 5 October

1997; and *New York Times,* 17 October 1998. Chinese president Jiang Zemin made a two-day visit to Tajikistan on 3 July 2000. The two presidents focused on bilateral cooperation, demarcating common borders and regional security. RFE/RL, 7 July 2000.

8. According to Interfax, 11 January 2000.

9. See Myron Weiner, "Political Integration and Political Development," in *Annals* 358, March 1965, pp. 52–64; Clifford Geertz, AThe Integrative Revolution," in Clifford Geertz, ed., *Old Societies and New State,* NY, Free Press, 1963, pp.105–57; Leonard Binder, "National Integration and Political Development," *American Political Science Review,* 58, September 1964, 622–31; and James A. Bill/Robert L. Hardgrave Jr., *Comparative Politics,* Columbus, Ohio: Charles E. Merrill Publishing Co., 1973, pp. 85–91. Ambassador Stephen Sestanovich made the comments in testimony before a House of Representatives International Relations subcommittee, 17 March 1999. RFE/RL, 18 March 1999.

CHAPTER ONE

1. For the historical background, see Richard A. Pierce, *Russian Central Asia 1867–1917,* Berkeley, CA: University of California, 1960, pp. 17–45; A. Lobanov-Rostovsky, *Russia and Asia,* Ann Arbor, MI: George Wahr Publishing Co., 1965, pp. 147–76; Basil Dmytryshyn, *A History of Russia,* NJ: Prentice-Hall, 1965, pp. 342–43, 359–60; Hugh Seten-Watson, *Russian Empire 1801–1917,* Clarendon Press 1967, pp. 438–45; Firuz Kazemzadeh, *The Struggle for Transcaucasia,* NY: Philosophical Library, 1951, pp. 5–7, 69–77. For the Soviet Union's decision to establish individual republics, see E. H. Carr, *Socialism in One Country, 1924–1926,* NY: Penguin Books, 1966, pp. 276–78, 282–92, 306–10.

2. Richard A. Pierce, *Russian Central Asia 1867–1917,* Berkeley, CA: University of California Press, 1960, p. 9.

3. For the history of the Turko-Moghul empires, see Owen Lattimore, "The Geographical Factor in Mongol History," *Geographical Journal* 91, January 1938, and Rene Grousset, *The Empire of Steppes: A History of Central Asia,* translated by Naomi Walford, New Brunswick, NJ: Rutgers University Press, 1970. According to Herodotus, the Scythians had the same social classes, that is, warriors, priests, and farmers as the Avestic and Achaemenid Iranians. E. H. Minns, *Scythians and Greeks,* Cambridge, 1913, and M. I. Rostovtzeff, *Iranians and Greeks in South Russia,* Oxford, 1922.

4. George Lenczowski, *The Middle East in World Affairs,* 4th Ed., Ithaca, NY: Cornell University Press, 1980, p. 46; see also, Firuz Kazemzadeh, pp. 23 and 135–38. Karl E. Meyer/Shareen Brysac, *Tournament of Shadows: The Great Games in the Race for Empire in Central Asia,* Washington: Cornelia and Michael Bessie/Counter Point, 1999.

5. Three campaigns (the first in 1838, the second lasting from 1840 through 1842, and the third in 1845) to capture Shamil, the leader of this group, cost Russians fifteen thousand casualties. He was finally captured in the campaign of 1859, which involved two hundred thousand soldiers.

6. E. H. Carr, *The Bolshevik Revolution 1917–1923*, NY: Penguin Books, 1966, pp. 334–44, fn.1, p. 337; and fn.1, p. 343. The Basmachi, who were also known as the Turkistan National Liberation Movement, began their anti-Russian activities in Tsarist time, and they played a key role in thwarting the Bolsheviks' attempt to reconquer Turkistan. The Basmachi movement cannot be separated from the earlier Muridun movement in Caucasus. H. B. Paksoy, "'Basmachi': Turkistan National Liberation Movement 1916–1930," in the *Modern Encyclopedia of Religions in Russia and the Soviet Union*, FA: Academic International Press, 1991, v. 4, pp. 5–20. The opposition in Kazakistan was known as the Qazaq Alash Urdu (Qazaq Alash Army). It consisted of conservative nationalists, who later split into two splinter groups, one of which joined the Bolsheviks. Included in the opposition were the Milli Firqa (Nationalist Party) in the Crimea and the Jadidi (Modernist) in Turkistan. Aman Berdi Murat "Turkmenistan and the Turkmens," in Zev Katz ed., *Handbook of Major Soviet Nationalities*, NY: Macmillan 1975, p. 265; Thomas T. Hammond, op. cit., pp. 61–70.

7. H. B. Paksoy, op. cit.

8. The existence of oil in Baku has been known since the eighth century. By the fifteenth century, oil for lamps was gathered from surface wells. Commercial exploitation of oil began in 1872, and by the beginning of the twentieth century, Baku's oil field was the largest in the world. Persia controlled the present site of Baku by the eleventh century, until Mongols captured it for a short time in the thirteenth and fourteenth centuries. In 1723, Peter the Great captured Baku, but it was returned to Persia in 1735. Russia captured the city in 1806, and in 1920, Baku became the capital of Azerbaijan.

9. Shirin Akiner, "Uzbeks," in *The Nationalities Question in the Soviet Union*, Graham Smith, ed., UK: Longman, 1990, pp. 217–18.

10. Nadia Diuk and Adrian Karatnycky, *The Hidden Nations: The People Challenge the Soviet Union*, NY: William Morrow and Company, Inc., 1990, pp. 164–69 and 185.

11. *Middle East*, March 1993.

12. The former Soviet republics in Caucasus and Central Asia are heavily dependent on the Russian Federation partly because they are geographically landlocked and have not been able to achieve economic independence. *Financial Times*, 16 August 1993.

13. *Middle East*, March 1993

14. Ibid.

15. Ibid.

16. *Far Eastern Economic Review*, 26 November 1992

17. *Economist*, 15 February 1997.

18. Ibid.

CHAPTER TWO

1. Azerbaijan (manat) January 1994; Kazakistan (tenge) 15 November 1993; Kyrgyzstan (som) May 1993; Turkmenistan (manat) November 1993; Uzbekistan (som), and Tajikistan on 30 October 2000.

2. Many corporations from the industrialized countries have negotiated contracts with these republics. For example, North America's gold producer, Newmont, has signed a deal to process ore from the Muruntao mine, the world's largest open-pit gold mine, which produces some seventy-five tons of gold annually. South Korea's Daewoo and Germany's Mercedes Benz are to build automobile factories in Uzbekistan. Meredith Jones, a British company, is spending about $8 million to build a spinning mill in Samarkand, Uzbekistan. Kazakistan has signed deals with France's Elf Aquitane, British Gas, and Agip of Italy to exploit the Karachaganak gas fields, and most recently, it has made an accord with six oil companies to explore other areas of the Caspian. Nozar Alaolmolki, op. cit., and *Economist*, 25 September 1993.

3. *Middle East*, November 1992.

4. *Swiss Review*, April 1993, Kazakistan received $3.2 billion in oil- and gas-related investments between 1993 and June 1998, and Azerbaijan's share has been $1.8 billion from 1994 through June 1998. Companies such as Unocal announced on 8 December 1998 that they were withdrawing from all Caspian projects except those based in Azerbaijan. On 9 December, Shell, Chevron, and Mobil signed a new agreement with Kazakistan in oil exploration in the Caspian Sea. RFE/RL, January 5, 1999.

5. *New York Times*, 23 May 1992 and *Financial Times*, 19 September 1997. In addition, Kazakistan has signed two agreements: (1) an estimated $5.58 billion accord with the British Gas Company, Agip and Statoil contract to explore and develop the 20 billion-cubic-meter Karachaganak gas field, and (2) an estimated $1.7 billion deal with United BMB of Turkey to develop four oil-fields and to build four gas-fired power stations at Aktyubinsk. These agreements may send Kazakistan on the way toward becoming a major twenty-first-century energy supplier. *Financial Times*, 3 November 1992, and *New York Times*, 20 March 1994. The following oil negotiations have been made: (1) In January 1997, American Mobil and UK's Monument Oil and Gas signed a memorandum of understanding to produce oil from a region of 20,000 square kilometers (8,000 square miles), covering much of western Turkmenistan's coast. (2) Two French oil companies, Total and Elf Acquitane, in January 1997, sealed an offshore oil deal with Azerbaijan, worth an estimated $2 billion. (3) In December 1996, Azerbaijan signed a deal with a consortium of oil firms including American Amoco and Unocal, as well as Japan's Itochu, to develop two offshore oilfields. (4) BP and Norway's Statoil closed a deal during the summer of 1996 to develop the Shah Deniz field. However, according to the BP Amoco PLC spokesman on 12 July 1999, the test drilling suggests the Shah Deniz field contains gas reserve of more than 400 billion cubic meters, which was a disappointment to the investors, since producing and transportation of gas is far more challenging, requiring companies to build expensive pipelines and seek out long-term customers. There is already enough gas in nearby Iran and Turkmenistan that the Shah Deniz gas would not be an attractive one at this time. (5) Malaysia's Petronas and the Chinese National Petroleum Corporation put bids for the Uzen oilfield, Kazakistan's second-largest field after Tengiz. (6) Last May, America's Mobil Corporation bought a 25 percent share in the Tengiz field, costing around $1.1 billion, while Russia's Lukoil snapped up a 5 per-

cent stake. *Economist*, 15 February 1997. In late January 1998, top White House expert on Central Asia, Jan H. Kalicki, flew to Moscow for an urgent meeting with senior Russian officials to salvage a multibillion-dollar American-Russian venture to exploit the Tengiz oil field. The Russian officials countered that the Americans were not straight, professing to partnership with Moscow in building the pipeline from Tengiz to the Black Sea while concocting a "Eurasian Transportation Corridor"—which the Clinton administration had announced in November 1997—that would bypass Russia altogether and still connect oil and natural gas lines from the Caspian to the European markets. *Washington Post*, 6 October 1998. The largest export pipeline is the western Kazakistan system that transports oil from fields in Atyrau and Mangistau in the northern Caspian region to Russia. This 1,800–mile pipeline runs from Uzen-Atyrau-Samara, and accounts for 75 percent of the nations's oil exports. Its oil export quota through this pipeline has been 150,000 bpd. The other export pipeline is the Kenkyak-Orsk line that transports oil from western Kazakhstan to Russia. Kazakstan [sic.] January 1999 United States Energy Information Administration.

   6. Interfax reported on 11 January 2000.

   7. "There are so many people around who do not want things to succeed," notes Peter Ryalls, vice president for operations at the Azerbaijan International Oil Consortium (AIOC). *Christian Science Monitor*, 18 August 1997. The TRACECA (Transport System Europe-Caucasus-Asia, informally known as the Great Silk Road) Program was inaugurated at a EU conference in 1993. This program encourages the development of a transport corridor connecting Central Asia to Europe. During September 1998, twelve countries (including Azerbaijan, Bulgaria, Kazakhstan, Romania, Turkey, and Uzbekistan) signed a multilateral agreement known as the Baku Declaration to develop the transport corridor through closer economic integration. Op. cit. Interfax, 11 January 2000.

   8. For centuries, outside powers, including Russia, Iran, United Kingdom, and Ottomans have battled over the Caspian region and its oil. Today, the struggle to gain influence in the region continues among Russia, Turkey, Iran, and the United States. This time, rather than fighting over direct ownership of the energy resources, they are fighting for oil pipelines. *Economist*, 4 May 1996. Russia, among all contenders, has the most powerful weapons to enforce its will. Perhaps most important, it also has economic leverage. Russia also has a legal weapon: the status of the Caspian Sea. Azerbaijan and Kazakhstan refer to it as a sea, while Russia and Iran have long argued that it is a lake. Russia, in other words, has the power to block all offshore deals unless it receives revenues from any republics that were to sell their energy supplies. Finally, Russia has significant power and inroads to invoke violence in any of these republics.

   9. A UN-sponsored convention on the Law of the Sea, which was signed in 1982, should take effect in the near future. Sixty countries need to ratify or accede to it for the law to be enacted. At the time of this writing, only fifty-five have signed the treaty. Among the states not willing to sign it are many Western industrialized countries, including the United States and Russia. William R. Slomanson. *Fundamental Perspectives on International Law*, NY: West Publishing Company, 1990, pp. 180–81. On 6 July 1998, Boris Yeltsin and Nursultan Nazarbaev signed a pact at the Kremlin, "dividing" the northern seabed into

Russian and Kazak sectors. The pact gives both nations equal access to fishing grounds and recognizes Kazakistan's claim to the oil near its coast. The five Caspian nations have long disputed who owns the rights to the resources. Azerbaijan, Kazakhstan, and Turkmenistan want the sea "divided" into national sectors to ensure that they can claim at least some of the oil. Russia and Iran wanted all the littoral states to share the resources. The Russo-Kazak agreement may open the way for other states to negotiate similar accords. *New York Times*, 7 July 998.

10. RFE/RL, 8 August 1997, *Economist*, 9 October 1999.

11. Russia agrees with these comments and Tehran's position in regards to oil exploration in the Caspian Sea. *Reuter*, 12 April 1997, and Internet, 12 April 1997.

12. *Economist*, 11 October 1997.

13. *Christian Science Monitor*, 18 August 1997.

14. *New York Times*, 24 January 1999.

15. Ibid. President Clinton, who was attending the meeting and was the force behind the pipeline route, greeted the signing of the agreements as "a historic event." But Russian Foreign Minister Igor Ivanov said that the United States resorted to "political pressure" to secure the multistate agreement. Officials at BP/Amoco PLC, the main oil company working in the Caspian oil fields, said early estimates of massive oil reserves in the region may have been overstated. Azerbaijan produces about 100,000 barrels of oil a day, about one-tenth of the 1 million a day that would be needed to make the project viable. Saudi Arabia, for example, pumps about 8 million barrels per day. Experts contend that it would cost billions of dollars to bring Azerbaijan's oil industry up to the level at which it could pump enough oil to make the project viable. Associated Press, 18/19 November 1999, and *Washington Post*, 9 November 1999.

16. As noted before, Kazak oil could be pumped via the Atyrau-Samara pipeline, which had the capacity of 200,000 bpd. Small amounts of oil could be shipped by rail and barge through Russia. In addition, oil is being shipped across the Caspian Sea from Kazakistan and Turkmenistan to the port of Baku for further transshipment westward by rail and via existing pipelines to the Black Sea. In 1996, Kazakistan signed an agreement to swap oil with Iran. The latter agreement involves a small amount of oil. *AFP*, 1 February 1999. In addition to the oil pipelines, companies involved need to make similar plans regarding the gas pipeline routes. The following are the route options: (1) through Russia; (2) through Eastern European Ports—Romania, Bulgaria, and Ukraine say they could send oil by barge or pipeline straight to Western Europe from their port on the Black Sea. (3) the eastern route through China—a feasibility study is due later in 1999 for a natural gas that would deliver fuel directly to China through Kazakistan. (4) An oil pipeline is also being studied through Georgia and the Black Sea—Some American companies favor this route for now, but Turkey objects to increased tanker traffic through Bosphorus. (5) through Turkey via Georgia—this one is favored and supported by the White House but is the most expensive route and the American companies need large amount of subsidies because of the expense. (6) through Iran—a pipeline through Iran would be the most direct and cheapest to offer oil to the customers in the Persian Gulf, but

the American government forbids investment of more than $20 million in Iran at the present time. The government of Kazakistan and Iran agreed in November 1997 to resume oil swaps between the two countries. (7) through Pakistan via Afghanistan—Pakistan would like to develop this route, but the condition in Afghanistan and the political system makes the route an impossible option at the present time. United States Energy Information Administration, December 1998 and *New York Times*, 24 January 1999.

17. *Christian Science Monitor*, 4 March 1999, Associated Press, 20 January 2000.

18. Ibid. The White House lobbied hard for the Baku-Ceyhan route, which fulfills its strategic goals of isolating the Islamic Republic of Iran and supporting Turkey, and maintains that the pipeline should cost no more than $2.4 billion to build. Granted for the White House, the main concern has been strategic, guaranteeing that any pipeline would skirt Russia or Iran. But this strategic move is very costly, if not unsafe, for the oil companies. "The oil companies had first hoped Washington would allow a shorter route through Iran, with an outlet at the Persian Gulf. But this was blocked by Washington's refusal to lift economic sanctions against Iran." *New York Times*, 21 November 1999.

19. *Washington Post National Weekly Edition* (hereafter, *WPNEW*), 16 June 1997.

20. Ibid.

21. *Economist*, 8 August 1992.

22. RFE/RL, 10 February 1994; *Christian Science Monitor*, 28 March 1994; and *Jamestown Foundation Monitor*, 4 October 1995.

23. Reported by the Russian news agency Itar-Tass, December 1992. *Manchester Guardian Weekly*, 21 March 1993. According to officials in Dushanbeh, the war claimed fifty thousand lives and more than sixty thousand Tajik refugees who may have fled into Afghanistan. The Tajiks in Afghanistan are among the thirty-six thousand or more refugees who fled from southern Tajikistan after the fighting commenced in December 1992. They oppose the former Communists who control the Tajik government, and the former Communists in turn accuse the refugees of being "Islamic fundamentalists." *Far Eastern Economic Review*, 28 January 1993, and *Economist*, 24 July 1993.

24. *New York Times*, 30 September 1992, and *Economist*, 24 July 1993.

25. Leaders of the Central Asian republics and the Russian prime minister, Viktor Chernomyrdin, met in Almaty, Kazakistan, on 4 October 1996 and discussed the situation in Afghanistan. At the meeting, President Nursultan Nazarbaev of Kazakistan expressed concern that the conflict is approaching the CIS border, and he condemned the human rights violations that followed the Taliban takeover of power in Kabul. President Askar Akayev of Kyrgyzstan, warned against intervention, as it would merely repeat the Soviet Union's mistake. President Islam Karimov's motion calling for open support of General Abdurashid Dostum's forces was voted down. *Manchester Guardian Weekly*, 2 August 1998, quoting *New York Times* and *Le Monde*. However, in an early August 1998 military campaign, Taliban forces were able to take over Mazar-e Sharif and other strongholds of the anti-Taliban Northern Alliance of General Dustam, Shi'ite armed groups, and Ahmad Shah Masoud. Security of the Cen-

tral Asian countries remains the primary goal of these governments. During their participation at the OSCE summit in Istanbul on 18 November 1999, the presidents of Kazakistan, Kyrgyzstan, and Uzbekistan called on the OSCE to do more to boost security in Central Asia. Karimove said regional security in Central Asia is as important as security in Europe, and he proposed the OSCE open an international center for fighting terrorism. RFE/RL, 19 November 1999.

CHAPTER THREE

1. *Economist*, 13 June 1992.

2. *Iran Times*, 6 Azar 1371 (27 November 1992), and *Ebrar*, 7 Teer 1371 (28 June 1992).

3. *Christian Science Monitor*, 25 August 1997. On 20 January 1997, Azerbaijan commemorated "Black January," when more than 130 people were killed and more than 700 wounded in 1990. Intervention by the Soviet forces helped the APF leader Abulfazl Elchibey attain power. *Daily Digest*, Open Media Research Institute, 21 January 1997; *Economist*, 16 April 1993; and *Manchester Guardian Weekly*, 18 April 1993.

4. In 1969, during the regime of Soviet Leader Leonid I. Brezhnev, Haidar Aliev became the Communist leader of the Azerbaijan Soviet Republic. Later, he was named to the Soviet Politburo in Moscow, the first leader from a Muslim republic to reach such a position. Mikhail Gorbachev forced Aliev from power in 1987.

5. *Economist*, 13 November 1993. Suret Husseinov, the leader of the coup, had to flee and has since been residing in Moscow.

6. *New York Times*, 21 September 1997. The issue of human rights was a topic of a seminar held in Georgia in late November 1999. The seminar provided highlights of the human rights situation in Armenia, Azerbaijan, and Georgia. Participants from the three countries agreed that current elections in these countries are "balloting charades." A representative of Armenia was quoted as saying that "'justice' is measured only by bags of money. All participants agreed that police brutality hits hard and that perpetrators are rarely, if ever, brought to justice." Today, people are still arrested and imprisoned for political reasons, mostly in Azerbaijan, and are held in "appalling conditions." Freedom of speech, press, and assembly differ among the three republics. However, governments of these countries do exercise power to clamp down on unfriendly printed and electronic media. RFE/RL, 30 December 1999.

7. Voice of America (VOA) reported the widespread unfairness of the election on 9 November 1995. *OMRI Digest*, 21 November 1995.

8. *Economist*, 6 March 1999.

9. Ibid.

10. *New York Times*, 21 September 1997, *Christian Science Monitor*, 13 October 1998. The remaining three candidates each polled less than 1 percent. *Economist*, 6 March 1999. The leaders of the Azerbaijan National Independence Party, Musavat Party, Democratic Party, and Azerbaijan Popular Front Party in an interview said they do not consider the results of the Octo-

ber 1998 presidential elections valid. RFE/RL, 8 September 1999.

11. Sophie Shihab "Thousands Killed in Karabagh War," *Manchester Guardian Weekly*, 13 February 1994.

12. Defense ministers of the two countries discussed the future of the station on 19 January 1996, during the CIS summit in Moscow. Russia's debt to Azerbaijan in 1996 was an estimated $18 million for the energy and services used by the station. Russian defense minister Grachev asked for a deferral of the debt payment, but Baku instead opted to have the debt counted against its trade deficit with Russia. *Jamestown Foundation*, 5 February 1996.

13. *Christian Science Monitor*, 25 August 1997.

14. Joint ventures in Azerbaijan as of 30 July 1992: Turkey fifty-one, Germany seven, Iran six, Sweden six, Great Britain five, Israel four, and the United States four. *Turan News*, 28 August 1992.

15. *Economist*, 11 July 1998, RFE/RL, 5 January 1999. The Azerbaijan International Operating Company (AIOC) signed an $8 billion, thirty-year contract in September 1994 to develop three fields—Azeri, Chiragh, and the deepwater portions of Gunashi—with total reserves estimated at 3 to 5 billion barrels. "Azerbaijan," United States Energy Information Administration, December 1998. *Turkmenistan-Economy-Bulletin* 99:154, 12 December 1999.

16. *OMRI Daily Digest*, 3 January 1997.

17. RFE/RL, 25 January 2000.

CHAPTER FOUR

1. *Christian Science Monitor*, 7 and 11 March 1994, and RFE/RL, 14 March 1994.

2. *Christian Science Monitor*, 11 March 1994. Of 176 deputies elected, there are 105 Kazaks, 49 Russians, 10 Ukrainians, 3 Germans, 3 Jews, 1 Uzbek, 1 Tatar, 1 Ingush, 1 Korean, 1 Pole, and 1 Ughur. Roza A. Unaybaeva, "The Development of Modern Kazakistan: The Foreign Policy of Independence," paper presented at the Annual International Studies Association (ISA) Conference, Washington, DC, March 28–April 1, 1994.

3. VOA, 31 August 1995.

4. *OMRI Daily Digest*, 8 December 1995.

5. *Jamestown Foundation Monitor*, 11 January 1996.

6. RFE/RL Newsline, 27 October 1999.

7. Ibid.

8. *Economist*, 28 November 1998, RFE/RL,30 November and 10 December 1998. Serikbolsy Abdildin of the Communist Party received 11.7 percent, Customs Committee Chairman Gani Kasymov 4.61 percent, and parliamentary deputy Engels Gabbasove less than 1 percent. The Central Elections Commission reports that 86.28 percent of the electorate turned out to vote. Judy Thompson of the OSCE on 11 January 1999 said the OSCE considers that "the election process was far from the standards which [Kazakistan] promised to follow as an OSCE member." A spokesman for U.S. State Department said on 11 January 1999, "The conduct of these elections has set back the process of democratiza-

tion in Kazakhstan [sic.] and has made more difficult the development of the important relationship between our two countries." RFE/RL, 11, 12, and 18 January 1999; *Washington Post*, 16 January 1999; *Christian Science Monitor*, 15 January 1999; and *Economist*, 16 January 1999. The election results were as follows: Otan Party, which supports Nazarbaev, received fifteen of the forty-seven seats contested in the second round giving it a total of twenty-three; the Civic Party, also supporter of the president, won three additional seats, giving it twelve. The Communist Party has three seats, the Agrarian Party two, and the Republican People's Party of Kazakhstan, one. RFE/RL, 27 October 1999.

9. *Jamestown Foundation Monitor*, 11 January 1996; Sidney Verba, "Comparative Political Culture," Lucian W. Pye and Sidney Verba, eds., *Political Culture and Political Development*, Princeton, NJ: Princeton University Press, 1965, pp. 516–60.

10. *Economist*, 5 December 1992.

11. The Almaty-based Giller Institute, under the direction of VCIOM in Moscow, conducted personal interviews with 1,199 adults in the republic eighteen years of age and older. It was commissioned by the USIA, "Opinion Analysis," USIA Office of Research and Media Reaction, 17 January 1995.

12. *Jamestown Monitor*, 4 October 1995.

13. He was replaced by Kanat Saudabev, Kazakistan's former ambassador to Turkey. RFE/RL, 19 April 1994.

14. *International Affairs*, 3–4, 1994, p 24. China is Kazakhstan's second largest trading partner after Russia. In 1992, Almaty's bilateral trade totaled $433 million, but it declined to $205 million in 1993, according to official figures. *Financial Times*, 26 April 1994.

15. Tuleutai Suleimenov, op. cit., 3–4, 1994, pp. 23–25.

16. *Iran Times*, 2 Aban 1371 (13 November 1992), *Economist*, 24 July 1999.

17. *Economist*, 13 November 1993.

18. RFE/RL, 26 January 1994.

19. The aid was described by U.S. officials as not only a reward for country's willingness to dismantle its nuclear weapons but also as a tribute to its progress in the privatization of its economy. Nazarbaev expressed his nation's interest to join NATO's Participation-for-Peace plan. RFE/RL, 15 February 1994, and *Christian Science Monitor*, 16 February 1994.

20. Tuteutai Suleimenov, op. cit., p. 27.

21. Reuters 20 July 1998, and *Economist*, 28 November 1998. The economic situation of Kazakistan deteriorated sharply following independence—similar to all other former Soviet republics—with GDP falling to 55 percent of 1991 levels by 1995, before beginning to grow slightly between 1996 and 1998. The change came about during 1994, when Almaty implemented a fiscal and monetary policy approved by the IMF. Kazakhstan January 1999 United States Energy Information Administration.

22. *Middle East*, November 1992; *New York Times*, 2 March 1993; and *Economist*, 28 August 1999.

23. *New York Times*, 23 May 1992; *Manchester Guardian Weekly*, 4 October 1992; and *Financial Times*, 3 November 1992.

24. *Economist,* 25 September 1993. However, recent information reveals that Tengiz crude oil is a light honey color, which is perfect for gasoline but contains a large amount of hydrogen sulfide that must be removed. Its removal would require extra scrubbers. Soviet geologists had discovered this oil field in 1979 in the northeast shore of the Caspian Sea. They called it "Tengiz," a Kazak word for "sea." It lies unusually deep, as much as three miles below a salt dome that itself was nine hundred yards thick. Soviet engineers spent more than $1 billion drilling dozens of wells before concluding that Western technology was needed. *New York Times,* 20 March 1994, and *Washington Post,* 6 October 1998.

CHAPTER FIVE

1. Safarbai Kushkarov (Khuskarov), a prominent resident of the city of Dzizak points out, "Under the Russians we lost everything and there was no respect for any of the ancient arts and skills of Central Asia." He attributes the overwhelming power of the long-standing and practicing Sufi school of thought in the region. *Far Eastern Economic Review,* 17 December 1992.

2. *Far Eastern Economic Review,* 19 November 1992.

3. Ibid.

4. *Plain Dealer,* 30 January 1998.

5. *Independent,* 17 February 1999; RFE/RL, 25 February 1999; *Agance France Presse,* 28 June 1999; *Economist,* 4 September 1999; and RFE/RL, 9 September 1999.

6. *Manchester Guardian Weekly,* 21 March 1993.

7. Interfax on 4 January 2000.

8. *Middle East,* July 1992.

9. *Far Eastern Economic Review,* 3 December 1992, and RFE/RL, 10 November 1999.

CHAPTER SIX

1. RFE/RL, 25 March 1998. The Kyrgyz Parliamentary Commission on Corruption in the gold industry is investigating the possible corruption, as reports indicate that the Kumtor facility far exceeded its budget in January 1998, during Apas Jumagulov's administration.

2. *Economist,* 20 February 1993.

3. *Reuters,* 28 August 1998

4. RFE/RL, 21 May 1998.

5. RFE/RL, 27 January, 3 September, and 3 December 1999.

CHAPTER SEVEN

1. Associated Press, 12 November 1999.

2. RFE/RL, 18 November 1999.

3. RFE/RL, 17 November 1999.

4. *New York Times*, 7 November 1993.
5. *New York Times*, 9 June 1992.
6. RFE/RL, 27 January, 3 September, and 3 December 1999.
7. Business Information Service for Newly Independent State (BISNIS), 5 August 1998, and RFE/RL, 8 November and 3 December 1999.

CHAPTER EIGHT

1. British Broadcasting Corporation (BBC); World Services, 15 January 1994; and *Economist*, 18 March 1995.
2. Associated Press and *Reuters*, 29 December 1999.
3. RFE/RL, 5 January 1999; "Turkmenistan," Energy Information Administration, September 1998; *Economist*, 8 January 2000.
4. RFE/RL, 21 October 1999.

CHAPTER NINE

1. Ian Bremmer, "Southern Tier Subregionalism," Center for Political and Strategic Studies (CPSS), 31 July 1997; John B. Dunlop, *The Rise of Russia and the Fall of the Soviet Empire*, Princeton, NJ: Princeton University Press; Pilar Bonet, *Figures in a Red Landscape*, trans. by Norman Thomas di Giovani and Susan Ashe, Woodrow Wilson Center Press/Johns Hopkins University Press; Ruslan Hazbulatov, *The Struggle for Russia: Power and Change in the Democratic Revolution*, ed. Richard Sakwa, UK: Routledge; Vladmir A. Zviglyanich, *The Morphology of the Russian Mentality: A Philosophical Inquiry into Conservatism and Pragmatism*, Lawson, NY: Edwin Mellen Press; Dimitri Simes "The Return of Russian History," *Foreign Affairs*, January/February 1994.
2. RFE/RL Newline, 16 March 1994.
3. RFE/RL, 30 March 1994. He pointed out that Uzbekistan is not prepared to join the NATO partnership of Peace Program. RFE/RL, 20 May 1994.
4. RFE/RL, 17 September 1997.
5. RFE/RL, 14 March 1994.
6. *Far Eastern Economic Review*, 25 February 1993.
7. The ECO was established in the early 1970s and consisted of Iran, Pakistan and Turkey. In 1992, the ECO was expanded to include Afghanistan, Azerbaijan, Kazakistan, Kyrgyzstan, Tajikistan, Turkmenistan, and Uzbekistan. Houman A. Sadri, "Integration in Central Asia: From Theory to Policy," *Central Asian Survey* (1997), 16(4), 573–86.
8. *Far Eastern Economic Review*, 25 February 1993. ECO member states met in Tehran on 26 January 1994. RFE/RL, 24 January; *Le Monde Diplomatique*, October 1998. See John K. Cooley, *Unholy Wars: Afghanistan, America and International Terrorism*, Sterling, VA: Pluto Press, 1999, especially chapters 1, 3, 5, and 10. On 19 July 1999, another UN-sponsored attempt was made to reach an end to war in Afghanistan.
9. Nozar Alaolmolki, *Struggle for Dominance in the Persian Gulf*, New York, NY: Peter Lang Publishing, Inc., 1991.

10. Besides those republics, Turkey has strongly expressed its dismay toward Tehran's activities in Turkey. *Middle East*, April 1993.

11. *Etela'at*, 15 Day 1370 (5 January 1992). At the beginning of the twentieth century, Tehran's population was about fifty thousand and reached over 10 million in 1998. Unemployment is estimated at 30 percent, over 50 percent of the country's population is under 25 years of age and more than 45 percent are under fourteen. Annual population growth is reported at 2 percent.

12. *Tehran Times*, 21 January 1999.

13. *Swiss Review*, June 1992; *Los Angels Times*, 7 January 1992; *Iran Times*, 23 and 30 Esfand 1370 (13, 20 March 1992); and 22 Shahrivar 1370 (13 September 1991). Iran had rescheduled $2 billion in debt payment. Iran's debt is placed at approximately $12 billion. The country is suffering from a serious shortage of raw materials and industrial parts because of the country's hard currency shortage. *Tehran Times*, 10 February 1999.

14. *Kayhan Havai*, 19 Tir 1370 (10 July 1991), and *Independent*, 27 June 1992.

15. *Kayhan Havai*, 19 Tir 1370 (10 July 1991), and *Independent*, 27 June 1992.

16. *Wall Street Journal*, 16 September 1991.

17. British Broadcasting Corporation (BBC), World Services, 13 August 1991. United Nations Security Council, 31 July 1991. Preliminary Report of the United Nations team, appointed by the secretary general in accordance with Security Council resolution 598 (1987).

18. *Wall Street Journal*, 16 September 1991; and *Economist*, 8 August 1998.

19. *Economist*, 8 August 1998, and *Manchester Guardian Weekly*, 26 July 1998.

20. *Iran Times*, 10 Aban 1370 (1 November 1991); *Washington Post National Weekly Edition*, 18–24 May 1992; and *New York Times*, 13 December 1998.

21. *Economist*, 13 June 1992.

22. *Iran Times*, 31 July and 2 September 1999.

23. Never have the mullahs stood in lower esteem. The young, especially, seem implacably hostile to Islamic values. The prominent clergy, Ayatollah Hussein Ali Montazari, wrote a letter to the most senior cleric, Ayatollah Golpayagani, and said when the time comes the people will not be making distinctions between activists and quietists, good mullahs and bad. "They will burn the wet with the dry." *Manchester Guardian Weekly*, 11 July 1993.

24. FBIS (Foreign Broadcasting Information Services), 26 October 1992; Houman A. Sadri, op. cit., p. 580. Ali A. Jalali contends that Iran's approach toward Central Asia, "so far has been guided by a policy of cautious engagement inspired mostly by geo-strategic consideration rather than ideological motives." *Central Asia Monitor*, April 1999; *Ettela'at*, 17 January 2000; *New York Times*, 17 January 2000; *Times*, 25 October 1999.

25. Bahgat Korany, "Defending the Faith amid Change: The Foreign Policy of Saudi Arabia," in *The Foreign Policies of Arab States*; Bahgat Korany /Ali E. Hillal Dessouki, ed., CO: Westview Press, 1991, pp. 323–24; and *New York Times*, 15 December 1992.

26. *Saudi Arabia*, winter 1991, and telephone conversation between the author and the Saudi Embassy, 2:00 P.M., 23 January 1990.

27. Peter Winkler, "Trouble in and around Egypt," *Swiss Review*, August 1992.

28. *U.S. News and World Report*, 8 October 1990.

29. The most dramatic declines in oil revenues occurred throughout the eighties. The Royal Dutch Shell Group reported in 1988 that annual Saudi Arabian oil earnings fell from an all-time high of $113 billion (U.S.) in 1981 to $23 billion in 1987.

30. *Middle East*, February 1992.

31. The revelation of U.S. and Saudi Arabia's involvement in oil marketing and pricing has embarrassed the Bush administration, as well as the United Kingdom, especially at the time of the Bank of Credit and Commerce International (BCCI) crisis. Edwin S. Rothschild, "The Roots of Bush's Oil Policy," *Texas Observer*, 14 February 1992; *Oil Daily*, 13 February–14 July 1992; *WPNWE*, 27 July–2 August 1992; *Financial Times*, 30 July 1992; *New York Times*, 30 July 1992; and *Washington Post*, 30 September 1998.

32. The oil industry, construction, and service sectors are dependent on foreign workers. Non-Saudis make up 25 percent of all teachers in the country. Even a greater number of public health workers are foreigners. Despite an attempt to change this in 1995, 84 percent of doctors, 80 percent of nurses, and 55 percent of pharmacists were still noncitizens. The figures were as high as 87 percent among general practitioners, 81 percent among dentists, 79 percent among gynecologists—obstetricians, and 71 percent of pediatricians. *New York Times*, 25 April 1993, and *Le Monde Diplomatique*, October 1998.

33. Fouad Al-Farsy, "King Fouad and the First Saudi Arabian Development Plan," in *King Fouad and the Modernization of Saudi Arabia*, ed. W. A. Beling, CO: Westview Press, 1980, p. 63.

34. *Middle East*, February 1992.

35. Quoted in ibid.

36. During 1999, the Saudi government beheaded ninety-nine people, the majority of whom were foreigners.

37. According to the *Washington Post*, one investment banker stated that he had inquired about arranging loans for Saudi Arabia by using the country's treasury securities as collateral.

38. WPWE, 18, 24 February 1991.

39. *New York Times*, 7, 15 October 1998; *Independence*, 23 November 1998; and *Los Angeles Times*, 25 November 1998.

40. *Washington Post*, 25 November 1998.

41. *New York Times*, 25 November 1998.

42. *New York Times*, 18 January 1999.

43. *Manchester Guardian Weekly*, 24 January 1999.

44. *Swiss Review*, May 1992; George Lenczowski, *The Middle East in World Affairs*, 4th ed., NY: Cornell U. Press, 1980, p.115; Kemal H. Karpat, *Political and Social Thought in the Contemporary Middle East*, revised ed., NY: Praeger Publishers, 1982, pp. 399–412, 433–43; *Middle East Journal*, Winter

1998, pp. 32–33. The author notes that the statement "peace at home and peace in the world," attributed to Ataturk could not be substantiated. Ibid.

45. *Middle East Report*, September-October, 1989, pp. 4–10, 22, 13–16.

46. This characterization was advanced by James Baker, former U.S. secretary of state, in a public (PBS) TV interview, 21 June 1992.

47. *Manchester Guardian Weekly*, 16 February 1992.

48. *Economist*, 24 October 1992.

49. *Milliyet*, 11 October 1992.

50. Tosun Aricanli and Dani Rodrik, eds., *The Political Economy of Turkey*, NY: St. Martin's Press, 1990; Henri J. Barkey, *The State and Industrialization Crisis in Turkey*, Boulder, CO: Westview Press, 1990; *Economist*, 24 April 1993; U.S. Department of State report submitted to the Senate Committees on Foreign Relations and on Finance and to the House Committees on Foreign Affairs and on Ways and Means, January 1998.

51. *Economist*, 25 July 1992; *Manchester Guardian Weekly*, 7 March 1999; *New York Times*, 16 May 1999; and RFE/RL, 16 July 1999.

52. *New York Times*, 20 May 1993. The visit by Ozal to Moscow resulted in the signing of a Treaty of Friendship, Good-Neighborliness, and Cooperation. *Middle East Journal*, Winter 1998, p. 36.

53. *Economist*, 24 April 1993.

54. *Washington Post*, 11 November 1992. The Amnesty International report additionally faulted the PKK for human rights abuses.

55. *Washington Report on Middle East Affairs*, March 1998.

56. Turkey's human rights record is poor. According to Amnesty International, six people died in police custody during the first six months of 1998, nine "disappeared" after being arrested, and twenty were victims of extrajudicial executions. Many of the victims were reportedly connected to the Kurdish-armed PKK movement, and others were critics of the state, military, and security forces. *Manchester Guardian Weekly*, 12 July 1998; *New York Times*, 15 October 1998; and *Washington Post*, 25 November 1998.

57. *Manchester Guardian Weekly*, 16 February 1992.

58. *Economist*, 27 November 1999; "A Case Study of the PKK in Turkey," *Foundation for Middle East and Balkan Studies*.

59. *Washington Report on Middle East Affairs*, January/February 1999, and *Christian Science Monitor*, 4 March 1999.

CHAPTER TEN

1. *Economist*, 24 July 1993.

2. *Washington Times*, 15 March 1994, and REF/RL, 15 March 1994; *New York Times*, 2 January 2000. The CIS was created in 1991 to promote political, economic, and military ties between the former Soviet republics.

3. First Deputy Prime Minister Oled Soskovets, former Joint Forces Commander Evengii Shaposhnikove and First Deputy Minister Andrei Kokoshin, RFE/RL, 14 March 1994.

4. *Economist*, 12 February 1994.

5. RFE/RL, 16 March 1994; *Washington Post*, 9 May 1999; *Washington Post*, 9 May 1999.

6. *New York Times*, 13 April 1994; RFE/RL, 26 January 2000; *Reuters* and *New York Times*, 26 January 2000.

7. RFE/RL, 30 March 1994, and *Economist*, 21 May 1994.

8. RFE/RL, 11 April 1994.

9. *Wall Street Journal*, 11 April 1997, and *Wall Street Journal Interactive Edition*, 14 May 1997.

10. "The Russian presence here is, for the time being, somewhat stabilizing," says George Adams of the International Rescue Committee. *Christian Science Monitor*, 12 May 1994. On 8 August 1998, the Russian Defense Ministry was quoted as ordering the 201st Motorized Infantry stationed in Tajikistan, to move close to the border with Afghanistan. *ITAR-TASS*, 12 August 1998.

11. Kazak Foreign Minister Kasymjomart Tokayev, on 10 August 1998, said the situation in Afghanistan should be discussed "immediately" by the foreign ministers of those countries that are concerned about the conflict. Tokayev referred to a statement adopted by Russia, Kazakistan, Kyrgyzstan, Tajikistan, and Uzbekistan in October 1996, after Kabul was captured by the Taliban forces. RFE/RL, 10–12 August 1998, and 19 April 1999.

12. Paul Goble notes that Moscow acknowledges that both the empire and the Soviet Union are "gone" and quotes Primakove as contending that "the present reality is such that sovereignty of the ex-USSR republics should not be subject to any doubt." He notes, "Primakove concludes, Moscow must do everything it can to bring 'the states formed on the territory of the former Soviet Union' closer together through economic integration and 'the creation of a single economic area.'" RFE/RL, 6 August 1998; WPWE, 21 September 1998; *Washington Post*, 13–15 January 1999; and *New York Times*, 2 January 2000. However, on 10 July 2000 Foreign Minister Igor Ivanov presented Russia's new foreign policy: "Our foreign policy resources are objectively limited, and they will be concentrated in the fields that are vital for Russia." At the same time, he stressed that Moscow will defend its national interests: "Russia was, is, and will always be a superpower." He noted that the foreign policy doctrine signed by President Putin late last month replaces a document adopted in 1993 under Boris Yeltsin. One of the main objectives of the new foreign policy will be "the development of friendly ties with key Asian states, primarily China and India." The new doctrine stresses the importance of further developing relations with Iran. *Washington Post*, 11 July 2000.

13. RFE/RL, 15 March 1994; *Financial Times*, 9 May 1994; and *Economist*, 14 May 1994. In contrast to the Russian economy, the Peoples' Republic of China is rapidly growing. *New York Times*, 9 January 2000, and *Christian Science Monitor*, 5 January 2000.

A P P E N D I X

The following information is compiled from the following sources: Europa, the U.S. State Department, and Radio Free Europe/Radio Liberty.

Azerbaijan: Haidar Aliev was born in the enclave of Nakhjevan (Nakhchevan) located on the border with Iran in 1923. He began his career working for the secret police at age 18. He joined the Communist Party of the Soviet Union (CPSU) in 1945. He later headed the KGB, the name for the secret police after the Second World War. In 1969, he became head of the Communist party in Azerbaijan. He led Azerbaijan for eighteen years, increasing the strength of the Soviet state-economy in the republic at the expense of local industrialization, while permitting widespread political corruption. He maintained a close association with the Soviet Communist party leader Leonid Brezhnev. He became a member of the Central Committee of the CPSU in 1971 and a full member of the Soviet Politburo in 1983. In the early years under the leadership of Mikhail Gorbachev, he continued his political ascent becoming Deputy Prime Minister of the Soviet Union. However, Aliev was expelled from the Politburo in an internal shake-up in 1987. He returned to his birthplace of Nakhjevan where he secured the position of head of the region in 1990.

Kazakistan: Nursultan Nazarbaev was born near Almaty, Kazakistan in 1940. He worked as a metallurgical engineer and trained at the Karaganda works, serving as party leader, his first political post. In 1979, he became secretary of the Central Committee of the republic's Communist Party. From 1984 to 1989, Nazarbaev served as chairperson of the republic's council of ministers and became the first secretary of the party central committee in 1989. Nazarbaev served as a deputy to the Supreme Soviet of the Soviet Union before he joined the Politburo of the Communist Party of the Soviet Union in 1991. Nazarbaev has ruled the country since 1989. Although he won a new, seven-year term on 11 January 1999, the election was rife with allegations of fraud.

Kyrgyzstan: Askar Akaev, president of Kyrgyzstan was born in 1944 in the Kyzyl-Baizak district. After graduating from the Leningrad Institute of Precise Mechanics and Optics, he pursued a career teaching at the Frunze Polytechnic Institute. In 198 1, he joined the Communist Party of the Soviet Union and served as head of the KCP Science Dept 1986–87. In the 1980s, he was department head of the Central Committee of the Kyrgyz Communist Party. In 1987, Akayev became vice president and then later president of the Kyrgyz Academy of Sciences. He was elected president of the Kyrgyz Supreme Soviet in October 1990, and then reelected in what was then the Independent Republic of Kyrgyzstan. Akaev adopted a democratic constitution and dissolved all Soviet collective farms. However, former Communist Party officials, relatives and friends acquired key government positions. Moreover, similar people were given the opportunity to obtain state properties for a token amount. In 1991, Akaev introduced a new political structure in which he attempted to reduce crime and corruption as well as worked to ease tensions between government supporters and opponents in the southern part of the country. So in 1996, as part of his anti-corruption campaign, Akayev dismissed several high officials. Among these officials was Jumagul Saadenbekov, a regional governor and former adviser to the president. However, in April of 1998, Akaev appointed Saadanbekov as Kyrgyz ambassador to Ukraine. His democratic image was tarnished in 1995, when he ordered a criminal investigation against two journalists because he felt they had insulted him. In July 1998, the Constitutional Court ruled that Akaev's first presidential term would not be counted therefore, he will be eligible to run again for the office in 2000.

Tajikistan: Imamali Rahmonov, president of Tajikistan was born in October 1952 in the town of Dangar in the Kulyab region of Tajikistan. After studying economics at Lenin State University in Dushanbe, he served in the Soviet armed forces. He was director of a state farm, rising from the mid-level Communist Party appointee position (*nomenklatura*). In November of 1992, Rahmonov was elected chairperson of the Culvert region government and then, during the height of the country's civil war, was elected chairperson of the Supreme Soviet. Rahmonov consolidated his power in 1992 through presidential elections and a referendum on a new constitution, and won the election with very little competition. Rahmonov heads a pro-Moscow government with a security force made up of members of the Kulyabi clan. He has been involved in a struggle with major opposition individuals and groups since he came to power. Among the opposition is the Islamic United Tajik Opposition, which operated largely underground until the peace accord, which brought a change in the name of the opposition to that of the Party of Islamic Revival.

Turkmenistan: The President of Turkmenistan and the head of the Democratic Party of Turkmenistan, Saparmurat Niyazov was born in Ashghabad February 19, 1940. He studied mathematics and physics at Leningrad Polytechnic Institute. From 1959–1967, Niyazov was an instructor with the All-Union Central Trade Union Council, and joined the Communist Party of the Soviet Union for the first time in 1962. After joining the Central Committee of the Turkmen Communist Party as an instructor in 1970, he became a deputy section head. From 1979–1984, Nlyazov served as first secretary for the City Committee of Ashqabad and became a member of the Central Committee of the CPSU in 1984. At the end of 1985, Niyazov was the head of the Turkmen Central Committee. Five years later, he was on the Soviet Politburo. While the Soviet Union was going through major changes in 1990, Niyazov became the chairperson of the Supreme Soviet of the Turkmen Soviet Socialist Republic. In October of 1991, 94.1% of the people approved independence in a referendum and created the Republic of Turkmenistan. He has become a cult figure in the country and in fact has been named Turkmenbashi (father of the Turkmen). Niyazov does not allow any political opposition in the country.

Uzbekistan: Islam Abduganievich Karimov, president of Uzbekistan, was born January 30, 1938 in Samarkand to a Tajik mother and an Uzbek father. He lost both of his parents at a young age. Educated at the Central Asian Polytechnic (studying engineering) and at Tashkent Economics Institute, he worked for Tashkent Chkalov Aviation from 1960–66 and for the Uzbek State Planning Agency (Gosplan) of Uzbekistan from 1966–83. He joined the Communist Party of the Soviet Union in 1964, but did not start public service until 1983 when he became the Minister of Finance for the Uzbekistan Soviet Socialist Republic. Karimov served as the deputy chairperson of the Uzbek Council of Ministers, eventually becoming the first secretary of the Communist Party Central Committee in Uzbekistan. At the time of the coup against Mikhail Gorbachev in August of 1991, Karimov was a member of the Soviet Politburo and the executive president of the Supreme Soviet of the Uzbekistan Soviet Socialist Republic. In 1990, he was elected to the Soviet Politburo. After the failed Moscow coup, Uzbek Communist Party separated itself from the Soviet party and changed its name to the People's Democratic Party of Uzbekistan. Karimov became the head of the party. With the collapse of the Soviet Union, the clans in the former Central Asian republics have increased their influence, and this is particularly true for the Uzbek government. In December 199 1, Karimov was voted in. He won eighty-six percent of vote, and became the President of the new republic. According to the 1992 constitution, a president may serve for a maximum of two terms. However, the Uzbek Parliament declared in August 1995 that the March 1995 referendum extending Karimov's presidential term meant he was still serving his first term. This would allow him to stand for election in 2000. Islam Karimov, who was born into a poor family, lacks a clan affiliation as the other Uzbek politicians such as Karim Khakulov, Alisher Azlzkhojaev and Ismael Jurabekov who are members of influential clans of Rashidov or Samarkandis. However, since independence, Karimov has used his presidential patronage shrewdly to position his allies in the key ministries of interior, defense and crucially, the SNB, which watches over state security. Karimov has used the threat of instability from neighboring countries to justify his iron-fist rule that tolerates no opposition or criticism. He narrowly escaped a series of bombs that went off in Tashkent during February 1999.

INDEX

SUNY series in Global Politics
James N. Rosenau, Editor

List of Titles